Life on the Railway

Life on the Railway

John Owen

Millstream Books

First published 1989

Millstream Books
7 Orange Grove
Bath BA1 1LP

This book has been set in New Baskerville type by Ryburn Typesetting, Halifax
Printed in Great Britain by The Amadeus Press, Huddersfield

© John Owen 1989

ISBN 0948975180

Contents

Acknowledgments

In compiling this work I am indebted to many people, who have assisted in diverse ways and without whom the book would not have been possible. It has been my good fortune to have met several former employees of the railway at Bath, all of whom have given freely of their time and experience. It is from these thoroughly professional and enthusiastic people that the inspiration for the book has come, and to whom it is principally dedicated. Particular thanks are due to:

John Barber	Cliff Smith
Fred Epps	Ted Smith
Norman Good	Frank Staddon
Ron Gray	John Stamp
Joyce Gunning	Harry Starkey
Fred Holmes	Jim Vowles
Ken Palmer	Bernard Ware
Verd Redwood	Norman White

With the historical research I should like to acknowledge help given by the staffs of Bath Reference Library; Bath Record Office; and the Public Record Office, Kew. I extend especial thanks to several photographers who have so generously supplied prints, and whose expertise has provided a valuable historical record in itself:

Hugh Ballantyne	Michael Mensing
Jack Blake	the late Ivo Peters
Robert Coles	Richard Riley
Brian Davis	John Stamp
Philip Kelley	Ronald Toop
Colin Maggs	Michael Tozer

I wish to thank Lens of Sutton; David & Charles (L&GRP Collection); Real Photographs/Ian Allan Ltd; National Railway Museum, York; Bath & West Evening Chronicle; Bath Reference Library (Bath Building Record); the Somerset & Dorset Railway Trust; and Marlene Witts for permission to reproduce pictures held in their collections.

For furnishing various plans, diagrams and details of Green Park and Weston stations, I am grateful to David Snelling of Mouchel & Partners and to Simmons Building Design respectively.

My sincere appreciation goes to my sister Hilary for her skill and forbearance in the massive task of typing the manuscript, while the unlimited access to a word-processor provided by Weeks & Powell Percy is gratefully acknowledged. Finally, and by no means least, I wish to put on record the considerable and vital contribution made by the publishers, Tim Graham and Alan Summers, in editing and arranging the material.

The forebuilding façade in July 1959, displaying the symmetrical, well-proportioned elegance typical of the Classical architectural tradition.
R C Riley

Introduction

In recent years the Somerset & Dorset Joint Railway has become something of a national cause célèbre – and rightly so! This is due in no small measure to the excellent work undertaken by the Somerset & Dorset Railway Trust. Compared with its illustrious neighbour, the Midland Railway's Mangotsfield and Bath Branch is relatively little known, and yet was an equally hardworking component of the railway scene in the city of Bath. Indeed, it had a longer history, just as complex a mode of operation, and as diverse a range of locomotive and stock working as the S&D. In many ways, it was the Midland's line which gave meaning and purpose to the S&D's Bath Extension Railway.

The Midland Railway (Bath and Thornbury) Act received the royal assent on 14th July 1864. Two separate undertakings were being applied for here: the 10-mile long double track Bath Branch from the main line at Mangotsfield, and the 7½-mile long single track Thornbury Branch from Yate. If the engineering works on the Bath Branch were to be unspectacular, they were certainly to be protracted. The approach to the city was relatively straightforward compared with the disruption, demolition and heavy engineering required to put the Great Western Railway through on the south side of the River Avon. Indeed, the Midland Railway was later to encourage development towards it rather than to cut through property which already existed. The impending arrival of a new railway caused much interest in the city. By the spring of 1869 all the river bridges were in position and there was great activity in the vicinity of Locksbrook and Lower Weston. The construction of Weston station and the Station Master's house were well under way, whilst between the level crossing and Osborne Road gangs of navvies were working on the cutting. A contemporary view of the scene in the *Bath Chronicle*, refers to 'a somewhat extensive cutting resounding with the noise of pick and shovel. On either side many men and lads are actively employed in excavating, while others are equally busy in loading numerous wagons, which are constantly being removed by attendant engines to the portion of the line and works adjoining the Bath terminus.'

The double line of rails had been laid throughout, the signalling installed and the intermediate stations at Weston, Bitton and Warmley all but finished (Kelston was in a less advanced state, and in the event opened slightly later). At Green Park, however, things were rather more behind. Although the station was a hive of activity, there was much to be done by way of the finishing touches. The platforms were nearing completion, but the canopy at the street entrance had not even been started, and the train shed was not yet finished. The site manager, Mr Turnbull, was making a sterling effort to get the station ready following the satisfactory outcome of the inspection of the line by the Board of Trade on 6th May. In spite of its incompleteness, the Midland Railway announced that it would open to the public on Wednesday 4th August. At the beginning of the week there was still no furniture in any of the rooms, while the western end of the train shed facing Green Park Mews had yet to receive its ornamental boarding, and thus remained open to the elements. The ironwork of the train shed was still being painted on the Wednesday, as was noted by the local newspaper reporter who was sent along to record the opening: 'The roof....is painted in vermilion, chocolate and white. The painting is still being carried on by means of an ingenious moveable stage, constructed by Mr J Green, the clerk of the works; it is so managed that trains can pass in and out without interfering with it.' Ready or not, the Midland Railway had arrived in Bath. The first train was due out at 7.40 in the morning, but well before then crowds of people were milling about on the platforms and in the street outside. A substantial train, consisting of 1st, 2nd and 3rd class carriages, it departed 8 minutes late, the third class carriages packed with Bathonians, most of whom had booked a penny ride just as far as Weston, thereby enabling them to return on the first service over from Bristol. This train was 10 minutes late – which was just as well, for had it been on time it would have spoiled the double!

The Midland Railway immediately set about publicising the new line and seeking to build up custom at the expense of the neighbouring GWR. This was achieved by instituting special cheap tickets and excursions. On Thursday 16th September 1869 a special was laid on to take the pupils of the Sutcliffe Industrial School to Bristol, where 'they were liberally supplied with creature comforts, and after thoroughly enjoying themselves returned to Bath in the evening. On their way to and from the station the boys marched four abreast, headed by their drum and fife band, and their clean and healthy appearance was the subject of general remark' (*Bath Chronicle*). Two weeks later the company provided an excursion to the Birmingham Great Onion Fair, held in that city's Aston district, the train leaving Bath at 5.30am. In mid November the local press announced that 'the Midland Railway Company have very handsomely acceded to the requisition of the sportsmen of Bristol and Bath, and granted hunting tickets at the single fare for the double journey'.

No sooner had the line settled into its routine than a major new railway initiative burst on the scene. Early in November 1870 it became known that the Somerset & Dorset Railway intended applying to Parliament in the next session for powers to build an extension to their existing line at Evercreech across the Mendip Hills to join the Midland at Bath. The proposed line marked a stormy episode in relations between the Great Western and Midland Railways. The latter's support of the S&D would enable them to drive a deep taproot into territory hitherto regarded as the preserve of the former. Not only did the GWR mount considerable opposition, but local interests and opinion were far from unanimous in support. In spite of these problems, however, the Bill passed through both Houses of Parliament, and The Somerset and Dorset Railway (Extension to the Midland Railway at Bath) Act gained the royal assent on 21st August 1871. Considering the topographical difficulties facing the engineers, the line was built in a remarkably short time, the first train leaving Bath at 7.25 on the morning of Monday 20th July 1874 (with few passengers and little ceremony due to the short notice given of the opening). The presence of the new trains had immediate repercussions on operating procedures at Green Park, as the *Bath Chronicle* noted: 'A considerable number of spectators .... watched the train as it left the departure platform of the Midland terminus, which arrangement caused some little confusion, as passengers for Bristol and the North had, in consequence, to start from the arrival side'.

This book attempts to explain the mode of operation of both the Midland and Somerset & Dorset lines in Bath, and aims to give an insight into the extensive nature of the work performed by a wide range of employees. In addition, it is hoped to highlight a way of railway life which has all but gone, and to explain something of the contribution made by a unique joint railway alliance towards the life of a unique city.

The façade of Green Park station in 1948. Although the railways had been nationalised at the beginning of the year, the canopy continues to display the names of the old companies. L&GRP; courtesy of David & Charles

1. Green Park Station

'Success to the Midland Railway' proclaimed the banner on the flag-bedecked frontage of George Stone's Ale and Porter Stores at the corner of Charles Street and James Street in the city of Bath. The date was Wednesday 4th August 1869; the event the opening of that Company's southernmost terminus station. Although there was not the formal ceremony, bands, ringing of Abbey bells and general holiday atmosphere that had greeted the Great Western Railway 29 years before, the event nonetheless possessed particular significance; for not only did it mark the opening of a new and imposing station in the city, it also heralded the arrival of a completely new railway company.

The realisation of the Midland Railway's long-cherished ambition to reach Bath called for something rather more imposing by way of a station building than a provincial branch line terminus might otherwise expect. The Bath Branch marked a prestigious addition to the company's network, and the architecture of the city itself set certain standards and challenges. It was also, perhaps, in the minds of the directors at Derby to demonstrate that their railway was a worthy rival to Brunel's Great Western across the city centre – a company whose territorial monopoly they had now broken. While the structure had to be functional, it was felt that the façade of the forebuilding on Seymour Street should not only be in sympathy with its immediate surroundings but also enhance them. The design for the buildings was produced by J C Crossley. He chose to adopt the Palladian architectural style for the façade – a genre favoured by John Wood the Elder who designed a number of Bath's Georgian buildings between 1725 and 1754. The contract for the construction

81   BATH. — Midland Railway Station. - LL.

Green Park station in the early 20th century. The pedimented window, top left, belongs to the flat where the refreshment room manageress lived, while that at the opposite end belongs to the room which was part of the Station Master's accommodation in the early years.

Marlene Witts collection

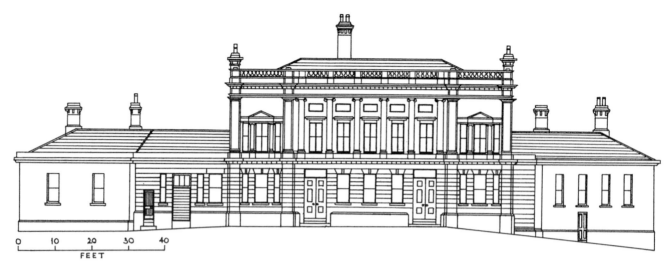

0　10　20　30　40
FEET

of the buildings was awarded to Charles Humphreys of Derby on 26th May 1868, the work to be executed in the local freestone (Bath Stone). The train shed, or overall roof, was put out to tender separately, the contract going to Andrew Handyside & Co of Derby and London. The main roof was to be of wrought iron and glass carried on segmental iron arches, with a subsidiary structure adjoining the north side. Even allowing for inflation, it is a sobering thought that a station which cost less than £16,000 to build from scratch in the 1860s cost something like £1¼ million just to restore in the 1980s.

The station was built in the angle of land between James Street and Green Park Buildings, with the front elevation on the short Seymour Street which connected the other two. A terrace of houses lined both sides of this street prior to the arrival of the railway, and it was to one of these that Jane Austen paid a visit in May 1801 whilst house-hunting: she was not impressed! The western rank of nine houses was pulled down in order to give access to the station. Throughout the book the name Green Park is used when referring to the station, as this is the title most readily called to mind by present-day Bathonians. However, when it opened it was simply known as 'Bath', and remained so designated in railway working timetables and on the platform

The forebuilding, east splay and Departure platform buildings viewed across Seymour Street in July 1960. A recent coat of paint has enhanced the details of the canopy.

R C Riley

nameboards for most of its life. In public timetables, such as Bradshaw, it became customary to give differentiating names where places possessed more than one station. Thus the Great Western appeared as Manvers Street and the Midland as Queen Square – perhaps the adjoining terraces of Green Park Buildings put up between 1791 and 1793 were considered less illustrious than John Wood's more up-market square of 1728–35 some distance away! The name Queen Square did not appear on platform nameboards, and it remained the general practice of locals and railwaymen alike to refer to the terminus as the Midland Station. It was only in June 1951 – Monday 18th to be exact – that the name Green Park was officially bestowed upon the station, with new nameboards being installed on the platforms and Seymour Street canopy to signify the fact.

Intending passengers entered the **booking hall** by way of one of the two entrances from Seymour Street, walking beneath the ornately-decorated glass and wrought-iron canopy (technically, a *porte-cochère*). The high, coffered ceiling of the booking hall was adorned with ornamental plasterwork, whilst the floor comprised large rectangular flagstones. On the south side (left-hand side on entering from the street) were the two windows of the booking office, with their high-bannistered hand-rails in front. The window on the left was used for ticket sales and that on the right for enquiries and telegrams. The windows were set in a wooden screen which ran the full width of the hall, and was supported at either end by a pillar (located on the booking office side). On the opposite side of the hall a door led to offices on both the ground and first floors of the north wing of the forebuilding. To the right of the doorway were wall-mounted noticeboards displaying timetables and posters. The booking hall was a cool place in summer and distinctly cold and draughty in winter. By day it was always somewhat gloomy, with the high windows and canopies both conspiring to shut out direct sunlight from the lower levels. During the hours of darkness it was dimly lit by gas light,

The wooden south wall of the booking hall seen not long before the closure of the station in 1966. The ticket window is on the left, while the word 'Enquiries' has been blanked-out on the other window.

Bath Building Record; courtesy Bath Reference Library

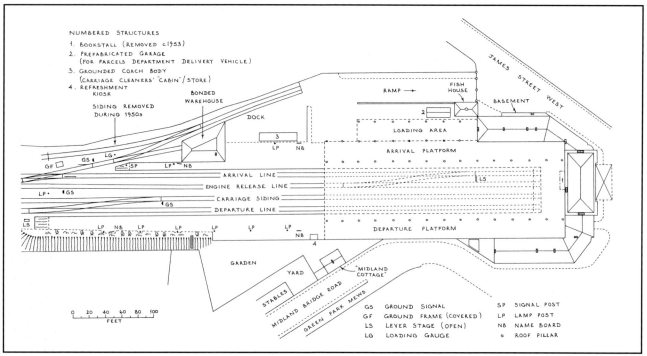

NUMBERED STRUCTURES
1. BOOKSTALL (REMOVED c1953)
2. PREFABRICATED GARAGE (FOR PARCELS DEPARTMENT DELIVERY VEHICLE)
3. GROUNDED COACH BODY (CARRIAGE CLEANERS' "CABIN"/STORE)
4. REFRESHMENT KIOSK

Scale drawing of Green Park station buildings and platform layout

the softly-glowing greenish-yellow pools of light from the few lamps alternating with strong patches of shadow to create quite an atmospheric effect. Looking straight ahead on entering the booking hall, one's eye was drawn to the Train Information Board centred between the two doorways leading to the platforms. With 'arrivals' on one side and 'departures' on the other, it was designed as a grid, each compartment having a surround of wood into which the appropriately inscribed enamelled panels could be slotted.

There were categories for place of origin or destination, time of train and notes/references (such as 'Saturdays Only'). It was an intriguing board to study, but towards the end it was not kept up to date, and so non-existent trains were shown, while the apparently large number of services over the old LMS line showed upon closer examination to be the same few for a whole range of destinations 'Change at Mangotsfield'!

Leaving the booking hall, the passenger walked out on to the platform **concourse**. This was constructed of wooden boards mounted on top of a masonry fascia. Occupying the space at the back of the concourse, between the two doorways, was W H Smith's bookstall. This was a feature of the station from 1907 until the early 1950s and did a sufficiently brisk trade before the last war to warrant a full-time manager and

assistant. Above the right-hand corner of the bookstall, in the centre of the roof span, was the station clock. Once a week a porter was delegated to wind it up; and it is a fact that, contrary to the normal reputation of station clocks, it kept remarkably good time!

The concourse was slightly lower than the platforms, with shallow ramps sloping upwards alongside the buffer stops. That part of the platform surfaces beneath the train shed consisted, like the concourse, of transverse wooden boards for all but the last few yards, the rest of the length out to the ramps being metalled. Looking along the tracks, the longer of the two platforms was on the left. In the days before the Somerset & Dorset appeared on the scene it was known as the Departure platform – for obvious reasons! This name continued to be used long after trains worked into and out of either platform. Some railwaymen referred to it as the 'long platform'; only from 1951 did it display an identification board proclaiming it as 'Platform 1' (and the 'Arrival platform' as 'Platform 2'). When the station opened, the platforms were of equal length (450 feet) but were soon extended. The presence of a Carriage/Horse Dock siding and line into the Bonded Stores on the Arrival side prevented that platform being lengthened to the Avon river bridge as on the Departure side. The river prevented any further extension, so that even the

A busy scene on the Departure platform around the turn of the century. The glazing in the train shed was destroyed in the Baedeker raids of April 1942, when many bombs fell on nearby streets but missed the station itself.   M J Tozer collection

long platform was only able to accommodate nine bogie coaches and a tender engine.

Although this was adequate for most of the trains using the station, the 'Pines' and summer expresses would overhang by three or four vehicles – making life difficult for even the most eagle-eyed train spotter! When it was known that incoming trains would be too long for the platforms, guards were instructed to walk through the rear coaches and request passengers who wished to alight at Bath to move along the train. During 1944 a plan was drawn up to extend the Departure platform across the river and so increase its capacity. War-time exigencies and the cost of modifying the bridge meant that it was a non-starter.

Passengers were informed as to which platform to go to by means of a slotted-post indicator at the front centre of the concourse. The time of departure was chalked up on a small wooden-framed black slate near the top of the post, while an arm-style board containing details of the stations served was slotted beneath, pointing to the appropriate platform. The boards carried pre-arranged details of all the regular services, which in Western Region days were written in cream letters on a brown background. They were kept in a rack at the base of the post and attended by one of the porters. One commonly used for Midland departures read: TRAIN TO BRISTOL. CHANGE AT MANGOTSFIELD FOR GLOUCESTER, BIRMINGHAM AND THE NORTH. Notice boards advising excursions, amendments to train times and the like were sometimes to be found near the indicator, the chalking of the boards and the indicator being delegated to porters with neat handwriting. Between 1956 and 1962 there was also a train-announcing system, but this was generally only used on summer Saturdays or for special announcements regarding late running of trains. The microphone for the system was in the ticket collector's hut on the Departure platform. A porter with clear diction would be put on this job, and it was always fascinating to hear the list of far-away places being reeled off.

Spanning the two platforms and intervening four tracks was the **train shed**. The 292-foot long structure was supported by 15 slightly tapered octagonal piers, the outside faces of which were set five feet back from the platform edges. This gave a main central span of 66 feet, with the

The Train/Platform Indicator photographed in 1965. The reduction in variety of services by this date is reflected in the paucity of boards stored at the base. The carriage tail-lamps seen on platform 2 are outside the doorway leading to the suite of staff rooms.

Bath Building Record; courtesy Bath Reference Library

Looking west from the buffer-stops at the end of the 19th century. Trains could always depart from either platform, but until the provision of a set of facing points by the signalbox in 1892, all incoming trains had to work into the Arrival platform, as in this picture. Note the interesting period rolling stock.   Marlene Witts collection

distance between rail level and the soffit of the arch being 41 feet. The arched iron ribs of the main portion of the roof above the tracks were surmounted by three stepped top-light smoke ventilators, glazed on the tops but open at the sides. Side aisles with a span of 23 feet covered the platforms; the roof here was timbered. An additional, slightly shorter overall roof adjoined the north side of the train shed to serve as a cabman's shelter and covered loading area. Most of the glass in the roof was destroyed in the blitz of April 1942, when a stack of bombs fell on Seymour Street and Green Park Buildings East. As part of the renovation of the station undertaken on behalf of the firm of J Sainsbury in 1981/2, the roof has been restored to its former glory.

One feature of note on the Departure platform for a great many years was a working model of Stephenson's *Rocket*. Housed in a glass case and mounted on a metal stand, its aim was to raise money for a railway charity at Derby. By inserting a penny in a slot, the locomotive's wheels would turn and the piston rod move back and forth. This fascinated youngsters, some of whom found that a strategically aimed blow with a clenched fist on the underside of the case had the same result as the penny. The platform staff got wise to this and arranged two projecting screws in an appropriate place: the effect was immediate! The more determined youngsters soon circumvented this when they found that a blow with a raised knee on the front of the frame made the model work; but as this was rather more obvious, and possibly painful, it was better to pay!

The Arrival platform possessed two buildings which were not part of the main suite of rooms : the **Bonded Stores** and **Fish House**. The **Bonded Stores** was a substantial ashlar stone building with ecclesiastical-style windows, and was situated at the river bridge end of the platform. It was used by HM Customs & Excise as a store and office. Vaults ran beneath the platform, the small barred windows belonging to these being seen at intervals along the platform face. Reached by a staircase next to the office, there were 27 cellars –

15

On Saturday 10th May 1958 the Gloucestershire Railway Society ran an excursion over the S&D, the first time a diesel multiple unit worked over that line. Features to note on the opposite platform include the cellar windows in the platform face; the parked cars beneath the cabmen's shelter; and the garage for the Parcels Department's town delivery van. Notice also the train announcement loudspeaker in the top right-hand corner of the picture.   Lens of Sutton

each measuring 26' 9¾" by 8' – so that the end wall of No 27 was in line with the eighth pillar in from the end of the train shed. Box vans containing wines and spirits were propelled into the store, uncoupled and securely locked in by the heavy wooden door which closed across the track. Barrels were conveyed to the relevant cellar by means of a rail-mounted trolley, a 2' 6½"-gauge tramway running the length of the central aisle of the vaults (the rails set in a concrete strip on an otherwise brick floor).

A large noticeboard on the east wall of the building proclaimed it as Bonded Stores No 2 (No 1 was located on the former Great Western main line in Bath West goods yard on the Lower Bristol Road). The officer in charge of the stores from the early 1950s was Mr J Fenwick. By 1960 it was rare for the stores to receive supplies by rail, and soon the track possessed that dark, almost grainy rust indicative of a long period of disuse. The attractive building survived for a few years beyond closure, but its redundant position within

the car park which succeeded the trains finally saw it succumb to the demolition men.

The two-roomed **Fish House** was a well-proportioned, airy and attractive stone building situated at the back of the cabman's shelter and adjoining the west end of the platform buildings. Designed to keep fish fresh in the days before electric refrigeration, this function had ceased by the mid 1930s. The occasional crate continued to be received at the Parcels Office, but in the main fish came into Bath by way of the Great Western. The driver of the Parcels Department's motor delivery van put the larger of the two rooms to good use, however, in the 1940s by keeping spares for his vehicle there (while the van itself was housed overnight in a large prefabricated garage erected immediately to the west of the Fish House). The room was also used to store a whole range of bits and pieces used by the station staff, and also to stack empty pigeon baskets. The smaller of the two rooms was used as a base for the passenger guards. Fortunately, the building

Ivatt 2-6-2 tank No 41243 passes the Bonded Stores as it sets off with the 5.45pm stopping train to Bristol. The sun highlights the Abbey tower and, to the right, the steeple of the original Holy Trinity church in James Street West. Built between 1819 and 1822, the main church building was gutted by fire in the Blitz, and the steeple was demolished soon after this picture was taken.   July 1959   R C Riley

survives today – beautifully cleaned and restored – and serves as the office for the Green Park shopping and market development.

Behind the bonded stores was the **Carriage and Horse Dock**, the siding which served it passing to the north of the stores at an angle and thereby giving that building its distinctive wedge-shaped appearance. An end-loading facility was also available here. In the days when horses for Bath Races were conveyed to the city in railway horse-boxes, any animals arriving from the Midlands or the North were dealt with in this bay. It was once a common sight to see stable lads leading horses from the station up Lansdown Hill to the race-course. The Dock had its own direct access to James Street West by means of a wide, sloping approach road. The high, wooden double gates and separate pedestrian entrance – which remain in use to this day – were kept open all night to allow Post Office vans to reach the platform with mail bags for the 2.40am train to Bournemouth,

and also for early turn staff arriving for work. Indeed, the main use of the Dock siding was for stabling vans for the 'Mail' and also for other parcels traffic.

Throughout the station's 97-year life, the platforms were lit by gas. The original lamps consisted of a cast-iron post surmounted by a large square-tapered glass case whose ventilator was decorated with a spiked finial. In 1953/4 they were replaced by the ubiquitous hemispherical glass lamp cases with enamelled caps. On the Arrival platform the new lamp cases were attached directly above the post by two side-mounted metal stays, whilst on the Departure platform the familiar swan-neck attachment was used. In both cases the original posts were retained. It was the job of one of the porters to light and extinguish the lamps every day, this being done by pulling a chain hanging from either end of the centrally-pivoted valve bar attached to the pilot light. From time to time

An elegant rebuilt Johnson 'Small' 4-4-0 loco waits with an S&D service in the mid-1920s. Notices and timetables for the LMS and S&DJR were displayed on separate boards, as may be judged from the mounting on the opposite platform.

L&GRP; courtesy of David and Charles

they required attention: cases needed to be cleaned, damaged mantles replaced, and pipes and valve gear checked or repaired. This was the job of the gas fitters, who had their cabin in the Midland Bridge yard. Latterly, this work was centralised at Bristol, and the gasman, as he was called, regularly travelled over to Bath. Indeed, his visits became more frequent as the system began to age and gas leaks became a constant problem. The main concentration of pipes and control valves was in one of the cellars beneath the west end of the Arrival platform. To gain access to this the gasman had to secure the permission of the officer employed in the Bonded Stores to go through his building and down the steps there to reach the vaults. When he had been down there for some time, the platform staff reckoned that he was always rather unsteady when he reappeared, being mildly intoxicated by the fumes from the stored spirits! Even today the walls of the cellars are coated in places with a dark film, resulting from the alcoholic vapours which permeated the air for several decades. The rails along which the barrels were run also remain *in situ*.

The cellars were a notable, if hidden, feature of the station, underlying all the rooms of the main buildings, most of the Arrival platform and half the Departure platform. The contract drawing of 1868 shows the provision of a kitchen, pantry and wine and beer cellars beneath the east end of the Arrival side platform and buildings for the refreshment room above, together with a barrel-rolling area from James Street. In the event the refreshment rooms were built on the other platform, and so the vaults were put to a variety of non-specific uses such as storing vast quantities of old notices and paperwork generated by the various offices above, and a wide range of materials used in the day-to-day running of the station (Station Stores). The station coal was stored in the cellar beneath the Station Master's office with a trap door and shute at the back of the platform, while lamp oil was kept in an adjacent vault. Some of the rooms had doors and/or windows giving out on to a street basement. On the Departure side, coal and bulky comestibles for the refreshment rooms were kept at the east end (with a trap door permitting direct deliveries from Midland Bridge Road) while the cellars between the Gents and the end of the train shed – with access to the street – were rented out to private firms. During the 1950s and 60s they played host to Bath Metal Plating Co and a firm of motor factors (first, F W Norman and then Spafax).

A few yards along Midland Bridge Road from the last of the cellars was Midland Cottage and the **Stables**. As the volume of traffic handled by the railway grew in the 1890s, so too did the number of horses needed to deal with the carrying to and from the city, yard and station. The existing stable accommodation provided by the Midland Railway was expanded in response to this, and in 1901 the company built a house at the station end of the block as a residence for the horsekeeper (later designated stableman). Known simply as The Cottage in the early days, it came to be known as Midland Bridge Cottage and finally Midland Cottage. The position of horsekeeper was held, in turn, by Messrs Metcalfe, Godfrey and Sargood. Oliver Sargood

held the job for over 20 years, but by the mid-1940s had fewer animals in his charge as the internal combustion engine was increasingly replacing traditional horse power. His successor, Harry Wiltshire, was one of the yard draymen and remained in the house to and beyond closure. The whole complex was demolished eventually to make room for Sainsbury's lorry delivery area.

Green Park closed its doors to passengers for the last time in March 1966. In many places disused stations become scenes of dereliction and creeping decay and for a time it seemed as though Bath was to be no exception. The obvious architectural merit and aesthetic value possessed by both the station buildings and train shed, however, means that Green Park has a story beyond closure. Indeed, just a few weeks before it closed the Bath Victorian Society, concerned lest it be demolished, mooted the idea of its possible conversion into an exhibition hall. The desire to preserve the generic Georgian identity of the city

The Midland Railway's stables at Green Park, with Midland Bridge in the background. The original stable block is nearest the camera.   June 1966   Colin G Maggs

centre from the ever-mounting pressures of road traffic directly threatened the station's continued existence. Bath City Council had given Professor Colin Buchanan the brief of analysing the city's communications problems and suggesting possible remedies. His report was published in 1966 and entailed the demolition of the station in order to build a dual carriageway feeder road into a vast interchange on the site of the Midland Bridge goods yard and motive power depot (linked with a tunnel under the city centre). Arguments raged for years over the merits and demerits of the scheme, and in the meantime the Council had turned much of the site into a car park. Concern over the physical state of the train shed caused the entrance through the booking hall to be closed, and as the years passed, the buildings began to deteriorate. Following local pressure, which culminated in representations being made to the Department of the Environment, the station gained the status of a Grade 2 Listed Building. This might arrest any plans for demolition, but could not prevent the continuing decline in the fabric of the building. By 1978 the situation seemed to be in a hopeless deadlock: the Council was stuck with a decaying, unprofitable shell; various pressure groups who wished ardently to retain the structure lacked the necessary funds; while interested organisations with the financial wherewithal had their plans frozen pending the outcome of a public enquiry (the Council had applied for Listed Building Consent to enable them to pull it down). The abandonment of the Buchanan Plan lifted the blight on the area, while local people continued to have ideas for the station, proposals ranging from a concert hall and conference centre to offices. The Council favoured a hotel development, while two well-known retail chains expressed a strong interest.

A breakthrough finally came at the end of 1979. The supermarket chain of J Sainsbury's reached an agreement with Bath City Council, who owned the station, and British Rail's Property Board, who owned most of the land to the west of the river. Part of the deal involved the restoration of the station buildings and train shed, this work being done in 1981/2. The task was both extensive and expensive, but the result is magnificent: with stonework cleaned and train shed reglazed, the platforms once again echo to the sound of footsteps – albeit to shoppers walking to and from their cars rather than trains!

Looking into the station across the southernmost of the twin cross-braced structures which comprise bridge 44 (over the River Avon). In the 1930s its weight restriction was eased by the addition of strengthening plates to the girders. This half of the bridge is still in use today as the vehicular access to Sainsbury's car park. The blunt, wedge-shaped bulk of the Bonded Stores is seen behind the signal.   26.4.59   P J Kelley

2. Green Park People

Many different functions were performed at Green Park, some of which were more obvious than others to the travelling public, but all of which were equally necessary to ensure the smooth day-to-day running of the station.

Station Master. The person most readily associated with railway stations in general was the Station Master. He was much more than a mere figure-head, being responsible for co-ordinating the work of the station on a daily basis, and for superintending its operation. All the paperwork pertaining to Green Park landed on his desk, from the working of trains, through amendments to Rules & Regulations, staff vacancies and promotions, requisitioning of sundry materials, to census information on passenger returns. Some of this work was duly delegated. His work brought him into contact with the various departments in his ambit and through this official contact with his staff, he developed a welfare function. His jursidiction extended to what might be called 'station limits', these being marked by Bath Junction's up S&D/down Midland home signals. He would only be seen by passengers during an occasional appearance on the platform: generally for the twice-daily visit of the 'Pines Express', the station's prestige train, for which he wore his gold-braided hat.

The first three Station Masters – Isaac Brooks, Samuel Halford and Charles Radway – all lived in at the station during each of their short terms of office. Viewed from the street, the right-hand wing of the forebuilding made up their territory, the ground floor being the office and the upper floor the living accommodation. In 1877 all of these rooms were required as offices following the transfer of the administrative headquarters of the S&DJR from Glastonbury. For the next 30 years men lived in tied company dwellings, for the most part in Hopmead House on the Lower Bristol Road in East Twerton. The new office accommodation was provided on the Arrival platform, in the suite of rooms at the top of the ramp.

As authority figures, Station Masters were respected rather than popular, having to maintain a certain distance. For example, during Arthur Exton's 10-year tenure from 1927 he certainly made an impression upon all who worked at the station. A man of few words, he possessed a definite presence; indeed, he was treated almost reverentially, staff making sure that they were seen to be busy when he appeared on the platform.

The railway at Bath possessed almost a family spirit. In any organisation employing hundreds of people there were bound to be grumbles and disagreements, but one of the most striking features at Green Park was the comradeship which existed within and between the various grades. Men had established ways of doing things, as well as unwritten rules, facts which were not understood by outsiders when they first moved to the city. This is illustrated by the incident of the 'Templecombe Apples' in the late 1950s. At the end of the growing season, the farmer who owned the orchard near Templecombe station took several boxes of apples to the station to be distributed among the railwaymen both there and along the line. Those ear-marked for the loco men of Bath were placed near the signalbox to await collection. They were loaded into the luggage compartment of one of the up local passenger trains, and word was sent along the line that they were on the way, so that when the train arrived at Bath a small group of men would be waiting to collect the largess and carry it to the shed. The sight of the men waiting around puzzled the new Station Master, and he asked them what they were doing. When they explained, they were duly informed that they would have to pay carriage on the apples, and were forbidden to take the boxes until payment had been made. His strictures were ignored! Arriving back at the motive power depot with their booty, the men informed Shed Master Morris of the contretemps and he went over to the station to 'talk the Station Master round'. This proved to be a difficult task and took a long time, but eventually he was won over – and even got some of the apples!

Green Park's last Station Master was George Robertson. His 50 years on the railway had taken him all over the country. Beginning as a telegraph clerk on the former Caledonian Railway in his home city of Perth, he transferred to the North British Railway in 1918 and worked at a number of stations in Scotland. In 1932 he moved to Grimsby, and five years later took up his first post as Station Master at Woodhead, an

The S&DJR Head Office staff in front of 13 and 14 Green Park in January 1928. Dissolution of the Head Office began in February of that year with various staff being stationed along the line from that time and the Accountant's staff moving to Waterloo Station. Second from the left in the third row back is Jack Loder who was killed in the S&D yard when loco 89 ran away on 20.11.1929.

Somerset and Dorset Railway Trust

isolated moorland location by the Derbyshire entrance to the famous Pennine tunnel. Promotion took him to jobs in Yorkshire, Nottinghamshire, Cheshire, Cambridgeshire and North London before his final posting to Green Park in 1960 (where he succeeded Bob Pearman). George retired in April 1965. For the remaining months of the station's life, it was administered by Bath's first Area Manager, from his office at the city's Spa station, the Station Master there, Albert Stowe, having also retired the same month. The Area Manager was Raymond Counsell, previously the Agent at the Western Region's Bath West goods yard on the Lower Bristol Road.

Station Master's Clerk. To assist the Station Master with the work load at busier locations, a salaried official was employed. At Green Park, his office adjoined that of the Station Master, both rooms sharing the same door onto the platform. While in a sense he could be seen as a deputy to the Station Master, a major part of his work at Green Park was dealing with staff matters such as the drawing up of rosters for the guards; invoicing staff privilege tickets and passes; dealing with requests for uniforms; and processing the more routine paperwork. Any correspondence with the public was also part of his remit. Between 1953 and 1963 this job was done by Ken Palmer, who then moved on to do similar work at the Spa station.

Booking Office Staff. The men who worked in the office were, like the Station Master's clerk, salaried employees. There were two booking clerks, one working an early, the other a late shift. The office opened at 6.00am and closed soon after 7.00pm on weekdays. On Sundays, a split shift was worked from 7.30 to 10.30am and from 6.30 to 9.30pm. Tickets would be sold at the beginning of these two sessions, the man remaining on duty for enquiries. The clerks covered the Sunday work on an alternating basis. If platform staff wished to apply for a vacancy in the booking office, they had to make a formal application and sit a written examination. The topics covered in the test included arithmetic, general knowledge, geography (mainly restricted to Britain and with a distinct railway bias), and an essay.

The only access the staff had to the booking office was through the door in the party wall between that room and the adjoining Parcels Office. Inside the booking office the fittings were gloriously Victorian, the only concession to the 20th century being a couple of electric lights. Behind the ticket/enquiry windows a sturdy counter ran the full length of the room, with extensive racks of tickets above and cupboards below. Green Park had an amazing range of destinations permanently in stock, due in the main to the nationwide travel undertaken by employees of the Admiralty and children at the various boarding schools in and around the city. The cupboards contained a range of items, collectively known as lock stock. The centre of the room was occupied by a large table while another table, that of the chief clerk, was situated beneath the window looking out onto Seymour Street. The office contained two safes, one for the chief clerk and the other for the two booking clerks.

The booking clerks came under the supervision of the **Chief Clerk**, who worked normal office hours. One of his daily duties was to take the station's takings to the National Provincial Bank at the top of Milsom Street. Regulations stated that two people were to make this journey, for security reasons. This was done in the lull following the departure of the 10.10am stopping train to Bristol and before passengers began arriving to buy tickets for the northbound 'Pines'. The second man would sometimes be the Station Master, but if he was otherwise engaged this duty would devolve on either the booking clerk, or if he was busy as well, the station foreman. The men left the station at precisely the same time every day – 10.30am – and always took exactly the same route, via Queen Square to Milsom Street. Such minimal concern for security would not be advisable today!

The chief clerk was responsible for completing the Weekly Revenue Account sheets. These were filled out separately for the S&D and LMS in the days before nationalisation, although both sheets were sent to Bristol. As far as the workforce was concerned, the most important job of the chief clerk was the payment of wages. This followed a time-honoured routine. Although wages were paid on Thursdays, the global wage-bill had to be worked out in advance and the figure sent up to Derby, who in turn forwarded a cheque to the Bath booking office for the required amount. The cheque arrived on a Wednesday, was paid into the station's account at the National Provincial, and the cash withdrawn. The individual wage packets were then made up at the station; only in the last few years, when Bristol was responsible for the wages, did the money come to Bath ready packeted. The Station Master's clerk joined the chief clerk on pay day to help him check all the individual sums of money. This was a mammoth operation, with the large table in the middle of the room being cleared to make space. Men at the motive power depot were paid from the small wages hut by the lane leading from Victoria Bridge Road. The chief clerk plus a minder carried the money from the booking office in a Gladstone bag, arriving at the depot for noon and remaining there for two hours to pay the men at a time of day when many were either coming on or going off duty. Men who could not report to the wages office between these times had to wait until 6.00pm, from which time they could go to the booking office window and present their brass pay tokens in exchange for their money. When the chief clerk arrived back from the shed, it was the turn of the guards and signalmen to be paid, the men reporting to the booking office window. The platform staff were issued with numbered brass pay tokens by the station foreman; these were handed in at the window in exchange for the pay packet. The tokens were placed in a stout wooden box and later on, a tally would be made against a ledger of names. The Goods Agent was responsible for paying his staff, and worked independently of the passenger station.

The last chief clerk at Green Park was Bob Gilham. Living in Wincanton he commuted by train every weekday. Latterly he shared the work with only one booking clerk who covered the early turn. As both a professional railwayman and a regular rail-user, he was one of the more vociferous opponents of the station's closure!

Every now and again auditors would descend, unannounced, on the booking office. The grey-suited individuals were not pleased when they turned up one day and were able to walk straight into the room – according to the rules the door should always be kept locked! Their visitations were unpopular more for their manner than any error that they might find, and when the Station Master learned of their arrival he always found some pressing reason to walk out to the Station signalbox, or anywhere, to keep out of their way!

By far the biggest earner on a day-to-day basis was the northbound 'Pines Express', especially during public holidays and the summer months. Sometimes the queue at the ticket window stretched right back through the booking hall and out into the street. When this happened, the booking clerk had to ask the chief clerk to help

out. He would open the enquiries window and work from there. During the 1950s it was commonplace to take £500 or more in about 20 minutes.

Most of the ticket sales were for more local journeys, and it is interesting to look at a range of day-return fares available from Green Park in 1962, the year in which the 'Pines' was routed away from the station:

Bitton	2/–	Midford	1/4
Oldland Common	2/3	Wellow	1/10
Warmley	2/6	Shoscombe	2/1
Mangotsfield	2/9	Radstock	2/6
Staple Hill	3/–	Midsomer Norton	2/9
Fishponds	3/–	Chilcompton	3/3
Bristol	3/–	Binegar	3/9
Yate	4/3	Masbury Halt	4/–
Gloucester	9/–	Shepton Mallet	4/9

The last significant demand for tickets came before the two closely-timed evening departures: to Bristol, with connections at Mangotsfield for the North, and to Bournemouth, leaving at 7.03 and 7.05pm respectively. With the departure of the Bournemouth train, the booking office closed on Mondays to Fridays. With only the 10.25pm stopping train to Templecombe requiring possible ticket sales there was no need to keep the office open. Before the booking clerk left, he gave a £1 float and excess-pad to a porter to deal with any late ticketless passengers. This porter had a key to the booking office where he put any takings and paperwork before locking up and going home. On Saturdays, the booking clerk stayed on duty to do the weekly account and so the office remained open: there was also an extra departure on Saturday evenings, namely the 9.45 to Bristol.

There may only have been one evening departure from Green Park after 7.05, but there were four arrivals: from Bristol at 7.44 and 8.50, from Binegar at 8.00 and from Bournemouth at 10.21. Tickets collected by the guard from passengers on these trains were handed to the station foreman who put them in a box in the porters' room until they could be taken to the booking office the next morning.

Booking the end of term arrangements for the boarding schools in the area was a major undertaking. The bursar of each school would send a list of requirements a few days before the end of term. As most of the schools finished at

The smartly dressed station staff in Edwardian times, posing in front of a variety of cabs. Note also the Midland Railway's horse-drawn parcels waggon and both companies' display boards.
Colin G Maggs collection

more or less the same time, there would be 300 names or more in total, with destinations all over the country (the GWR Station received similar lists). Preparations began a day or so before the end of term as everything had to be ready, checked and paid for by the requisite day. Once the tickets had been made out and costed, the school was notified and it in turn despatched a cheque for the required amount. This worked well providing schools did not change their minds. All too often though phone calls would be received asking for changes to be made, as parents would be collecting a child – or not, as the case might be! This caused the booking office staff a good deal of trouble. At 5.00 on the evening before the tickets were required, the booking clerk closed the ticket window and, together with the chief clerk, went through all the ticket details, hoping that everything tallied.

School traffic was predictable and lucrative, if periodic. Admiralty traffic was also a large revenue earner. It was obviously smaller in volume at any one time, but was spread right through the year and was often long-distance.

Details of the ticket requirements were telephoned into the booking office in advance, so that the tickets would be ready when needed.

Parcels Department. The Parcels Office at Green Park was always a busy place. The original office had been located on the Arrival platform, but as part of the drive initiated in 1930 to effect economies, the decision was taken to move personnel out of offices at 13 and 14 Green Park Buildings (acquired in 1902 and 1877 respectively, and which dealt with commercial matters). The slimmed down operation was now wholly concentrated at the station. This move entailed a major reshuffle in the use of a number of rooms and involved the Parcels Department moving into the suitably modified former Ladies Third Class Waiting Room, fronting the concourse at the end of the Departure platform. With a total of four waiting rooms in the original station building, economies here were obviously easy to effect. Indeed, this Ladies Room had already been altered once before, having begun life as the general Second Class Waiting Room, its redesignation following the Midland Railway's

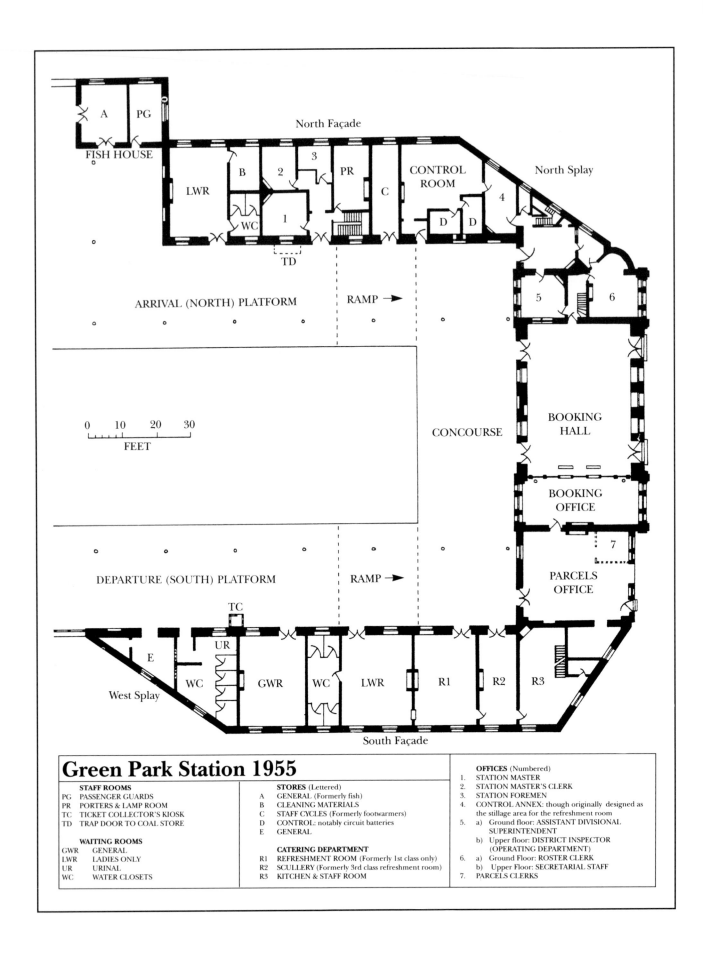

Green Park Station 1955

STAFF ROOMS
PG   PASSENGER GUARDS
PR   PORTERS & LAMP ROOM
TC   TICKET COLLECTOR'S KIOSK
TD   TRAP DOOR TO COAL STORE

WAITING ROOMS
GWR GENERAL
LWR LADIES ONLY
UR   URINAL
WC   WATER CLOSETS

STORES (Lettered)
A   GENERAL. (Formerly fish)
B   CLEANING MATERIALS
C   STAFF CYCLES (Formerly footwarmers)
D   CONTROL: notably circuit batteries
E   GENERAL

CATERING DEPARTMENT
R1 REFRESHMENT ROOM (Formerly 1st class only)
R2 SCULLERY (Formerly 3rd class refreshment room)
R3 KITCHEN & STAFF ROOM

OFFICES (Numbered)
1. STATION MASTER
2. STATION MASTER'S CLERK
3. STATION FOREMEN
4. CONTROL ANNEX: though originally designed as the stillage area for the refreshment room
5. a) Ground floor: ASSISTANT DIVISIONAL SUPERINTENDENT
    b) Upper floor: DISTRICT INSPECTOR (OPERATING DEPARTMENT)
6. a) Ground Floor: ROSTER CLERK
    b) Upper Floor: SECRETARIAL STAFF
7. PARCELS CLERKS

abolition of the second class category in 1875. Before German bombs blew out the window and roof glass in 1942, the waiting and refreshment rooms had their designations indicated in embossed window glass.

With the Parcels Office in the south wing of the station, it became practical to provide direct access to the street, and it was now that the staff and van-delivery doors were put in (these were recently modified to form the pedestrian entrance to the present-day Green Park market and Sainsbury's supermarket). Members of the public visiting the office called at the main, high double doorway leading from the platform concourse (in later years, the smaller of the two street doorways was kept permanently locked). A bell-push summoned someone from the office, which was always full of parcels of all shapes and sizes, together with left luggage and items of lost property. Much of the south wall was taken up with shelves, while a weighing machine took up part of the crowded floor area. The staff had a well-tried system – known only to them – for creating order out of seeming chaos! The office hours were from 6.00am until 10.00pm, Mondays to Saturdays. The men who worked here came under the supervision of the **chief parcels clerk**, who worked conventional office hours. His staff consisted of a **parcels clerk**, **parcels porter** and a **junior parcels porter** on each of the two shifts. Their work involved the constant sorting and moving of parcels; getting them ready for specific trains; storing them for collection by the public, or for dispatch by the road delivery vehicles. When the office closed for the night, a parcels porter remained on duty for a further hour to deal with the 10.15pm 'Perishables' to Derby and with any traffic from the last passenger train up from Templecombe (10.21 in Bath).

Two parcels **vanmen** were employed at the station. In the inter-war years one man operated a petrol vehicle for delivery to the more distant suburbs and outlying districts, whilst the other drove a horse-drawn waggon for addresses in and around the city centre.

A glass and wood screen in the north-east corner of the main room served as the clerks' office, the chief clerk's desk looking out onto the street. The chief clerk kept his accounts separately from the booking office and also dealt independently with the bank. However, he regularly used to visit the booking office in order to get change, and so the connecting door was not kept locked. The parcels staff worked entirely within their own territory, the handling of parcels to and from trains being the responsibility of the platform staff. One of the well-known parcels porters of later years was Walt Morgan. He transferred to Green Park from his previous post as porter at Weston when that station closed in 1953. He was a keen gardener and had lovingly tended the extensive borders at Weston, an activity he now undertook at Green Park. In addition to keeping the flower border on the Departure platform, he also mounted floral displays on the concourse behind the buffer stops. His efforts went a long way towards gaining the station an award in the Best Kept Station competition, and continued a long-established tradition. In earlier years, one of the passenger shunters, Harry James, with others, expended much time and energy on the displays. A passenger was so impressed by them that Harry was told he could order whatever he wanted – within reason – and the bill would be paid. This offer was gratefully accepted!

Within a year or so of the station's opening in 1869, the Midland Railway Company set up a town office for the receiving of parcels and goods at 24 New Bond Street (the GWR's receiving office, incidentally, was at No 20). The facility also dealt with passenger enquiries and ticket sales. The office had its own permanent agent, while one of the junior parcels porters at the station was required to attend to the cleaning of the rooms first thing in the morning. In 1924 the LMS moved the office to 5 Union Street. Nine years later the company decided to discontinue running an independent town facility, in a drive to effect economies, and instead shared an agency with the GWR at 20 New Bond Street. This office was now a much busier place and so employed two agents; one to deal with passengers and parcels, and one with goods.

The Parcels Office also employed an **excess luggage collector** whose job was to check the weight of luggage against that actually paid for, and stick 'excess' labels on those which had been undercharged. Much of the work in the office concerned 'left luggage' or 'luggage in advance'. Mention has already been made of the sudden increase in traffic occasioned by the end of term at the various boarding schools in the area. This thrice-yearly event had a much more bulky manifestation in the Parcels Office, especially at the end of the summer term when everything had to be taken home at the beginning of the long holiday. Great volumes of trunks and cases began to arrive at the office, and had to be got ready for dispatch by the appropriate train. The necessity of handling large volumes in a short space of time made it impractical to send the railway's own van to the school: it would have to make too many trips. Thus, for example, for many years the removals firm of A G Workman of Claude Avenue conveyed the luggage from Monkton Combe School in one of their lorries. Some of the trunks from this school were so heavy that one former porter remarked that the boys must have been taking home a whole year's collection of completed woodwork projects!

Platform Staff. Responsibility for the areas of the station used by the public devolved upon the porters, supervision of whom was performed by a foreman. One foreman covered the early turn and another the late. They directed the work of the porters, deciding on such matters as sweeping of platforms, cleaning of waiting rooms, posting notices and all the other minutiae necessary to the running of a station. They were also in charge of the carriage cleaners, passenger shunters and station stores, the latter involving everything from the issue of signalmen's dusters to chalk for the notice boards. The last two foremen, both with many years in the job, were Clement Bartholomew and Arthur Rowett. Their office was across the passage from the Station Master. As with the booking clerks, these men took it in turns to work the Sunday split shift, for which they were paid time and three-quarters!

Station foreman Clement Bartholomew retired in 1962 and was presented with a clock by his colleagues. They are, from left to right, Bernard Ware, Bert Ilot, opposite-turn foreman Arthur Rowett, two junior porters, Clement Bartholomew, Norman White and Station Master George Robertson.   Bath & Wilts Chronicle & Herald

Porters were often given a specific responsibility such as lighting the lamps or collecting tickets from people detraining from expresses in the summer. Also, if the booking office staff were very busy they would refer passengers' enquiries to the porter on this last-named duty. During the last war, Joyce Ainsworth was one of a few women recruited to the station staff to ease the manpower shortage. She was known to all as Rose, because she always wore a buttonhole in her uniform tunic, and stayed on after 1945 to become a familiar figure at the ticket barrier. She and her colleague, Gladys Jones, were mainly responsible for the Ladies Rooms, one of which was on each platform.

Of all the tasks a porter had to do, one of the most hectic was the handling of parcels. The favourite train for dispatching those destined for the Midlands and the North was the 'Pines'. However, the men had to be quick, for as soon as the appointed time of departure was reached, the guard whistled up 'train ready to leave'. Luggage doors were hurriedly closed and the right away given. Any parcels which had not been loaded in time were left on the platform.

In its British Railways days, Green Park had six passenger porters, three per shift Mondays to Saturdays, and three shift porters who worked consecutive eight-hour shifts on weekdays and also took it in turns to cover the Sunday split shift. Because the shift porters were called upon to assist the passenger shunters and perform additional duties, they were paid slightly more than their six colleagues. In later years, this grade was staffed by George West, Percy Noad and Bert Ilot. Two of the passenger porters also received slightly higher pay for their additional responsibility as **lampmen**. The lamps which they tended were not the gas lamps at the station but the paraffin lamps illuminating the signals and the tail lamps of the carriages. The signalmen were far too busy to leave their boxes to replenish the signal lamps and clean the coloured spectacle lenses on the signal arms/discs. The white paraffin used for this job was kept in corrugated iron lamp huts near the signalboxes. This work was always done on Tuesdays, the oil lasting through the full seven days. To save walking back to the lamp hut between attending each signal, the lampmen would very often hang up to 12 lamp cases on a long shunter's pole and carry them round on a circuit. This was especially the case at Bath Junction where the signals were well spaced. The Junction's S&D up distant signal was

the farthest one to be attended, being right out near the Co-op siding in Oldfield Park. On a pleasant day in spring or summer the lampman might decide to walk out there, but he would often opt to go out on the banking engine of the 11.20 freight to Evercreech, dropping off on the way back from Combe Down tunnel. Before the closure of Weston station in 1953 a porter did the signal lamps there. After that date, the work was transferred to the Green Park men. The lamp room at the station was off the porters' room, and it was here that the carriage tail lamps were dealt with. The lamp oil was kept in the cellar beneath.

One of the annual rituals at Green Park was the arrival and stowing of the station coal. A requisition for coal was sent each year to Gloucester and towards the end of September or early October the allocation would arrive, attached to one of the regular freight workings via Westerleigh. The delivery to the station was made last thing on a Saturday night. The yard shunting engine would propel a loaded ten-ton coal wagon right up to the buffers on the Arrival line. As the Sunday services to and from Bristol were worked by tank engines, its presence there would not interfere with the running round of the locos. On Sunday morning two volunteers reported to unload the truck, and although it was hard work it was a chance for porters to earn a bit of extra money.

In the autumn the coal supply might look ample, but in a cold winter it dwindled all too rapidly, and in every year in fact usage seemed to exceed supply. Staff found themselves having to cadge coal from sympathetic loco crews, a practice at which they were adept and had plenty of opportunity, with engines spending some time near the buffer stops! Station coal was frequently a contentious issue on the railway: the men reasonably expected to have an adequate supply for their comfort as well as that of the passengers in periods of cold weather. The Station Master's clerk could try to requisition for an additional delivery later on in the winter, but Gloucester seemed to want to account for every lump.

During the racing season, pigeon specials were a feature of the railway at Bath. Trains would regularly work from the Midland to the S&D, some of these being very heavy. The birds were accompanied on the trains by 'convoyers', people whose function was to feed and water the pigeons en route, supervise their dispatch, note the time of release and telephone the home branch of the

Racing Pigeon Federation. With anything from 10 to 20 birds in a basket, they travelled down generally from the North on Friday night, in readiness for a Saturday race. When the release point was Bath, the vans were worked into the Midland Bridge Road yard, and the birds freed from there, and before 2.00pm if possible, in order to give them sufficient hours of daylight. Failing that, they would have to be kept overnight and released the next day. The older, more experienced birds raced in late May and June, and the younger ones in August and early September. Training flights were also organised in the early summer for new birds, these being over shorter distances, smaller in quantity and with the pigeons being released from Green Park. The procedure was for a porter to release the birds and record the time, this then being notified to the appropriate club. The only instruction issued as to the chosen moment of release was that it was 'all right if you can see the hills'! Empty pigeon baskets were stored in the Fish House, until they too were returned to their home base, rather more slowly than the birds! Local pigeon clubs – such as Bath Central Flying Club and Bath Premier Homing Society – also organised events of their own requiring birds to be dispatched by train for release elsewhere. The most favoured time for this was a Friday evening when members would set up trestle tables on the covered roadway near the Fish House ready for the exodus. As the birds arrived they were individually checked and recorded, and then placed in the ready-labelled baskets. Porters then loaded these into the two or three vans which had been marshalled in the Carriage Dock. These were duly attached to a local passenger train – generally the 7.03pm – as far as Mangotsfield, where they were transferred to a northbound service. Once the trestle tables had been taken down, the porters were required to sweep up the inevitable mess that accompanied the pigeons!

The porters' room was situated on the Arrival platform, and afforded a refuge for the men between periods of activity. Integrated within it was the lamp room. This was really little more than a corridor partitioned off from the main room. It was a dark, cramped sort of place and not unnaturally smelt strongly of oil, but served its purpose. Between the porters' room and the Bath Traffic Control office was a small room – more of a wide passageway really – which from 1869 until the first decade of the present century was the store for footwarmers. Passengers could hire these sturdy, oval shaped cans for their journey in the days before carriages had steam heating, and it was the job of one of the porters on each shift to attend to the boiling water used in the warmers. When footwarmers ceased to be necessary, the room was used for parking staff bicycles.

The canopy standing in front of the forebuilding on Seymour Street was once the pitch of two outside porters who carried or wheeled passengers' luggage from the station to destinations in the city centre. They were often required to convey luggage across the city to the Great Western station. Travelling salesmen were a major source of work for these men, arriving in considerable numbers and usually well-laden with sample cases. These porters were not employees of the railway, but rather paid a retainer to the company for the right to ply their trade. They were not permitted into the concourse to tout for business: any carrying on station limits was the preserve of the platform staff. When it came to the question of possible tips, lines of demarcation had to be strictly observed (not that railway employees were supposed to solicit tips!). By the middle of the last war only one outside porter remained, and he too disappeared from the scene soon afterwards.

In addition to the outside porters, there were a few other people who gained a livelihood at the station without actually being employees of the railway. In the early days, cabmen would wait for custom beneath the shelter adjoining the Arrival platform. Here, passengers and luggage could be transferred from rail to road under cover. Cabs bringing people to the station dropped them off beneath the canopy in front of the booking hall. In later years, a permanent taxi stand was located here. One of the drivers, Bert Owen, found that he had enough custom for his large Buick taxi in the mid 1930s to make it worthwhile to cover Sundays as well as weekdays. He later transferred to the Abbey stand, and after the war there were no official station taxis.

Passenger Shunters. The job of these men involved coupling and uncoupling engines from trains or empty stock, as well as working the three lever frames which permitted shunting movements at the station. Although there were three shifts to be covered on weekdays, there were only two shunters. The figure of Jack Watley ducking out from beneath buffer beams and strolling to the lever frame, pulling off his

A view along the Arrival platform, c1910. Advertisements and notice-boards were a prominent feature of the station at this time, and covered almost every piece of prime open wall. W H Smith's large bookstall is seen at the rear of the concourse. Notice the horse-drawn transport waiting beneath the cabmen's shelter to the left of the picture. M J Tozer collection

heavy-duty gloves as he did so, is another of the well-remembered images of Green Park. His opposite number was Sidney Broad, who had gained promotion from his previous job of goods yard shunter. The third turn was covered by one of the shift porters, who acted as relief to the two regular men. As firemen did not have to couple/uncouple their engines, there was plenty of walking about for the shunter to do, especially when two trains were in the station at the same time, both with engines at each end. A major part of the duties of the shift porters was to assist the shunter at such busy times. One man would be near the buffer stops to uncouple the engine there and operate the Arrival line lever frame; and the other would be near the river bridge to attend the locos and work the frame there.

The station possessed three lever, or ground, frames: one working the engine release road points on the Arrival side; another controlling the points from the carriage siding on the Departure side; and the third working the points connecting the engine release road with the platform line and dock siding. The first two were simply open lever frames, but the levers in the latter were housed in a substantial wooden cabin, on the outside wall of which was a bell rung by the station signalbox to alert the shunter that his services were about to be required. All three lever frames could only be operated when released mechanically by the Station box signalman, i.e. the signalman had first to pull the appropriate lever in the signalbox to unlock the levers in the ground frames.

The work of the passenger shunter fluctuated between periods of great activity and relative quiescence, but with shunting operations between trains he was not idle for long. In spells of cold weather he would often visit the porters' room in between trains 'for a bit of a warm', as the ground frame cabin had no stove. Only on summer Sunday excursions did firemen have to couple and uncouple their own engines; at all other times a shunter would be on hand. The period between about 11.00pm and 5.30am was quietest; indeed, the station itself was closed and doors to the street locked. Only the 'Down Mail' on the S&D departed between these times, at 2.40am. To cover this working as well as late night and early morning shunting, a shift porter was employed. Having dealt with the coaching stock of the 8.50pm from Templecombe (10.21 in Bath), and marshalled the mail vans in the dock siding, there would be a gap of about three hours when nothing happened. The shift porter was kept on duty to keep an eye on the vans before the arrival of the GPO personnel and also to couple the engine when it arrived from the shed. He also swept out the empty coaches in the carriage siding ready for the more detailed attention of the cleaners.

The carriage cleaners' cabin consisted, appropriately, of a grounded coach body on the Arrival platform. The first, with a clerestory roof, appeared about 1930; it was later replaced by the coach seen here to the left of Ivatt 2-6-2 tank engine No 41241, about to leave with the 5.45pm stopping train to Bristol.   R E Toop

Carriage Cleaners. With coaching sets often out on a two-day cycle before they returned to home base, carriage cleaning was a necessary job. Several sets of coaches were stabled overnight; some at the station and some in either of the two sidings adjoining the Midland, or top, shed. Bath had responsibility for cleaning S&D stock only, and this would be stabled at the station. The Midland coaches were attended to at Bristol. The cleaners booked on at 5.30am. Two women, Polly and Evelyn – 'a couple of real characters' – were brought in to do the carriage interiors during the last war and stayed on afterwards. They used the grounded coach body on the Arrival platform as a mess room, to which they retired for a breakfast break. They always had a cup of tea on hand and a yarn for any porter who happened to have a few minutes free. They also had a small stores hut behind the wall of the platform, near the doors of the bonded warehouse.

Their first duty was to clean the coaches which would work over to Bristol attached to the 7.01am – these forming the 9.03 through train from there to Bournemouth. The stock forming the 8.15 Bath to Templecombe then received attention. A break was now possible before dealing with the S&D arrivals at 8.42 and 10.46.

The coach exteriors were cleaned by a male employee, one of the porters. A line of water taps was provided on either side of the carriage siding. The coaches' windows were cleaned daily, but the coach bodies less frequently. He was also responsible for filling the tanks which supplied the lavatories.

Carriage and Wagon Examiner. A man had to be on call to deal with a range of matters relating to passenger rolling stock, from wheel-tapping and examination of brakes, to inspection of couplings and steam pipes. Three men covered this work in consecutive eight-hour shifts, combining duties at the station with those in the goods yards. Dickie Weeks was one of the old hands at this job, while Eric Mogg followed his father in the C&W Department. The men had a cabin at the station, in the dock siding near the bonded warehouse. Another cabin was situated near the Station signalbox, being more conveniently placed for work in the Midland Bridge Road yard. Examination of assembled freights as well as dealing with problem wagons kept the men very busy; it was sometimes difficult to find time to have a meal break. When, in 1958 the Western Region took over the management of Green Park, the C&W examiner had to cover Bath Spa station as well. Occasionally an urgent phone call would be received saying that there was a problem with a coach on a service train at the Spa, and the examiner had to make his way across the city to deal with it.

Refreshment Room Staff. Situated at the concourse end of the Departure platform were the refreshment rooms. Walking through the high double doors leading from the platform, the passenger entered the main room, formerly the First Class Refreshment Room with its long, high serving counter and circular customers' tables, all marble-topped. A second doorway, nearer the Parcels Office, led into what had been the Third Class Refreshment Room. From about 1930, only the larger First Class room was used by the public, the other being used by the staff as a collection point for dirty crockery, as it contained a sink. The water for any tea served in the refreshment room was drawn from the urn kept on the counter in this back room. Leading off from the south-east corner of the room was the large kitchen in which the staff had their meal breaks.

The staff consisted of a manageress and an assistant, both of whom lived in at the station, a waitress and a cellarman. The Catering Department was administered from Gloucester, with occasional visitations to see that all was well.

The staff accommodation was reached by a staircase which led up from the staff room along a dark passageway to the two rooms in the south wing of the forebuilding (to the left of the booking hall when viewed from the street). The manageress lived in the first floor room which looked out onto Seymour Street, while her assistant had the room which looked out onto the station concourse. Without the benefit of a coal fire, or even the provision of an electric power point, conditions were distinctly chilly for much of the year and bitterly cold in the depths of winter. The manageress had the compensation of receiving any morning sunshine, but the train shed blocked any direct light to her colleague's room which, despite its three big windows, was bleak and unwelcoming. The fittings, such as they were, had to be contained in just the one room; there was not even the comfort of an easy chair. A shared toilet was situated near the top of the stairs, although each room did have its own bath, which was screened off by a wooden partition and was supplied by a gas-powered geyser. Partly because of the primitive facilities there was a fairly rapid turnover of staff. The last incumbent as manageress was Miss Mundy.

The working day began at 8.00am from Monday to Saturday, and went on until about 6.00pm or even later at busy times. Each of the employees had a rotating half day off. The first task was to light the gas in the urn and make the sandwiches. There was little in the way of hot meals to be prepared due to the nature of the traffic using Green Park station: shoppers and commuters, being essentially local, would generally only require a drink or a light snack. One of the duties of the manageress was to order the regular bulk supplies like tea, biscuits, sugar and so on, whilst the staff themselves went out to buy fresh fruit and vegetables from Wetten & Norris in nearby Kingsmead Square. The cellarman saw to the fire and did the fetching and carrying, as well as attending to the bar.

There were two notable periods of intense activity. The first concerned the 'Pines' in the interwar years. An almost daily ritual then was the preparation of luncheon hampers. Although the 'Pines' conveyed a restaurant car, some first class passengers preferred to reserve a compartment and order a hamper, Bath being the obvious place to deal with this as the train arrived around noon. The manageress would receive a phone call earlier in the morning, after the train had left Bournemouth, giving details of the number and contents of the hampers required. When the train arrived she and her assistant would be waiting on the platform. The guard directed them to the compartment(s) concerned, and made sure that everything was satisfactory. One guard who had a monopoly of the 'Pines' roster was Fred Toller. In his immaculate uniform, complete with buttonhole, his customer relations technique was highly polished, so that after the hampers had been delivered he got the tip and not the ladies!

The other time when the Catering Department was stretched to the limit was on summer Saturdays, so much so in fact that part-time staff had to be taken on to help out. The staff were kept so busy that they barely had time to have anything to eat themselves. All the expresses to and from the Midlands and the North had an enforced stop at Green Park in order to change engines. This stop-over was turned to advantage by the staff, and on a hot day the demand for their services approached something of a clamour, especially with southbound trains when people had been sitting in a stuffy compartment for three, four or five hours. The refreshment

In this view, taken on 5th July 1959, the by now little-used refreshment kiosk stands out clearly in its new coat of Western Region paint. Behind it is the roof of Midland Cottage, the residence of the company's horse-keeper. An Ivatt 2-6-2 tank engine waits with a 3-set of Southern (Maunsell) coaches for departure to Bristol. R C Riley

room itself was supplemented by the wooden kiosk on the Departure platform and by a trolley for use on either platform. When a train ran into the former, the two women in the kiosk would already have the cups lined up on the counter and a large teapot ready and waiting: they knew what to expect! Carriage doors flew open and there was a stampede towards the kiosk. Cups disappeared as soon as they were filled; one person pouring, and one taking the money. A crowd would still be milling around even when the guard blew his whistle for train ready to leave. People who were still to be served waited until the last possible second, rushing back to their seat either empty-handed or with the tea slopping into the saucer. Crockery left on the trains eventually found its way back to Bath, but often in a sorry, sticky state.

The trolley was used largely for trains using the Arrival platform. In later years, the kiosk was rarely used as the trolley allowed much greater flexibility, but, like the rest of the station, was painted every five years or so as part of planned maintenance.

Even towards the end of the station's life the refreshment room did a brisk trade, Miss Mundy paying in plenty of cash each day. Indeed, this was often a cause of comment by the booking office staff, who enquired how many cups of tea she had managed to get from each tea bag. The jest was not appreciated!

Control Office. The function of Control was to have an over-view of all train movements within a prescribed territory, with the intention of keeping everything running smoothly. The Bath Traffic Control District extended from Warmley on the Midland Line to Broadstone (where the S&D met the Southern Railway), and included the Highbridge Branch. Before the opening of the Bath Extension in 1874, the S&D was administered from Glastonbury, on the former Somerset Central Railway. This location quickly ceased to be convenient when it became clear that the main axis of trade was shifting to the new line. Thus in 1877 the Control staff – known as crossing agents, due to their important role in arranging the crossing of trains on the then single track line – moved into what had been the Station Master's offices at Green Park. Many railwaymen continued to refer to the staff as crossing agents long after the Midford to Templecombe section had been doubled. From 1930 onwards the Control office was situated at

Some of the station staff, c1938, posing under the iron ribs of the train shed. Note the ornamental display which was a feature of the station concourse in the 1930s.

Colin G Maggs collection

the concourse end of the Arrival platform, facing the refreshment rooms.

The office was at the hub of links with stations, signalboxes, engine sheds and sundry offices and individuals. Details of the late running of trains, for example, would be telephoned to Control, while that office in turn advised on amended schedules, special workings and other more routine matters. Liaison was necessary with all those concerned with operational matters: signalmen, shed foremen, guards, shunters and Station Masters. The two daytime shifts were manned by a **deputy chief controller** and two **assistant controllers**; while on the night shift it was only necessary to have one man on duty. The **District Controller** worked normal office hours and had ultimate responsibility for the management and running of trains. This particular job was held by Jim Payne between 1955 and 1958, although was now classified as Assistant Divisional Superintendent. In 1958 the post was absorbed into the Bristol office, and Jim moved over to Avonmouth as a goods inspector.

The personnel at Bath Control, or at least their voices, were known to staff throughout the district, and because of their lengthy tenure they had a sound understanding of both general and particular aspects of the railway's operation and idiosyncracies. Typical of their friendly working relationship, combined with professional expertise, was Henry Ware. Having gained experience in various posts at several locations on the S&D, he spent 31 years in the Control office at Bath and consequently knew the whole Line thoroughly, from the mode of operation at each location to the personnel involved. He worked as a deputy chief controller from 1950 until his retirement in 1955 and was renowned for keeping things on the move on the busiest of summer Saturdays when hesitation or indecision would result in trains queuing up for occupation of the station or the single line to Midford. The Western Region of British Railways took over the lines to Green Park in 1958, and just four years later closed the Control office there. Train movements were then overseen from Bristol.

Two other administrative posts existed at Green Park, and were accommodated in offices in the north wing of the forebuilding. The room on the first floor, above the Assistant Divisional Superintendent and looking out into the station, belonged to the **District Inspector**. For a great many years, right down to the end of the 1950s, this post had been held by Harry Helps. He had responsibility for guards and signalmen, and although he was a stickler for rules and regulations and gave the men a thorough grilling, he was always fair and genuinely had the men's interests at heart. Guards would periodically be summoned to his office and spent what seemed to be an interminable time answering questions on all matters to do with their work – often on minor or obscure details! He made such an impression on his victims that his reputation had spread well beyond his territory – even as far as the Midlands. His district actually extended from Warmley, through Bath to Burnham-on-Sea and Blandford Forum. He frequently travelled the line examining signalmen on rules, interviewing and assessing men who were applying for posts as signalmen, and undertaking an annual assessment of the men already so employed. When he was spotted on a train by a signalman, word was quickly passed along the line, a fact which Harry realised – indeed, when he had finished at one box he would often tell the signalman where he was going next, and depart with the rejoinder, 'You can put me on line'. His successor for the last few years was a Mr Freeman, who transferred to the city from Gloucester.

The ground floor room at the front of the forebuilding was occupied by the **chief roster clerk**. His work involved drawing up the weekly rosters for the platform staff and signalmen, and also all the relief duties to be covered. For many years this was the preserve of Bert Hazzard, who at one time had the services of an assistant to help with the masses of paperwork. Bert was a most amenable person and would try and change an inconvenient relief roster if requested.

The various offices inevitably generated a good deal of paperwork. To cater for the clerical work, a secretaries' office was provided (on the first floor, overlooking the street). In later years just two typists were employed on this work: Pam Salter and Jean Flowers.

Passenger Guards. Bath-based guards working on passenger and parcels trains had their headquarters at Green Park station (while the goods guards' room was in the Midland Bridge yard). This was the smaller of the two rooms in the Fish House, nearest the main station building. It contained the usual equipment lockers and notice boards, as well as a long table in the middle of the floor at which men would fill out their journals. As the guards' room contained only a small stove by way of heating, it was usual in the winter for the men to collect their equipment and walk along to the porters' room

to write up the journals, as there was a real fire here and the chance of a cup of tea and a chat. Booking on an hour or so before the first train in their roster was due to leave, this gave time for the journals to be prepared : number and type of vehicles, weight of train and traffic details. Some of the data could only be completed at the last minute when the train was actually in the platform (as with the through workings between Bristol and Bournemouth). On certain trains, notably specials and Sunday excursions, guards were asked to make as accurate an estimate as possible of the number of passengers. The work of the guards was overseen by the District Inspector, who examined the men once a year on rules and regulations relating to the working of trains, such as emergency procedures and the protection of trains.

With the exception of the 'Pines' and summer excursions, guards on most passenger trains working into Bath were required to collect the tickets of passengers terminating their journey at Green Park. For all sorts of reasons, guards would need to issue tickets to passengers on the train. In later years, some of the smaller stations like Oldland Common were only staffed on the early turn, while some were reduced to unstaffed halts (like Midford and Wellow). In these situations passengers had to buy their tickets from the guard. In the absence of platform staff, the guard had also to collect tickets and often turn out platform lamps.

Travelling Ticket Collectors. Whereas guards were concerned with issuing or collecting tickets at either end of a passenger's journey, the travelling ticket collectors were more interested in checking the validity whilst in transit. Two such men worked from Bath, covering the S&D as far as Templecombe and also the Highbridge Branch (the former LMS line was covered by men from Bristol as far as the local stopping trains were concerned, although the Bath men covered the 'Pines' as far as Gloucester). One of the regular turns involved leaving Green Park on the 9.55am S&D semi-fast to Bournemouth, and travelling as far as Evercreech Junction. Here, the man joined the northbound 'Pines' on which he travelled as far as Gloucester. He then returned home on the southbound 'Pines'. Walter Adams did this job for many years and was a familiar face on the 'Pines', although with the exception of that express the effectiveness of the work lay in its random nature. Visits to 'the Branch' were only very occasional.

3. The Motive Power Depot

The term **Motive Power Depot** is frequently used synonymously with Engine Shed, but in Bath's case this would hardly be appropriate. The presence of two initially independent railway companies brought about a more complex evolutionary development in locomotive accommodation and servicing, and so the term is more widely taken to cover not one shed but two, as well as a whole range of assorted sidings and facilities.

When the Midland Railway opened its Mangotsfield & Bath Branch, a modest m.p.d. was adequate to deal with the essentially local nature of the traffic before the arrival of the Somerset & Dorset. The stone-built shed contained just two lines – or roads in railway parlance – complete with servicing pits. To the rear of the shed was the office accommodation. This too was modest, given that Bath shed in 1869 was a sub-shed of the company's main

General view of the m.p.d taken from the top of the water-softening tower on Bath Loco's last day – hence the unusual lack of activity. The piecemeal development of the S&D shed complex gave it a bulky if somewhat patchwork appearance. The boat road is clearly seen, curving sharply away behind the tender of the Stanier 8F on the left of the picture (48760), the tender itself standing on the connection between the fitting shop and No 7 road. The siding leading into Stothert & Pitt's is also clearly visible.   Sunday 6th March 1966   Hugh Ballantyne

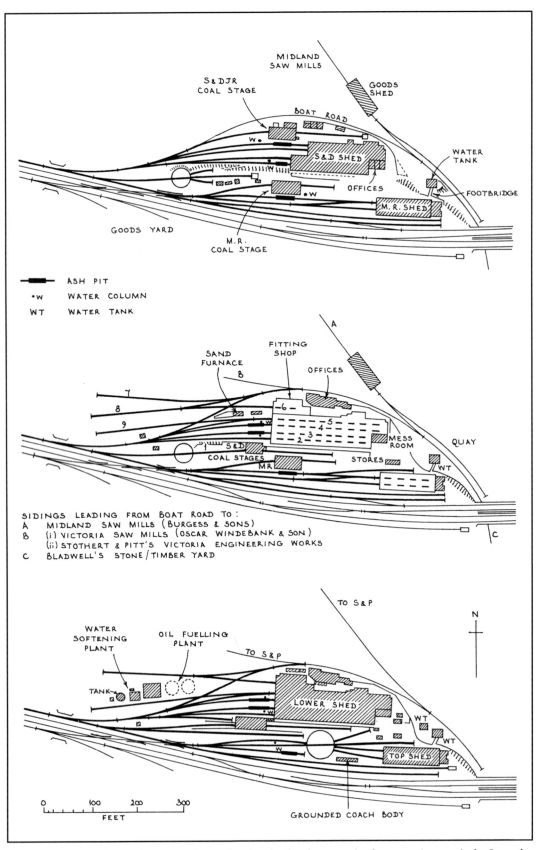

Scale drawings of the motive power depot showing its development in the years (respectively, from the top) 1884, 1902 and 1950

One of the 1925 batch of the S&D 2-8-0 class 7s, 53810, being turned on Bath shed's 60' turntable. A table was installed here in 1935, replacing the earlier 46' version, which had been located on the approach to the coal stage. The later table was renewed in 1960.   26.6.62   R C Riley

operation in the area at Bristol. As a separate undertaking, the S&D provided its own locomotive and office accommodation, even after the leasing agreement of 1875 by which the Midland became responsible for motive power. The original two-road timber shed was enlarged by adding an extra two roads (later known as Nos 2 & 3) in 1878, and the structure was further extended six years later. The S&D also possessed its own coaling stage, with even the coal itself coming from a different source to that used by the MR (namely, a softer Welsh coal rather than the harder northern variety). Only the turntable and water were jointly used. It was only in 1928 that the anomalous situation of two independent sheds providing locomotives for a joint undertaking was removed, when the Midland shed came under the control of the S&D's Locomotive Superintendent based at Bath – a post which later became known as Shed Master. The two coaling stages remained in use, which if

not absolutely essential was operationally convenient. Bath's 46' turntable was not only too short for the Class 7 2-8-0 freight engines which first appeared in 1914, but was also poorly placed and a cause of congestion. Thus in 1934 the ex-Midland coaling stage was demolished in order to make room for a 60' turntable, which was installed in the following year. From then on, it was only possible to reach the Midland shed by means of the turntable. Even after the merger, locomen generally continued to refer to the sheds as either Midland or Dorset, and only gradually did the terms 'top' and 'lower' sheds begin to creep into common usage for the ex-Midland and ex-S&D sheds respectively. The term 'lower' certainly had meaning when the River Avon periodically flooded and all the tracks became submerged. Although this was not usually to a very great depth, it was sufficient to incapacitate the shed and disrupt routine – especially that of the ash-pit men who were not

On the far left is the siding which played host to the Permanent Way/Breakdown train, the inscription on the coaches reading MP BATH. Next come the two turntable roads, with a water column in between. This arrangement allowed one engine to take water while another turned, without having its exit blocked. The tank engine is standing over the ash pit, this siding being the customary base for the top shed ash wagon. Alongside the shed is the Gas siding, which took its name from the fact that in the days when coaches were lit by gas, the tank wagons which replenished their reservoirs were stabled there. Finally, next to the running line, is Tommy's siding. This is thought to have taken its name from Thomas Smith who for many years early in the century undertook running repairs to vans parked on the siding specifically for that purpose. A crossover once connected the siding with the main line in front of the vehicle seen in this picture.   26.4.59   P J Kelley

Access to the shed was by means of the turntable. A back road and short spur to the north of the shed were similarly reached. The stone-built shed measured some 120 feet by 40, and was constructed over a vaulted basement which acted as a store (and served as an air-raid shelter during the last war). The grounded coach body was used for Mutual Improvement Classes.
                                                                                                        June 1965   R E Toop

On the right of the picture is the coal road. The brick-built coal stage seen here replaced an earlier wooden structure in 1954. The short siding in front of the stage was officially labelled No 1 road, although was rarely referred to as such. It served as the base for the lower shed ash wagon; and is followed, in turn, by roads 2–5, i.e. the shed roads. Standard class 5 No 73019 is standing on the approach to the boat road and astride No 6 road which led into the fitting shop. The corrugated-iron structure seen to the right of the loco marks the site of the sand furnace. 26.4.59   P J Kelley

expected to become submariners! The variation in level also meant that there was a short but steep incline from the lower shed up to the loco road on the bridge over Victoria Bridge Road. With rails wet after rain, locos could slip themselves to a stand when being worked by an unsuspecting crew; while engines going on shed had to be careful not to run in too fast as there was little room to correct errors of judgement.

The locomen's mess room, known to generations of railwaymen as The Cabin, was situated behind the lower shed at the end of Nos 2 and 3 roads (having been the office accommodation of the S&D operation in the early days).

From time to time, on Sunday mornings, men were required to attend Mutual Improvement Classes, lectures lasting for up to three or four hours on a whole range of subjects from Rule 55 to Vacuum. These meetings were usually held in The Cabin, although sometimes the venue was the grounded coach body near the Gas siding.

Administration. The administration of the depot consisted of more than the men who worked on the footplate, so that the most fundamental division of staff was between Footplate and Non-Footplate Grades. Men would move up through each grade, but remained mutually exclusive on either side of this divide.

The man at the top of the hierarchy was the **Shed Master**, a post which had variously been known as Shed Foreman and Locomotive Superintendent. He occupied the easternmost of the suite of offices between the lower shed and the boat road. As a continuous operation on weekdays, someone had to be officially in charge at all times. Thus the depot was covered by three consecutive eight-hour shifts: midnight until 8.00am, known as the Early Turn; 8.00am until 4.00pm, the Day Shift; and 4.00pm until midnight, the Late Turn. The day shift was always worked by the Shed Master, a man with sound mechanical expertise as well as operational knowledge. In more recent times this post was

Harold Morris, Shed Master from 1956 to 1966, pictured in his office. Above the S&DJR Gradient Diagram is a picture of Alfred Whitaker, Bath's renowned Locomotive Superintendent from 1889 to 1911.   J Stamp

held, in chronological order, by Tom White – a man who had the enormous respect of locomen – followed by Arthur Elliott, Derek Webb and Harold Morris. A Welshman by birth, Mr Morris moved to Bath from Bristol in 1956, and thus had the unenviable task of superintending the depot in its declining years. His personality and experience was such that he was deservedly popular with the men, no mean feat considering his whole career to date had been on the Great Western! The small depot at Radstock, as a sub-shed of Bath, also came under his jurisdiction, although the daily supervision there was left to a chargehand.

The other two shifts were worked by foremen on an alternating basis to allow for a fair share of night work. The two men who held this post for the last few years were Fred Holmes and Cyril Bruton. Neither were native Bathonians, but after some initial coolness from colleagues, became popular figures by virtue of their professional commitment. Hailing originally from Stoke-on-Trent, Fred was a driver of many years standing on both the Bath Branch and S&D, and had a keen interest in all aspects of his work, both administrative and practical. Cyril, from Wolverhampton, endeared himself to people by virtue of his demonstrative language: he might have been difficult to understand at times, but knew what he was doing! One of their immediate predecessors on the 4.00 to midnight shift was Tom Rudd. As a short and very portly gent – never without a flat hat – he cut a distinctive figure which, together with his manner, made him one of the depot's colourful characters. Notable amongst his idiosyncracies was a predilection for drinking tea directly from the pot. Having brewed the tea, he added the milk to

Beneath the coal stage, on No 2 road, is 7F No 53804; with 4F No 44561 on No 3 and 53805 on No 4. Water columns were provided between roads 2 & 3 and 4 & 5, with ash pits on Nos 3 & 4. Notice the telephone by the foot of the lamp post; it was used by enginemen to communicate with the signalman in the Station box. Although the coal stage possessed 3 coaling points, it was only able to deal with one tender engine at a time due to its restricted length.   31.7.59   P J Kelley

the pot and then drank the liquid through the spout! His stentorian voice was another – and inescapable – feature: he could be heard all through the shed. For example, he could stand in the far inside corner of the lower shed, call for the fitter, and be heard by him at the extreme opposite end of the building. Tom was also a stickler for time-keeping, and kept the afternoon cleaners on their toes. During their shift, the men were allowed a half-hour break, at the exact end of which Tom was there ushering them back to their duties.

The foremen kept a log, a document which makes fascinating reading as it gives an insight into the day-to-day running of the shed. The entries cover an enormous field, from the mundane to the major; from the regular to the unusual. Thus, for example, on 2nd February 1960 comes the entry: 'Electric lamp near 4 & 5 points needs new bulb'. On 1st October, a more weighty matter is recorded: '53804 derailed on coal road at 3/50, Breakdown men sent for at 4/0, only two arrived, Hutton and Trim. Owing to the large amount of spillage difficulty was experienced placing packing & ramps. Engine rerailed by 6/30, thanks to Fitter Brennan, & good work by coalmen digging out spillage in a

confined space against the loading platform.'

Some of the entries related to correspondence with other sheds, the most common type of request being exemplified by the following: (a) 27th May 1961 'Phone message from Radstock Loco saying that they had no engine oil or lubricator oil for engine booked out early Monday morning, could some be sent today, Saturday'. (b) 18th October 1961 'Barrow Rd requests the loan of a fireman on Thursday next (19/10) to be at Barrow Rd by 10/0 if possible'.

During the summer it was an essential part of the late turn foreman's job every Thursday to prepare the locomotive diagrams for the coming Saturday. This was no simple task, for not only were a large number of engines involved, but the weekly number and timings of the north-south special and relief trains varied, making a standard formula impossible for all but the regular services. Even then, late running could cause major problems, and an ample Spare Link had to be available. The following extract shows a typical summer Saturday in 1958 and reveals the intensity of the operation, with 15 locos needing to be prepared for departure from Bath between 2.35 and 4.10am, all but one of the trains being double-headed.

* 2.35	45006	B'mth 5.00 – 8.40 ex B'mth – Bath, 11.14. Loco
* 2.35c	75071	Evercreech 3.32 – LE Loco, 5.10
* 2.40	73047	B'mth 7.29 – 9.55 ex B'mth – Bath, 12/25. Engine then 2/30
* 2.45	73019	B'mth 5.18 – 10.05 ex B'mth – Bath, 12/45. Engine then 3/57
* 2.45c	40601	Evercreech 3.43 – AR 9.36 ex Evercreech – Bath, 10.31; then 12/0 AR
3.02	53810	B'mth 5.38 – 7.40 ex B'mth – Bath, 9.54. Loco
* 3.02c	40697	Evercreech 4.02 – LE Loco
* 3.15	73087	B'mth 6.00 – 9.25 ex B'mth – Bath, 11.45. Engine then 2/52
* 3.15c	40698	Evercreech 4.18 – 10.15 AR ex Evercreech – Bath, 11.14. Loco
3.25	44775	B'mth 6.10 – AR 7.40 ex B'mth – Bath, 9.54
* 3.25c	40700	Evercreech 4.30 – LE Loco
3.45	73116	B'mth 6.20 – 12/20 ex B'mth – Bath, 2/54. Loco
* 3.45c	44096	Evercreech 4.48 – LE Loco
* 4.10	73049	B'mth 6.44 – 10.35 ex B'mth – Bath, 1/00. Loco
* 4.10c	44560	Evercreech 5.14 – LE Loco, then 9.05 AR
6.55	76017	ex last Up. B'mth 11.07 – 1/08 ex B'mth – Bath, 4/22. Loco (engine then 7/05)
8.15	44523	B'mth 1/57 – 5/30 ex B'mth – Templecombe
* 8.15c	40697	Evercreech 9.28 – 12/06 AR Everc – Bath, 1/00
9.05	73051	B'mth 11.48 – 2/45 ex B'mth – Bath, 5/11. Loco
9.05c	44560	Evercreech 10.01 – 11.23 AR Everc – Bath, 12/25
9.55	75071	B'mth 12/54 – 3/40 ex B'mth – Bath, 6/56. Loco
10.32	53800	B'mth 1/17 – 4/10 ECS ex B'mth – Bath, 7/45
10.32c	40700	Shepton 11.19 – LE Evercreech – 1/35 ex Everc AR – Bath, 2/10. Loco
12/00	34042	ex 8.00 B'mth – Bath, arrive 10.14.
12/00c	40601	T'cbe 1/20 – LE Evercreech – AR 3/06 ex Everc – Bath 4/22. Loco
12/24	34040	ex 8.16 B'mth – Bath, arrive 10.31
12/24c	T	ex T'cbe, arrive Bath 10.14 (AR 8.00 ex Everc)
12/58	73050	B'mth 3/40 – LE Bath. Loco
12/58c	44096	Evercreech 1/49 – LE Bath. Loco
1/10	40696	ex 7.12 B'mth – Bath, arrive 10.59
2/12	34099	ex 9.45 B'mth – Bath, arrive 11.56 – 7/25 ex B'mth – Bath, 9/53. Loco
2/12c	T	ex T'cbe, arrive Bath 11.45 (9.25 Up)
2/30	73047	B'mth 5/15 – 10/30 goods ex Poole – Bath, 3.29
2/30c	T	ex T'cbe, arrive Bath 12/45 (10.05 Up)
2/52	73087	B'mth 5/35. Remains for Sunday duty No 5
2/52c	T	ex T'cbe, arrive Bath 11.56 (9.45 Up)
3/30	34105	ex 11.12 B'mth – Bath, 1/49
3/30c	44422	ex T'cbe, arrive Bath 1/49 (11.12 Up)
3/57	73019	B'mth 6/23 – 8/30 ECS ex B'mth – Bath, 11/00
3/57c	40698	Evercreech 4/53 – 10.05 AR ex Everc – Bath, 11/00
4/21	73049	B'mth 7/23 – 10/00 ex B'mth – T'cbe, 11/26
4/21c	44557	ex lst Up, arrives Bath 8.42 – T'cbe, 5/38. Loco
4/37	44417	ex 8.48 B'mth – Bath, 1/35
7/05	76017	ex 6.55 arrives Bath 4/22
10/25	T	ex T'cbe, arrives Bath 4/59

10.10	45229	Bristol	12/50	45075	Cleethorpes
10.25	42868	Sheffield	1/05	44966	Manchester
10.45	45591	Liverpool	1/55	44775	Sheffield
11.25	73142	Bradford	2/18	45006	Derby
11.50	44920	Manchester & Liverpool	3/05	45265	Nottingham
12/05	44747	Manchester	5/28	44828	Bristol
12/35	44757	Leeds	9/58	44814	Bristol

Notes
*	Locos booked out twice
c	Coupled engine, i.e. pilot
T	Templecombe shed to provide loco
AR	Assist Relief working as pilot engine
LE	Light Engine
ECS	Empty Carriage Stock
Loco	Motive Power Depot

Apart from the variety of destinations in the Midlands and the North, what is also interesting is the wide geographical catchment of the motive power provision. For example:

(a) The 10.10 to Bristol was worked by a Black 5 from Rose Grove, Burnley (24 B).
(b) The 10.25 to Sheffield by a Crab from Agecroft, Manchester (26 B).
(c) The 10.45 to Liverpool by Jubilee class *Udaipur* from Crewe North (5 A).
(d) The 12/35 and 5/28 departures by Caprotti class 5 and Black 5 respectively from Leeds, Holbeck (55 A).
(e) The 9/58 to Bristol by one of Saltley, Birmingham's (21 A) Black 5s.

Rosters could work perfectly well on paper, but in reality even the best laid plans could be upset. Although particular events could not be predicted, their general occurrence could at least be anticipated – hence the facility of spare engines and men. This was generally a straightforward substitution, but could sometimes produce unusual pairings between trains and locos. A few examples from 1960 may be of interest:

(a) On 22nd January ex GW pannier tank No 3742 failed with a front left-hand washout plug blowing, and so her shunting duties had to be performed by 4F No 44560 (these engines were more at home on the banking turns).
(b) On 9th March 2-6-2 Ivatt tank engine No 41242 failed at Bristol with a suspected broken air valve, and so 4F No 44520 worked the 8.10pm passenger train from Temple Meads to Bath. Being a Saturday evening, and with the tank marooned at Bristol, the shed foreman at Bath had no option but to book the over-powered Standard class 5 No 73028 to work the Ivatt's first diagram on Monday morning, which was the 7.01 passenger to Bristol.
(c) Newly arrived 9F No 92206 was officially failed at 4.00am on 6th July due to a badly leaking washout plug in her smoke box, and consequently 4F No 44559 was booked to take out the 9.55am to Bournemouth.

In order to cover the work of the Shed Master and foremen when they were not on duty – as on rest days, annual leave or through illness – some of the footplatemen were designated **deputy foremen**. These could be either drivers or firemen, the men being approached by the Shed Master and asked if they would be willing to do the work. On the credit side of the balance was the inherent status of the job and the cleaner, less strenuous working conditions, but on the debit side was the lack of overtime pay resulting from fixed hours.

The atmospheric interior of the lower shed, showing the trussed timber roof and gas lights. The locos on shed in this picture are Standard class 4 2-6-0 No 76026 and Stanier 8Fs 48309 & 48760.   27.2.66   J Blake

The Non-Footplate workers came under the direction of the appropriate foreman. Thus, the various craftsmen were supervised by the **foreman fitter** who, like the Shed Master, worked a day-time 8-hour shift. In the early and mid-1930s, the foreman fitter was Lew Adams. A keen member of the St John Ambulance Brigade, he was widely respected by dint of his professional competence. Unfortunately, he suffered from arthritis, and before the outbreak of war his health had deteriorated to the point where he was forced to give up the job. For some years, he had been joined in the fitting shop by his brother George, and it was he who now became the foreman, a post which he held until the closure of the depot. The shift work was covered by two 12-hour turns, with the change-over times at 6.00am and 6.00pm. The men were allowed an hour's meal break during the shift, to be taken between the third and fifth hours of duty. Each fitter, including the foreman, was accompanied by a fitter's mate. Two of the regular teams comprised Ernest Bolt (fitter) with Frank Beazer (mate); and Reg Iley (fitter) with Stan Charlton (mate). Stan's particular responsibility was that of

brake-block fitter (generally referred to as brakesman). He was nicknamed Digger by his colleagues, after the brand of tobacco he constantly chewed. Every four or five days the brake blocks on the S&D freight locomotives required changing, such were the demands made by the steep Mendip gradients, and this generated a good deal of work for the fitter.

A number of craftsmen were needed to ensure that locomotives remained in good running order. Parts had to be made, repaired and fitted, and faults detected, requiring specific skills and experience. Much of this work was done in the fitting shop between No 5 shed road and the boat road. The forge, for castings and the like, was the preserve of the blacksmith and his assistant. The last blacksmith was Albert Manley, who looked every inch the part, solidly built with powerful, muscular arms! His assistant was Bob Clothier. Other craftsmen included a turner, carpenter and tin-smith.

From 1935 any heavier repair work was centralised at Barrow Road, Bristol, but in spite of this there was always plenty of work at Bath. Indeed, in the early 1950s a new and very

46

The latter-day office staff at the m.p.d. From left to right: Stuart Davis, general assistant; Ernest James, senior wages clerk; Harold Morris, shed master; Bert Merrett, chief clerk, who succeeded George Curnock early in 1962. The suite of offices occupied a rather confined space between the lower shed and the boat road.   J Stamp

expensive Skoda lathe was ordered from Czechoslovakia. It was railed over from Bristol on a 60-foot low-loader one Sunday morning, and manoeuvred through the shed sidings and into the fitting shop.

The locomotive cleaners were directed by a **foreman cleaner**. His cabin was situated at the end of No 3 road in the lower shed. For the quarter-century before 1946 the foreman had been Lew Chalker. On his retirement, the post was taken up by Fred Trim, who had previously worked in the stores. He remained in the post until the depot closed. His hours were from 6.45am until 2.45pm, after which time the cleaners took their orders from the Shed Master or foremen.

Materials for use by footplate and non-footplate gangs alike were kept in the storeroom, adjoining the lower shed: oil, paraffin jelly, tallow, cotton waste, brushes, detonators and the like. The lamps mounted on the engines were also kept here. One storeman was on each of the three turns. In the days when the S&D shed was supplied separately, the spares van travelled up to

Bath from Highbridge every Friday with requisitioned items for the store.

Office Staff. Men booked on and off duty in the time office at the lower shed, situated between the locomen's signing-on lobby and the Shed Master's office. It was manned continuously, except for a few hours on a Sunday, the shift work being covered by the **time clerks**, two per shift. Essentially, the work of the office was divided into two sections; one dealing with the men's rosters and the other with their wages. Whereas the shed foreman drew up the engine allocations, or diagrams, the enginemen's duties, or rosters, were drawn up by the **chief roster clerk**. He and his assistant had overall charge of the making out of the rosters and the completion of time-sheets, and both worked normal office hours. The simple pairing of drivers and firemen on a rolling cycle of duties was used wherever possible, but men might not be available for duty for a whole series of reasons: annual leave, illness, visits for eyesight tests, arriving too late on duty, and the taking of owed rest days, and so on. Details of the rosters were written out longhand in the Train

Arrangements Register and the details notified to the men by way of a notice board in the locomen's lobby. With 79 drivers and 69 firemen on the books in the late 1950s, this was quite an undertaking, with any amendments being written in the Register in red ink and rest days stamped in (RD) in correct rotation. The complexities of working out these arrangements may be illustrated by looking at just one driver in Link Three for a 16-week period at the end of 1958. It shows the variety of work undertaken on both the Midland and Dorset lines, with a basic eight-week cycle and a rolling rest day every fortnight. By moving links as the opportunity arose, men would simply substitute a different cycle, but over the years build up a detailed knowledge of every turn covered by the m.p.d. The details shown below are taken from an old Train Arrangements Log rescued from a bonfire at the shed following closure in 1966.

WEEK ENDING	M	T	W	T	F	S	FIREMAN	NOTES
30.8.58	11/29	11/29	11/29	11/29	11/29	11/29	DM	a
6.9.58	11.00	RD	11.00	11.00	11.00	10.32A	DM	-
13.9.58	7/05	7/05	7/05	6/27	6/27	2/52A	DM	b
20.9.58	6.30	6.30	6.30	6.30	RD	6.30	HL	c
27.9.58	7/18	7/18	7/18	7/18	7/18	7/18	DM	-
4.10.58	RD	4.00	4.00	4.00	4.00	4.00	DM	-
11.10.58	2/10	2/10	2/10	2/10	2/10	2/10	DM	-
18.10.58	2.40	2.40	RR	2.40	2.40	RD	DM	d
25.10.58	11/29	11/29	11/29	11/29	11/29	11/29	WW	-
1.11.58	11.00	RD	11.00	11.00	11.00	7.05B	DM	-
8.11.58	7/05	7/05	7/05	6/27	6/27	6/27	RW	-
15.11.58	6.30	6.30	6.30	6.30	RD	6.30	RW	e
22.11.58	7/18	7/18	7/18	7/18	7/18	7/18	RW	f
29.11.58	RD	4.00	4.00	4.00	4.00	4.00	RW	g
6.12.58	2/10	2/10	2/10	2/10	2/10	2/10	RW	-
13.12.58	2.40	2.40	2.40	2.40	2.40	RD	RW	-

EXPLANATION OF TRAINS

2.40am	S&D	Mail/Freight	A	Assisting Engine (pilot)
4.00am	MR	Freight	B	Banking Turn
6.30am	MR	Freight	RD	Rest Day
11.00am	S&D	Freight	RR	Road Refresher
2/10pm	MR	Freight		
6/27pm	MR	Freight	DM	D Massey
7/05pm	S&D	Passenger	HL	H Lambert
7/18pm	S&D	Freight	WW	W Weston
11/29pm	MR	Freight	RW	R Williams

a   Driver also worked 7/47pm S&D passenger on Sunday.
b   On Tuesday, driver was switched to work 7/18pm S&D freight. J Prince drove the 7/05.
c   HL fired Monday to Thursday only; another man covered Saturday.
d   J Barber drove the 2.40am on Wednesday to cover RR.
e   T Davis covered for RW on Tuesday.
f   WW fired instead of RW on Monday.
g   In the event, the driver was reallocated to 7.05 banking turn Monday to Friday with RD on Saturday, due to the illness of the banker's driver. As the banking turn fireman (A G Hobbiss) remained on that roster, RW was reallocated to 6.55am S&D passenger.

One of the time clerks would be responsible for chalking up details of each duty number, together with the allocated driver, fireman and guard. Each driver possessed a wallet-style folder into which the roster cards were inserted, informing him of all the details of that particular turn of duty.

In addition to the routine of endless paperwork, the essential task of the **senior wages clerk** was the weekly payment of wages. For a great many years the monies were paid out from the small wages hut which was situated at the boat road end of the footpath which sloped up from Victoria Bridge Road. In pre-war days the men were paid on a Friday, but this was afterwards brought forward one day. The senior wages clerk went to the station booking office late on a Thursday morning to accompany that office's chief clerk with his Gladstone bag full of money to the hut, where the wages were paid out between noon and 2.00pm. Footplate crews had a time-card system to book on and off duty, and so on pay-day gave their works number to the senior clerk, who then counted out the money loose. Only relatively late on was the money put into envelopes. For security reasons it was decided to do away with the wages hut, the men then being paid from the drivers' lobby at the lower shed. With less men employed at the very end of the shed's life, this method was further changed, the men having to report to the station booking office.

The non-footplate personnel were issued with an oval brass check, or token, with their works number stamped on it. This was kept in a compartment-style rack on the time board inside the office. Coming on duty, the men had to collect their check and put it into a slotted box. Following the regime determined by the shift patterns, it was a regular duty of the time clerks to empty the box and record the numbers against the names in a ledger. The checks were then put back in the rack for the men to collect when next they reported for duty. Men who for one reason or another failed to report, were identified when a tally was made between the daily roster and the check numbers. The names of absentees were entered in a separate log.

Water Supply. With an allocation of 40–50 engines, not to mention visitors, and its operation on a 24-hour basis from Monday to Saturday, the m.p.d. had a huge thirst. The principal supply of water was that which was piped down from Devonshire and Combe Down tunnels, through 6" and 9" diameter pipes respectively. The occurrence, collection and tapping of this water is described in the chapter on the tunnels. This copious source was, not surprisingly, referred to as tunnel water, and while generally consistent in quality was not always sufficient in quantity to meet the needs of the shed during busy periods like summer Saturdays, or after a prolonged dry spell. To supplement this supply came river water. Water was drawn out of the River Avon by means of a suction pump situated on the left bank below the boat road, and went by way of a 4" diameter pipe to the water tower. The original tank on its masonry base was joined by a second structure in the early 1930s. The valve for the pump was situated inside the door of the fitting shop.

While it was a useful, even essential, source at busy times, water from the river was dirty compared with the naturally-filtered if rather hard water from the tunnels. Dirty water could lead to problems with priming in locomotives, the dangers of which are described later in the book. The intake pipe from the river was fairly high in the bank and so if the Avon was low in summer, it would be exposed above the water level and consequently be inoperative. If the combined tunnel and river water supplies could not meet demand, then there was a third source: namely city water. As this was metered and had to be paid for, it was to be used only as an absolute last resort. At times when the situation became serious the Shed Master or one of the foremen would delegate someone to walk to the station to turn on the city water at the stop valve which was situated a few yards from the buffers on the Arrival platform. There was a meter set in the plinth of the forebuilding at pavement level between the two entrances on Seymour Street. Periodically one of the foremen would have to walk out there to take readings. From the valve a 6" diameter pipe carried water to the tower at the shed. As with the tunnel pipes, the city pipes were hidden from view, except where they crossed the Avon on bridge 44 (although even here they were housed in wooden casing and ran in the narrow gap between the two girder bridges). So precious was the city supply that there was an indicator in the shed office which showed 'City Water On/Off', and an entry was made in the foreman's log book: thus on 28th July 1961 the man on the 4.00pm to midnight turn recorded 'city water turned on 6.00pm. Turned off 10.00'. This must have been a particularly thirsty period,

The substantial bulk of the water-softening tower dominates the right-hand side of the picture. The gibbet-like winch, or 'mash crane', stands gauntly against the sky. The wooden hut in front of the tower was a tool store-cum-workshop for the fitter who dealt with repairs to rolling stock, principally the replacing of brake blocks. It was known as Jack Usher's Cabin, so long was that individual the incumbent. The train is the north-bound 'Pines', with 2P 40564 piloting 34042 *Dorchester*.

14.7.51   the late Ivo Peters

for the next day it had to be switched on again at 8.30am right through until 3.00pm.

From whatever source, the water was taken to the tanks situated near the Midland Shed. In the case of the tunnel water the source was at a greater height above datum than the top of the tower, so that there was a natural head which allowed the water to feed in by gravity. The input pipes led into the tank near its top edge, the water passing through straw filters before draining into the tank. The tank itself was stocked with trout, which fed on the algae on the sides and thus helped to keep it clean. They clearly thrived in this environment and grew to quite a size!

From the tower, water was piped off to the softening plant at the end of No 9 road. When water was extracted from the tower, and the level dropped, so too did the huge four foot square floats which opened the intake valves and drew in replacement water from the tunnel pipes. The level of water in the tank was shown on a tank indicator. When the water level became very low, a warning bell on the tower sounded.

Barring problems, maintenance was carried out just once a year, on a winter Sunday when the need for water was at its lowest. Any engines requiring water – notably the Bristol 'local' – had their tenders or tanks filled early in the morning, for the work would normally start at around 8.00am and last until about 6.00pm.

Water Softening Plant. Originating in limestone country, the water supplied by the tunnels was hard, and created a nuisance in the furring of pipes and tubes in locomotive boilers. In order to soften the water, a massive black cylindrical tower was built in the early 1930s on the Victoria Bridge Road end of the triangle of land occupied by Nos 7, 8 & 9 roads. The local hard water was piped to the plant from the two reception tanks, and after treatment the soft water was stored inside the softening plant itself. From here pipes led to the water cranes at the two sheds and by the Avon river bridge. The plant was in the charge of one man and an assistant, and was worked as an eight hour, day-time shift. Their job was to prepare a chemical cocktail to add to the water to reduce the furring. The ingredients comprised lime, iron sulphate, soda-ash (sodium hexameta-phosphate) and an anti-sticking agent. The resultant brew resembled a barley wine, a rich reddish-brown colour.

When the mixture was ready in its vat, it was winched to the top of the tower by means of a roof-mounted crane, and poured into the water tank. Great quantities were required each day due to the large water consumption at the m.p.d. The treatment was certainly effective, but produced a substantial amount of sludge, which had to be removed on a regular basis. This was achieved automatically. Set in the base of the tower was a 200 lb cylinder of air. At hourly intervals this injected a blast of air into the plant with a tremendous force, sufficient indeed to

50

blow the sludge out into the sludge-pit. The motor started up with a tremendous noise. On the siding adjoining the water softening plant, an old loco tender or two would be stabled, and it was into these that the sludge would be disposed. To lift the sludge from the pit into the tender, a mechanical device was employed, known to Bath locomen as the mangle. This was so named as it was worked by two men turning a handle on either end of a drum which moved a continuous chain belt mounted inside a tube. Discs fixed at regular intervals along the chain drew the sludge through the tube and upwards, ultimately spilling out of the end overhanging the tender. When the tenders were full they were taken away to Gloucester to be emptied. The most favoured train for this was the 11.29pm freight to Westerleigh, from whence they would be worked forwards on a main line service.

The work at the plant was physically demanding, from the manhandling of bags of lime and working the mangle, to the long climb up the ladder to operate the crane. It also required skill, a knowledge of exactly how much of each ingredient needed to be added and when the concoction was ready – there was no computerised

Looking east along No 7 road at the ex-S&D shed. The base of the water-softening tower is on the extreme right, while the flat-roofed store building belonging to the plant is behind the 2P (which still carries her pre-nationalisation number of 568, and the letters LMS on the tender). Behind the 4-4-0 is an Ivatt Mogul, or 'Doodlebug', with the two oil storage tanks towering above. A Stanier Black 5 brings up the rear.   8.10.49   the late Ivo Peters

The short-lived and unused oil-storage tanks are seen behind one of Bath Shed's venerable large-boilered 7Fs, No 53807. The flat-roofed building on the left is the store belonging to the water-softening plant. 21.4.51 the late Ivo Peters

quality control in those days! Between 1939 and 1944 Thomas Hilton was in charge of the plant, being succeeded for the remainder of the decade by Sid Thursfield. Sid lived at 2 Albert Buildings, literally in the shadow of the tower. He was a popular and conscientious man but sadly had a fatal heart attack after climbing the ladder in the course of his duty.

Oil Fuelling Plant. In the summer of 1946 it was announced that 27 of Bath's engines were to be converted for oil-burning as part of a new Government policy. Men came down from Derby to plan details of the new plant and to discuss the phased changeover that the scheme would require. The new oil depot was to be on some of the land occupied by Nos 7, 8 & 9 roads, the spaces between which had previously been used from time to time to stack coal reserves. These sidings were now to be rearranged to allow for the erection of two large circular storage tanks, mounted on concrete bases. No 7 road was moved slightly nearer the footpath and No 8 was taken out altogether in order to make room. The tanks were duly put up, but the pumps and valve gear were not installed, even though they had been delivered. The two engines which had been converted for oil firing – two of Stanier's Black 5s – had to be supplied from an oil tank-wagon stabled at the buffer stop end of the coal road. An announcement came at the end of 1947 that the plan had been officially abandoned due to a national lack of funds. The two black tanks stood empty and useless for four or five years, until they were eventually dismantled and sold for scrap. The two circular bases remained *in situ* like giant concrete pancakes.

4. Locos and Locomen

PART 1: FOOTPLATE GRADES

In seeking to gain an insight into the routine which existed at Bath shed, it may be useful to approach this on a rising scale of seniority, following the route taken by an aspiring school-leaver whose ambition was to become an engine driver.

Call Boys and Bar Boys. On the Midland Region boys could start work in the Locomotive Department at the age of 14 (on the Great Western it was 16; one of the many differences between the two companies). Apart from general duties like sweeping floors and making tea, certain specific duties had also to be undertaken. On the 10.00pm to 6.00am shift this involved calling crews who were due to book on from about midnight until 6.00am. The call boys had to knock-up train crews an hour or so in advance of their booking-on time, a duty which took them all over the city in the course of a night. On reaching a house they were supposed to knock loudly at the door and call out the roster and booking-on time, not leaving until the man had acknowledged. Some boys were rather more purposeful in this than others, as disturbed neighbours would attest! One or two boys even called out the state of the weather! When crews had to be called for trains which were closely timed and the booked men were spread widely around the city, a young fireman or passed cleaner would be volunteered by the foreman to help out.

Things went well enough when the boy knew his geography of the city, but a youngster recently started who was only familiar with his own district, could encounter problems.

In the late 1920s the foreman decided to catch out a rather impetuous youth. He told him to make a call at a house at the top of Bath Lane, a location which had changed its name to Dartmouth Avenue some 30 years before. The boy confidently set off, only to realise that he did not know where Bath Lane was. As many men lived in Twerton or Oldfield Park, he set off in that direction. While wandering through Oldfield Park he came across a policeman and enquired of him, but he was singularly unhelpful, saying that it was the boy's job to know these things. Sensing that the house must be somewhere in

Widcombe or Larkhall, he set off for the east of the city – with no success. Eventually he returned to the shed to admit defeat, to be told that 'It's off the Brickyard; I'd've told you that if you'd asked me'. The boy learned his lesson, but the driver was late for work!

In the early 1920s the S&D suspended the practice of calling for a while for men who lived beyond a certain, quite small radius of the motive power depot. This was a so-called economy measure, as it meant that fewer boys needed to be recruited. The Midland, however, continued to call. This led to the anomalous situation where two men who lived almost next door to each other in Railway Place (opposite Bath Spa station), received different treatment. One worked on the Midland and the other on the S&D. Both were due on duty at about the same time, but only the Midland man was called. His colleague overslept and missed the turn (and his pay). When the LMS and the S&D amalgamated for operational purposes, an agreement was made whereby former S&D men need only work on the 'Dorset' if they wished, whereas Midland men could be called upon to work either line. Calling was still an issue which was exercising minds, and so in an effort to rationalise manpower in the new joint enterprise, a calling zone was delineated, this actually being marked on a street map displayed in the shed office. The areas in which men were to be called all lay south of the river. Thus a curious situation subsisted for many years in which men living right out at Odd Down or Combe Down would be called, whilst colleagues living just across the river and much nearer the shed would not!

The other specific job of a newly-started lad was that of **bar boy**. From time to time the fireboxes of engines needed cleaning: clinker and grime had to be cleaned from the fire bars at the bottom of the grate. On the Midland, firemen had to clean their own fires, unlike the GWR where fire droppers were employed solely for this purpose. The fire had to be dropped in order for the bars to be removed, this being done by shovelling out the contents of the firebox with a long-handled shovel. Once the bars had been removed and cleaned, it was the job of a bar boy to crawl into the smokebox through the stoke hole to put them back again. Although the bars

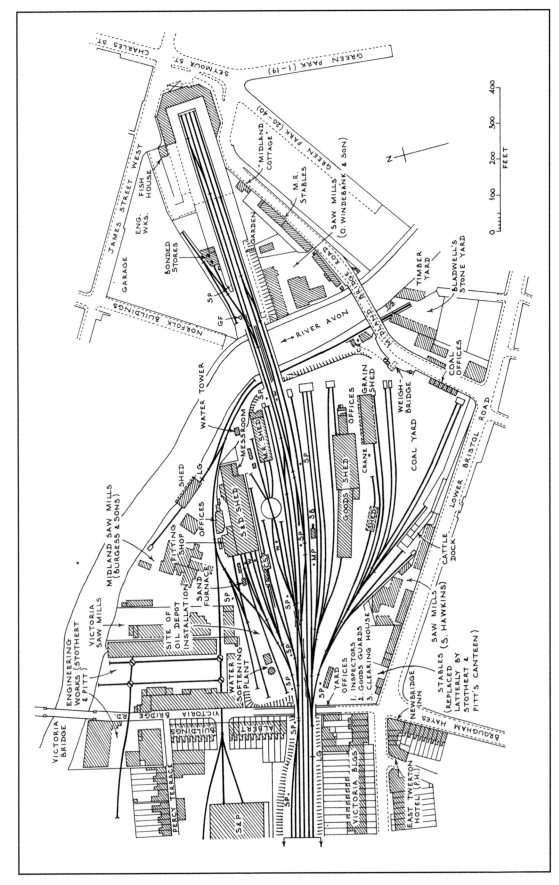

Composite track layout diagram for Green Park station, motive power depot and sidings

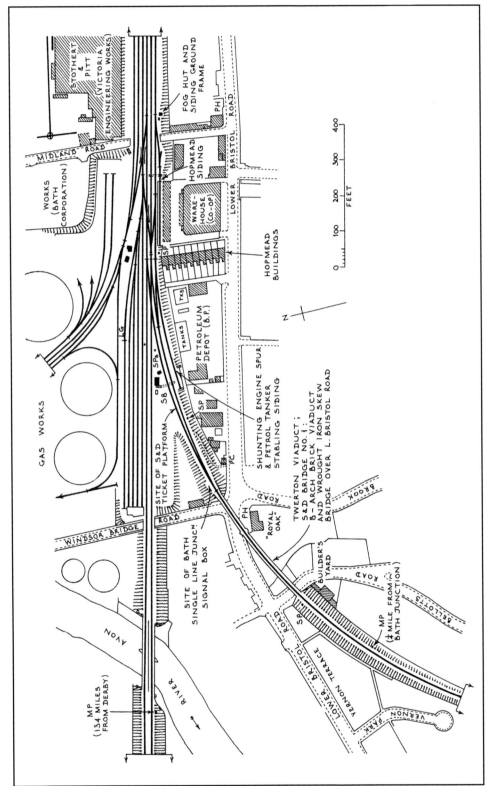

Composite track layout diagram for the Midland and S&D lines and sidings at Bath Junction

had definite upper and lower edges, and lugs to ensure equal spacing in the grate, a new boy could make 'a right mess of it' until they knew what they were doing, with bars being put in upside down and insecurely anchored. This work would be done on cold engines in advance of a Monday morning when the steam raiser would have a busy time preparing a number of locomotives for the start of a working week. Before the steam raiser got to work, the boys would be sent into the firebox to clean the brick arch and also the smokebox crown.

Cleaners. Depending on vacancies, a boy might expect to advance to the job of cleaner at around the age of 17 or 18. This entailed a good deal of elbow grease in getting the engines spick and span. The combination of a ball of cotton waste and paraffin jelly were the tools of the trade, teams of young men being allocated to a certain number of locomotives. They came on duty at 6.00am and 8.00am and at 1.30pm and 10.00pm. As with other grades they had a rolling rest day every other week, but at least had no Sunday work. They were organised by a foreman cleaner from his cabin at the end of No 3 road in the lower shed. With the run-down in manpower in the last years, the work of this grade was the first to suffer from the lack of recruitment.

Passed Cleaners. After a year or so as a cleaner, men would hope to take the next step up the ladder. Having learnt the basic Rules and Regulations applying to work on the footplate – notably Rule 55 on the protection of trains – a cleaner put in for a verbal fireman's examination. If he passed, he would be available for work as a spare fireman should an opportunity arise, as during the summer peak period or Bank Holidays. In many ways, cleaners and passed cleaners could virtually be jacks of all trades, helping around the shed and assisting on the coal stage.

Firemen. The length of time a passed cleaner had to wait until he could fire on a regular basis depended upon local vacancies and changes in the pattern of train working. A number of men who joined the railway not long before the last war found that promotion was fairly rapid. If vacancies arose at other sheds on the LMS men could put in for them, but they had the option to move or stay where they were, whereas on the GWR men were expected to move. In 1934, a man in his first year of firing was paid 57/- a week (£2.85), the minimum age for this being 18.

When a fireman booked on for duty in the time office, or signing-on lobby, his first job was to inspect the fire and water in his booked engine. Following this, the sandboxes were checked and the lamps attended to. Whether the engine had been put in steam from cold, or kept simmering from a previous turn of duty, one of the preparation gangs would have kept an eye on it, so what the fireman had to do was to build up the steam pressure and get the engine ready for the road. Before and during the last war, firemen had always to attend to this, the time allowed depending on the class of the locomotive. Thus a 7F for example was given an hour, while for a 2P, 3F or 4F it was 40 minutes. Added to this was 15 minutes walking time and 10 minutes for coaling. In later days, this final preparation was still frequently undertaken, but on some rosters men booked on only 15 minutes or so before taking the engine off shed.

When the engine returned to shed, a further allowance was made in the calculation of hours. If another crew were taking over, the fireman going off duty did not need to dispose of the fire, and so had 15 minutes for booking off. His colleague, likewise, did not have to work on the fire to anything like the same extent; his extra time came at the end of the shift when the engine had to be disposed on shed. This entailed shovelling out the smokebox and throwing the contents on the ground for removal by a shed labourer later. If the fire needed to be kept in for the next day, he would pull back some of the coals into a corner of the smokebox. The exercise of shovelling out was tedious and could be time-consuming if the fire had not been allowed to thin down before coming on shed. During and after the last war the practice grew for firemen to lift the fire bars – with a fire iron – and knock the fire through the grate into the ash pan, where it could either be shovelled off or hosed off into the ash pit. Sixty minutes were allowed for disposing a large engine such as a 7F, and 30 minutes for the smaller classes of engine.

The Ivatt 2-6-2 tank engines and many of the Standard engines shedded at Bath were fitted with self cleaning smokeboxes, this being indicated by a plate bearing the initials SC beneath the oval shed number plate on the smokebox door. The device consisted of a cage-like mesh fitted to the inside of the smokebox which was designed to trap 'smokebox char'. Its function was to reduce the frequency with which the smokebox required to be cleaned, and also to make the servicing much easier. Quite often the gaps between cleaning were too great, especially on visiting engines in summer – and on opening the smokebox door the fireman would often be confronted by a wall of ash and cinders.

When working back to Bath on S&D freight trains, firemen tried to have a bright but low fire by the time they reached Midford, as they did not want to spend a long time in the shed afterwards disposing of a large fire. The drawback with this was that if they had to stop at a signal or missed the single line tablet at Midford signalbox and the train consequently had to stop, it meant a cold start with a small fire up to Combe Down tunnel. With the train labouring by the time it got to the tunnel, a consequently unpleasant crawl through the restricted bore would give the crew a hard time. Conversely, if the fireman still had a big fire at Midford, the driver would help him to get rid of it by some heavy-handed regulator work. Opening the engine right up, the exhaust blast sharpened up to a bark, sending cinders and lumps of burning coal showering out of the chimney. At night this made quite a pyrotechnic display, while one fireman related how they would 'do it for a lark; to show off' in the summer if they saw people picnicking or walking in the fields below Summer Lane and De Montalt!

Firing was a definite art. No two engines steamed in exactly the same way and so the method of firing had to be varied accordingly. Firemen became conversant with individual engines. Thus for example 0-6-0 4F No 4146 (later 44146) 'liked a shallow fire with the flames dancing; but with not too much up front otherwise you had trouble'. Some engines were unpredictable, such as 7F No 53810, which would steam really well one day and then give the fireman problems the next. The Bulleid West Country Light Pacifics were also erratic, a tendency made worse in that Bath firemen were unused to their wider but relatively shallow fireboxes. They had to modify their technique substantially, finding it difficult to 'fire around the corners of the box'. Some firemen found that the most effective way of spreading the fire was to build up a large mound in the centre of the box and allow the vibration of the engine to disperse the periphery of the hump in all directions. Firemen found these engines very demanding; indeed, they consumed so much fuel that when leaving Bath they would already have a big fire and as much coal on the tender as it could take: the coal was piled so high that it had to be gauged to make sure that there would be adequate clearance for the restricted bores of Devonshire and Combe Down tunnels!

Yet other locos had reputations as constantly poor steamers, and this called for continuous vigilance and skill on the part of the fireman. Despite his efforts, if steam pressure continued to fall, a train might well have to stop in order to get the pressure back, to have a 'blow up', in railway parlance. One fireman actually had the fire go out on him on Standard class 5 No 73001 on the 10.15pm 'Perishables' at Bitton one night, blocking the up line for several hours while the fire was relit and built up from scratch!

To an observer the trials and tribulations being experienced on the footplate were often not appreciated, as when for instance a poorly-steaming freight was just about managing to keep moving with Masbury Summit on the Mendips in sight and the welcome down grade thereafter. All of a sudden the dogs of the Mendip Hunt burst through the fence at the top of the cutting and began swarming across the tracks. The Hunt Master appeared and remonstrated with the crew for not stopping; his dogs might be killed. As the train was travelling at less than walking pace, the driver did not feel moved to accede to his request – the dogs were better able to move than his engine!

Where locos were known to be poor steamers, some drivers would resort to the use of a razor (these devices being known also as a chopper or jimmy). This piece of metal was so called because it resembled a cut-throat razor and when an engine was reported to be steaming badly the driver would turn to his fireman and say 'we had better cut her throat then'. It was fitted with two wire clips to enable it to be wedged over the blast pipe, and was often held in place with either a heavy brake block or secured with a nut and bolt. This had the effect of increasing the sharpness of the blast and certainly improved the engine's performance. No 53806 regularly had her throat cut! The razor was an invaluable if highly unofficial piece of equipment for many drivers; young firemen who were not used to this practice and did not know that one had been fitted, became somewhat fearful at the frightful noise the engine made when going through the tunnels on the way out of Bath. Many locomen knew when one had been fitted because the exhaust was accompanied by a distinctive whistling sound.

Passed Firemen. After three years of firing, or a

minimum number of turns of duty, a man was deemed to have sufficient experience to be considered for driving, subject to his passing an examination. If successful, his weekly wage in the mid 1930s rose to 72/– (£3.60), a figure which 30 years later had crept slowly up to the sum of 284/– (£14.20). Interestingly enough the way the examination was conducted varied between the different regional divisions of British Railways: nationalisation did not bring standardisation. In 1950 the management of the motive power at Bath passed from the Midland Region to the Southern. Outwardly there was no change: the engines continued to be Midland, although their shed code plates were changed from 22C (Bristol Division) to 71G (Eastleigh District). The Southern Region continued to be responsible for administration until the end of 1957, and under their regime the test was entirely written and verbal, with no footplate assessment. An inspector travelled up to Bath from Eastleigh to conduct the examination, and if a man was passed by him he had then to report to Swindon on the Western for an eyesight test and general medical before being confirmed in the new grade. When the Western Region took over in 1958 the test was entirely practical – as it had been in LMS days – involving the firemen taking a driving test with an inspector in the cab and also answering a series of verbal questions. This further reassignment involved yet another re-coding of Bath's engines; this time from 71G to 82F. Once classified as a passed fireman a man could apply for posts as a driver when vacancies arose. If a man was prepared to move, he could get promotion quickly when prospects at his own shed were limited.

Drivers. These men were at the top of the tree, although there were different grades (or links) even here: from driving shunting engines through freight to local and express passenger trains. A top link man was paid 90/– (£4.50) a week in the mid 1930s, big money by railway standards! A man had to be 23 years old before he could become a driver. The term link was applied to differentiate the various categories of work and at Bath they were often referred to as gangs. In order to understand the wide range of work undertaken at Bath shed, the various links worked in 1958 are taken by way of illustration.

Link One. This was a passenger link, Bath's top link in fact, and was known at the depot as the passenger gang – in contrast to the other passenger link (seven) involving the local stopping trains to

Bristol which were mainly worked by tank engines and thus known as the 'tanky gang'. Link One consisted of eight sets of men and in 1958 covered the following trains on an eight-week repeating cycle as follows:

Week 1: 9.55am to Bournemouth; worked as far as Templecombe.
Week 2: 3.20pm stopping train to Templecombe.
Week 3: 12.01pm northbound 'Pines' as far as Gloucester.
Week 4: 4.37pm stopping train to Templecombe.
Week 5: 8.15am stopping train to Templecombe.
Week 6: 1.10pm stopping train to Templecombe.
Week 7: 6.55am to Bournemouth; worked as far as Templecombe.
Week 8: 10.15pm 'Perishables' to Derby as far as Birmingham.

Each of the above involved a booked return working.

The times at which men booked on and off duty depended upon the amount of preparation/disposal required for the engine concerned and upon any other duties which were included in the roster. Generally, men would book on anything from 45 minutes to an hour and 50 minutes before the departure of the train shown in the table above. The traditional practice was followed whereby early turns alternated with late.

One of the great fascinations of the steam engine is that every one seemed to be an individual; indeed, they could be looked on more as anthropomorphic than mechanical! It is hardly surprising, therefore, that locomen often had likes and dislikes when it came to particular classes of engine or even to individual locomotives.

The loco which predominated in Bath's top link in the 1920s and '30s was the 4-4-0 class 2 tender engine, commonly referred to as the 2P class. They were descended from, and often rebuilds of, early Midland engines. No 629 (later 40629) was a firm favourite with many drivers, while 633 had its supporters and critics in equal numbers. Their effective performance depended as much on the expertise of the crew as the mechanical soundness of the machine, as was attested by the appearance of the 4P compound class during the last war. Some drivers did not fully appreciate the principal of compounding – there were three cylinders instead of two – and as they treated them as a simple two-cylinder 2P, this gave their firemen a hard time! They were not suited to the nature of the work over the S&D as there was not the opportunity for them to run fast for long stretches, and so they soon disappeared.

Oliver Bulleid's West Country Pacific *Wilton* passing the top shed with the 7.05pm stopping train to Bournemouth West. This engine had been allocated to Bath m.p.d. between 1951 and 1954, and continued to make appearances for several years after her re-allocation (remaining in original unrebuilt form).   29.5.63   Hugh Ballantyne

The range of engines used in Link One was relatively small until the late 1930s, and locomen had the chance therefore to drive them with consummate skill. Then a number of new classes of engine began to appear on the scene; from the Black 5s and West Country Pacifics to the Standard classes 4, 5 and 9. Other engines also made rather more brief appearances, like the Horwich Crab and Ivatt Mogul. Bath's locomen certainly had variety and plenty of scope to develop and demonstrate their skills.

The one loco which brought forth most criticism from drivers was the Bulleid Pacific in its original, streamlined form. The variety of nicknames applied to these engines by Bath footplate crews is perhaps indicative of their lack of favour: 'tin lizzies', 'channel packets', 'spam cans', 'green-backs', or simply 'green 'uns'. Men admitted that on a straight, level road they ran well, achieving high point-to-point speeds. However, the S&D was anything but straight and level in its northern section; the only place where they could really show their paces was in the vicinity of Bailey Gate on the fast length between Corfe Mullen and Blandford Forum on the Dorset section.

One problem to which they were prone was slipping. On wet, greasy rails difficulty might well be expected, but they were liable to bouts of slipping even when running at speed on dry rails. The area around Wellow was a bad place for this; enginemen felt that the motion on the series of curves here was unbalanced, and without any warning or apparent reason the engine would suddenly lose her feet – somewhat disconcerting when they were travelling at 50 to 60 mph. When slipping occurred in Combe Down or Devonshire tunnels the conditions on the footplate were appalling.

Following trials over the S&D in March 1951, four of these engines were allocated to Bath shed. In some quarters this event was viewed with serious reservations as men remembered an earlier incident when one of the Pacifics had first appeared on the line. This had been in 1948. On Saturday 6th November, Bournemouth Town Football Club were playing Bristol City in an early round of the FA Cup at Ashton Gate. Two 'soccer specials' were organised from Bournemouth and district to take the large numbers of supporters to Ashton Gate station via the S&D. The first train originated in Christchurch with Southern men working it to Broadstone where an S&D crew were waiting to take over. The latter had travelled down from Bath earlier in the morning and viewed with certain unease the sight of the 12-coach train arriving in the charge of a Pacific – still sporting Southern Railway livery and its pre-nationalisation number of 21C149 (later 34049) *Anti-Aircraft Command*. Although the crew soon found that the engine was steaming badly, it made a reasonable attempt at the more easily-graded section between Broadstone and Evercreech Junction. With a heavy train of 420 tons the driver was growing apprehensive about the engine's ability to cope with the climb to Masbury Summit. At Evercreech the train stopped for the loco to take on water and for 2P No. 40505 to couple up and assist as pilot on to Bath. The driver's fears soon proved well founded. Between the Junction and Evercreech New station the Pacific struggled, with the comparatively light 2P making sterling efforts to keep the formation moving. The next three miles to Shepton Mallet were on a rising gradient of 1:50, and the performance here was chronic: it took an hour and a half! The engine barely moved between each feeble exhaust blast, the train proving too heavy for the pilot alone to manage. The fans were growing increasingly agitated, while the special following behind was correspondingly delayed. Limping into Shepton Mallet the train stopped to take on water again as the exertion of the climb had drastically lowered the level in the tender. During this stop the fireman worked hard on the fire in an effort to raise steam pressure.

If the crew and passengers were concerned at the train's late running, so was Control at Bath. The consternation at the state of affairs was indicated by the heavy presence of top brass on the platform when the train finally reached Green Park. The only explanation the experienced driver could give was poor steaming. Another engine was booked to take the train on to Bristol, but by the time the fans in the following special got there, the match had already kicked off. There was, in the words of the driver of the Pacific, 'one hell of a row'.

To complete the story, the return trip that evening with the same engine was also not without incident. The powers that be had evidently decided that it would be wiser to let the other train run ahead of that hauled by *Anti-Aircraft Command*. The second train was timed to leave Bath ahead of the last down stopping train between Bath and Bournemouth, but the guard was unhappy at the way in which the train was marshalled. S&D regulations permitted only two coaches to be conveyed to the rear of the guard's vehicle, but on this train there were five. He informed the station foreman that the formation would have to be reassembled. As this was probably the first time carriages with buck-eye type couplings had worked into Bath, the foreman did not think that the passenger shunter would be able to deal with it. A Southern Region inspector travelling on the special was becoming concerned at the delay – the morning had been quite enough – but the guard was adamant. The District Controller now joined the scene. The suggestion was made that an extra brake-coach be added to the rear, but this would take time and increase the load to thirteen vehicles. In the end the guard was formally ordered to work the train, the Controller taking the responsibility for overriding the rules! The train left Green Park half an hour late, with the engine making heavy weather of the banks in spite of the efforts of the pilot engine in front. The climb from Radstock was painfully slow, so much so that as they crawled through Midsomer Norton the inspector's earlier agitation turned into out-right frustration and then desperation when the guard told him that they had another six miles of the climb to the summit still to go!

Another notable, and notorious, feature of these engines resulted from the enclosing of the chain-driven valve gear, centre connecting-rod and crank axle in an oil bath. Leakage from the bath was commonplace and men complained of heavy oil loss during a journey. The sharp swing to the left at Bath Junction on southbound S&D trains sent oil showering over the ballast. It was not unknown for the oil bath to catch fire. The sinuous nature of the line south of Bath exacerbated the tendency of the oil baths to leak and by the time a loco reached Masbury, there was oil everywhere. The steep down grades on either side of Masbury Summit found out another problem: poor braking power. With the brakes firmly applied in an effort to control the train, the temperature underneath the cladding of the engine rose higher and higher, and this combined with the oil which had oozed out from the bath quite commonly caused fire to break out. It was easy to tell when there had been a fire as the paintwork on the cladding was blistered.

Although many drivers have their horror stories of the 4-6-2s, the majority of journeys were incident-free, and on the positive side the engines gave a smooth ride and ran well when on the level. They possessed such innovations as electric lights in the cab, which greatly helped the firemen at night, and steam-operated firebox doors.

Links Two, Three and Four. These were all freight links, or goods gangs as many Bath men referred to them. Whilst the name is self-explanatory, it covered a wide spectrum of turns, from the local shuttle trips with a 4F to Westerleigh to the longer, more demanding trips with a 7F over the S&D, or a long distance freight to the Midlands. Additionally, the 6.05pm and 7.05pm S&D passenger departures were included. Each link contained eight sets of men and covered the following workings on an on-going sequential pattern, early turns alternating with late:

Link Two
Week 1:	3.30am	S&D	freight
Week 2:	10.50pm	S&D	freight
Week 3:	9.23am	MR	freight
Week 4:	6.05pm	S&D	passenger
Week 5:	8.55am	S&D	freight
Week 6:	9.15pm	MR	freight
Week 7:	5.50am	S&D	freight
Week 8:	12.35pm	S&D	freight

Link Three
Week 1:	11.29pm	MR	freight
Week 2:	11.00am	S&D	freight
Week 3:	7.05pm	S&D	passenger
Week 4:	6.30am	MR	freight
Week 5:	7.18pm	S&D	freight
Week 6:	4.00am	MR	freight
Week 7:	2.10pm	MR	freight
Week 8:	2.40am	S&D	'Mail'

Link Four
Week 1:	4.50am	MR	freight
Week 2:	Spare*		
Week 3:	VAR*		
Week 4:	8.55pm	S&D	freight
Week 5:	VAR*		
Week 6:	2.00pm	S&D	freight
Week 7:	5.00am	S&D	freight
Week 8:	6.27pm	MR	freight

*These turns will be explained under Links Five and Six

Much of the work on the Midland line was performed by the old faithful class 4s, the Fowler-designed 0-6-0 tender engines, and before the war by the Deeley rebuilds or 3Fs. These were rarely seen at Bath in later years, except perhaps occasionally as pilots on summer expresses.

The one loco which really belonged to Bath shed is of course the 2-8-0 class 7. These powerful engines were built specially to haul heavy freight trains over the Mendip Hills between Bath and Evercreech. In 1914 Bath S&D shed took delivery of six of these engines: Nos 80 to 85 (BR Nos 53800–53805). They had been designed by the Midland Railway's Chief Mechanical Engineer Sir Henry Fowler, and built at the company's Derby Works. They were fitted with tender cabs and were right-hand drive – a fact which had external expression in the placing of the ejector gear on the right-hand side of the boiler. Footplate crews did not like the tender cab as it made the job of taking the fire irons off the tender somewhat difficult. By 1920 they had all been removed.

In 1914 the 7Fs were the heaviest engines on the line, and had pride of place. As the bridges over Midland Road and Victoria Bridge Road in Bath were not strong enough to take the engines, they were unable to work into the m.p.d. While the bridges were being strengthened, the engines in the interim were stabled and maintained at Radstock, but as 'Bath engines' a cleaning gang was sent out from the home base to attend them. When working into Bath, tender first, they had to stop short of the goods line into the Midland Bridge Road yard, uncouple, and pull forwards onto the Midland main line and allow another loco which had been waiting on the goods line to couple up to the train and draw it along the siding. Whilst waiting for the change of engine the brakes of the guards van were usually sufficient to hold the train, although a few wagon brakes could be pinned down if it was felt desirable. This inconvenience was only short-lived, but even when the 2-8-0s were able to work into the m.p.d., the turntable was not long enough to be used by them; so the convention was to work chimney first out of Bath and tender first back. Running tender first into an icy, squally north wind in winter was most unpleasant for the footplate crew – the tender cabs perhaps had not been such a bad idea after all! The Avon river bridge at the station was not strengthened at this time, and consequently the 7Fs were prohibited from crossing it.

In 1925 a further five 7Fs were built for the S&D by Robert Stephenson & Co of Darlington. These had larger boilers – 5' 3" diameter instead of 4' 9" – and were left-hand drive, Nos 86 to 90 (BR Nos 53806–53810). At first all engines were fitted with cast-iron blocks. On particularly heavy trains, when the brakes needed to be firmly applied, the

A fine study of one of Sir Henry Fowler's 7Fs, 53806, captured in this panned shot storming up the 1:50 bank past the site of the former brickworks in Oldfield Park with the 2pm freight to Evercreech Junction. Notice the tablet-catcher on the tender for use when running tender-first. No 53806 was the last of the 1925 batch of this class to be fitted with a small boiler (August 1955). She was taken out of service in January 1964.   6.8.63   Hugh Ballantyne

blocks could be almost completely worn away and it was by no means uncommon to damage the steel wheel tyres. It was necessary for the blocks to be changed virtually every day, and each of the three shifts at Bath m.p.d. had a brakesman on duty whose sole function was to change the blocks. The cast-iron blocks were later replaced by Ferodo blocks. However, the first type of these to be used had a tendency to grip the wheels too tightly – even under light application – and gave off a powerful smell. They were improved later.

Designed to meet the demanding nature of freight work on the Mendip section of the S&D, the 7Fs were not intended to be used as passenger engines; indeed, they were not fitted with carriage steam heating equipment. The demands made on motive power at Bath shed during summer Saturdays in the 1950s and early '60s were such that they were of necessity pressed into service. Initially, this was very much as a last resort, but it became increasingly common to see them on local trains and as train-engines or pilot engines on expresses at peak weekends. The need for, and suitability of, the class 7s was restricted to the summer months, although they could very occasionally be used *in extremis* at

other times when nothing else was available. In the depths of winter this can hardly have been popular with the passengers, but a cold train was better than no train. When used for long journeys, the engines could sometimes run rather hot, especially at the front end. The customary groaning sound emitted by the motion could become disconcertingly loud. The engines possessed lubricators: large boxes mounted on the running plate behind the raised section over the cylinders. They were often referred to as the 'firemen's friend'. They were self-acting as the locomotive moved, and providing the motion was kept well lubricated, it would save on coal and water and thus ease the fireman's job. When the groaning became too loud for comfort, the handle on the lubricators would be given a few extra manual turns whenever possible in an effort to prevent hot running.

Link Five. Classified as a freight link, this was actually Bath shed's spare gang. The designation 'spare' was applied to a variety of extra or substitute work. Men were occasionally required to work additional trains such as holiday relief specials, excursions, ballast trains and the like. With engines requiring periodic maintenance or repair, there was much movement between the depots at Bath, Templecombe and Barrow Road. During the summer months this was increased by the borrowing of engines to cover additional rosters. Spare sets of men were used extensively to effect these movements. The second type of work covered by this link was that of absent colleagues (excluding rest days). Men might not turn up for duty for all sorts of reasons, some of which were known in advance – like medicals, eye-sight tests, annual leave and notified illness – while others either failed to report without prior notification or were too late on duty to work the rostered train. As it was important that trains ran as scheduled, it was necessary to have a reserve of men who could be called upon at short notice.

In the mid-winter months, six sets of men were assigned to this link during a 24-hour period, with a four-hour overlap between each eight-hour shift to ensure continuous availability. Thus the first gang booked on at 2.00am, followed by others at 6.00am and 10.00am, then 2.00pm 6.00pm and 10.00pm. For the bulk of the year, however, the link was made up to 12 sets. This allowed a much greater density of cover. By drafting passed cleaners into the relief link, the necessary restructuring could be achieved.

By its very nature, the work was varied and did not follow any set pattern, other than the usual alternation of early and late shifts. The actual daily regime depended upon the reason for any particular job being done. Thus, taking October 1958 as an example, one passed fireman found himself filling in for a regular driver in Link Three who was taking his annual leave. This entailed the spare man working Bath's turn 22A: the 6.30am Midland freight from Monday to Thursday and again on Saturday; whilst on the Friday – which was the rest day for that particular roster – he had to cover the 7.05am banking turn (No 21B) at short notice.

The turns listed as VAR in both this link and Link Four were used to cover rest days taken by drivers and firemen in any of the links. As rest days were tabulated well in advance of the completion of any particular week's Train Arrangements, the turns were fixed – if highly varied. Thus in one week in late October for example, one team found themselves rostered for the midnight banking turn on Monday morning; the 8.55am S&D freight to Evercreech Junction on Tuesday; the 9.23am Midland freight to Westerleigh on Wednesday; 5.50am pick-up goods on the S&D on Thursday; and 6.55am S&D

passenger on Saturday (Friday was a rest day). Variety indeed! The allocation of VAR workings was relatively infrequent in Link Five during the summer months, as the two turns were distributed amongst 12 teams of men.

Link Six. As with Link Five this was also classified as a freight link, although referred to at Bath as the loco gang, the work actually being classified under the title relief.

Unlike the rosters outlined above, the eight turns in this link followed a set pattern. In order to prepare, dispose and move engines on shed, men were required throughout the day, the timings of the shifts reflecting the distribution of the work to be done, as some periods were busier than others. The first turn began, curiously, at one minute past midnight, then at 3.00am, 9.20am and 11.00am; 12.15pm, 3.00pm, 3.45pm and 8.00pm. In addition to this, the banking/ shunting link provided two relief turns: 4.35am and 2.30pm. With each shift lasting eight hours, there was obviously a good deal of overlap, notably in mid-afternoon when six teams were on duty simultaneously – this being the time of day when a number of engines which had gone out in the morning were now back on shed and either required preparing for a new turn of duty, or disposing, while other engines had to be got ready for the rosters which began in the evening.

The driver in the team moved the engines about the depot as required. Thus the gang would coal up the locos at the coal stage, fill the tender with water and position the engine in the correct running order ready for duty. The favourite location for stabling the engines was the gas siding, then Tommy's siding or the boat road. On summer Saturdays all three locations would be crammed with engines. The prepared locos were then chalked up on the noticeboard in the lower shed for locomen's information. Some men got this particular turn of duty off to a fine art, especially on a winter Saturday evening when there was not much to get ready and only little to dispose of, and would finish the work well inside the eight hours – and there was always the added incentive of a quick visit to the *Newbridge Inn* at the bottom of Brougham Hayes!

Taking the 3.00am–11.00am relief as an example of the work to be covered in one shift, the first duty for the men was to dispose of the engine which had arrived in Bath with the 9.28pm Poole to Bath freight (2.39am in the Midland Bridge Road yard). One hour was allowed for the disposing of a 7F, Black 5 or

Snow-plough engine for the winter of 1954/5 was Bagnall-built 0-6-0 tank engine 47465, seen here positioned over the ash pit at the top shed, and next to the ash pit wagon.   27.2.55   Hugh Ballantyne

Standard class of tender engine, and 1½ hours for a West Country Pacific. Clinker and ash had to be shovelled out of the smokebox, ash emptied from the ash-pan into the pit, and the fire cleaned. Their second duty was to walk to the station at about 6.00 in order to take over the engine of the 12.37am Leicester parcels (due into Green Park just after 6.00). They relieved the parcels crew on arrival, as the men had left Bath at 10.15 the previous evening and had thus completed their set turn of duty. The passenger shunter was on hand to uncouple the engine and the 3.00 relief men performed the necessary shunting of vans at the station. The engine was generally taken to the shed at about 8.00 where it was coaled, watered and had the fire cleaned ready for its return north with the midday 'Pines'. The engine would then be left to await the arrival of the men from Bath's Link One at 10.30, releasing the relief men to dispose of an engine which had worked in from Westerleigh, their third and final task.

Whereas most engines only required the attention of the loco gang for a few hours, there was one exception: the snow-plough engine.

During the mid-winter months, one of Bath's 0-6-0 shunting tank engines was fitted up with a snow plough front and back, which entailed removing buffers from their beams. The loco was kept in light steam and generally parked on the short siding leading from the turntable at the top shed. It was the job of one of the loco gangs to attend the engine in order to make sure that the fire was clean and water tanks sufficiently stocked so that she could be got ready quickly if her services were required. Sometimes this task was overlooked, especially early in the winter when the engine had probably not been used for days on end. This, indeed, was the situation at the beginning of the atrocious winter of 1962/63 when Fowler 3F No 47557 was the snow-plough engine. There was an unexpected and quite heavy fall of snow on Boxing Day, and it was decided to send the engine over the line to Evercreech Junction and back to make sure that the road was clear. When the men assigned to this working climbed aboard the engine, however, they found the boiler pressure low and the fire in a terrible state. Much of it had to be thrown out and built up again almost from scratch before the engine could leave the depot – very late that evening. Fortunately it was not really required as the snow fall had not been as heavy on the Mendips as had been feared, but it served as a warning, for only four days later there was another heavy snow fall. Being a Sunday there was little disruption to services, and a chance to clear the lines. No 47557 set off in mid-morning to clear the line to Mangotsfield, and then departed with the intention of clearing the tracks to Evercreech – a destination she was not to reach, as she became utterly and completely stuck in a deep drift at Winsor Hill. Unable even to move their engine backwards, the crew took refuge for the night in a nearby permanent way hut. The next day the tank engine was pulled out of the drift by a 7F which had been sent to find her, but because of the need to attend to the slight damage caused by her 45 mph impact with deep snow, her role as a snow plough engine devolved upon sister loco No 47496 – and a very demanding role that proved to be in the Arctic blizzards of the next few days!

One of the regular duties of the loco gang was to fill the sand-boxes on engines, which often necessitated drying out the sand first. This was done in the sand furnace housed in the corrugated hut between Nos 5 & 6 roads. On a cold winter's day this was a popular job, as the sand-heating plant provided a pleasantly warm refuge. The cleaners often went in there as well, and would stay for as long as they thought they could get away with it – and at least the foreman cleaner knew where to look for them when they were needed!

When a driver was about to take an engine off shed, he would satisfy himself when starting his turn of duty that everything was in order with the locomotive, for once he was beyond shed limits it became his responsibility if anything went wrong. Until that time, any faults or deficiencies could be put down to the loco gangs!

The personnel in the loco gang changed from time to time. They often included passed firemen who undertook the role of driver, while passed cleaners were also brought in at busy times to work as firemen. This link was also used as a light duty for men who were not 100% fit. For example, eyesight tests were carried out regularly and if men were not passed A1 they might be asked to do a stint in this gang. Men with high blood pressure or recovering from injury or long illness would also be put in this link pending a return to full health.

At busy times, or when a number of men in other links were away for one reason or another, personnel in the loco gang would have to cover driving or firing turns which could not be met by the spare link. This was particularly the case in July and August when passenger traffic was at its peak at weekends, and many locomen liked to have their annual fortnight's holiday. Such was the volume of work on summer Saturdays that the m.p.d. would borrow men from Radstock. With a lull in freight activity over the S&D to clear the decks for the procession of holiday expresses, the normal demand for banking and shunting attended to by Radstock locos did not exist for much of the day, and so the sub-shed had men to spare. As many as four men would travel into Green Park on the first up stopping train of the day, which left Radstock at 8.16 and was due into Bath at 8.42. Their contribution was always most welcome and one of the Radstock men in fact literally made an impression on Bath shed on one occasion.

In the last chapter mention was made of the short but steep incline between the loco road and the S&D shed. In August 1959 an incident occurred which demonstrated the dangers of this bank for the unwary. One of Radstock's older drivers had travelled up to Bath to give assistance to the loco gangs on one of the busiest Saturdays of the year. Though a driver of many years' standing, he was more used to his own shed's assortment of tank engines and, to a lesser extent, the 4Fs and 7Fs assigned to local freight work. The deputy foreman on duty that day asked him to move an engine which had worked up from Bournemouth that morning and which was positioned over the ash pit on No 3 road at the lower shed. She was to be moved over to No 2 road, coaled up ready for her return trip, and then taken back to No 3 road to await her turn of duty. There was nothing out of the ordinary in such a manoeuvre, but on walking out to the job the Radstock man found himself facing one of the rebuilt Bulleid West Country Pacifics, a class which was making its first appearance at Bath in this form. It was a good bit heavier than anything he was used to, and the cab layout was unfamiliar. Undaunted, he set off and backed the engine beneath the coal shutes. With the coaling complete, he moved off No 2 road and out onto the incline in order to clear the points before setting back. So far so good. Putting the loco into reverse, the heavy engine began to move backwards, slowly at first, but then more quickly

Irresistible force, in the form of a 7F's tender, meets an immoveable object: the foreman cleaner's cabin at the end of No 3 road. The only masonry in the lower shed was used in the locomen's messroom, the end wall of which is visible behind the timbers; it also required repair which included the provision of a window.   August 1959   J Stamp

as momentum built up on the incline. She entered the shed line obviously rather too fast and on reaching for the steam brake, the driver found to his dismay that it came on only sluggishly as boiler pressure was low. The Pacific rolled relentlessly along the track, failing to slow sufficiently to prevent it buffering up to two wooden ash wagons which had been berthed by the shed entrance for the convenience of the shed labourers. Continuing ever backwards, the wagons were pushed before the loco into the shed itself. Right at the end of the line, against the buffers, was a 7F. Driven ever onwards, the ash wagons crashed against the 2-8-0's buffer beam and promptly disintegrated into a mass of splintered wood and tangled metal. Unfortunately, things literally did not stop there. The jolt caused by the impact, together with the continued progress of the West Country, pushed the 7F right through the wooden buffer-stops and on across the shed floor, the buffers of the tender crashing through the foreman cleaner's cabin and coming to rest against the back wall of the shed – behind which was the enginemen's messroom. Fortunately the wooden cabin was empty at the time, while the noise of destruction in the shed meant that the men in the messroom beat a hasty retreat – through both the door and the window – rather than wait and see what was causing the approaching havoc. The back of the shed was covered in ash and wooden wreckage, while the driver was covered in embarrassment! When the damaged back wall was rebuilt, a large window was incorporated so that the men had a view into the shed – just in case!

Link Seven. This passenger link, consisting of four sets of men in 1958, was commonly referred to as the tanky gang, and worked the passenger trains between Green Park and Bristol. Allowing for the rolling fortnightly rest day, the men in this link worked Mondays to Saturdays, the roster showing the same sort of rotation pattern described earlier, i.e. alternating morning and afternoon turns. The cycle began with the 6.20am, and was followed, in sequence, by the 5.45pm, 7.01am and 2.05pm. The two Sunday turns – 7.55am and 7.05pm – were covered by other teams of men. Subject to covering annual leave, drivers for the Sunday work were always taken from Link One. As there were eight men in this link they would have to work a Sunday turn once every four weeks, alternating between the morning and evening departures. The firemen for these trains followed a different roster cycle,

although in the main were also drawn from Link One, and included passed firemen and occasionally passed cleaners.

This link was considered another of the light duty links and was ideal for older men or men who were not completely fit. It was also a useful testing ground for young firemen and passed cleaners. Over the years the men in this link drove all sorts of tank engines. The locomotive most commonly used on the Bath–Bristol locals from the early years of this century to the 1940s was the 1P Johnson 0-4-4 class, although by no means all of these trains were booked out to tank engines. They were replaced by more modern engines designed by Sir William Stanier or Henry Ivatt for the LMS. In the former category was the 0-4-4 push-pull tank (2P) which was tried out on the Bath Branch just after the war. Two of these engines were delivered in December 1946, Nos 1902 and 1903 (later 41902 and 41903). No 1900 arrived at the end of March 1947 and 41904 early in 1949, these engines performing shunting duties at Bath as well as working the Midland locals. They gained a reputation as poor steamers and had a voracious appetite for water. When used to bank freight trains to Combe Down tunnel they could just about make the climb, but the water would be right at the bottom of the gauge glass. They were better on the easier gradients between Bath and Bristol, but were not popular. All four were removed in October 1949, and most drivers were not sorry to see them go. A similarly unsuccessful engine had been the 4-4-2 Tilbury tank class tried out on the Bath Branch in 1936. There was a unanimous sentiment that this engine was just not suited to the work, and the visit was short lived (indeed, only a matter of months).

The departure of the 0-4-4 tanks was phased with the appearance of two new classes of 2-6-2 tank engines, namely the Stanier class 3 and the Ivatt class 2. The former had in fact been around since 1935, but only now turned up on the Bristol locals. The three which regularly worked the trains were shedded at Barrow Road and not Bath, and consequently their appearances were restricted to the few rosters handled by the Bristol depot. It was more usual to find the slightly smaller Ivatt tank engine at the head of one of these trains. Four of these last-named engines were delivered from new to Bath towards the end of 1949, Nos 41240–3. Although the first of these was actually transferred to Barrow Road in September 1953, the Ivatts came to have a near

The Bath-based Ivatt tanks worked mostly on the Midland line with the exception of the 6.05pm out-and-back stopping service to Binegar. Here, No 41243, with its customary Midland 2-set, passes the well-kept gardens off King George's Road in June 1954.
R E Toop

monopoly of the regular workings on the line between the autumn of 1953 and the appearance of the Standard class 3 2-6-2 mixed traffic tank engines in 1958. While Barrow Road had four of the Stanier tanks in the mid 1950s – 40116, 40120, 40164 and 40174 – it became increasingly rare to see one of these engines on the Bath Branch.

The Ivatts were ideally suited to the work demanded of them, and gave sterling service. The three remaining after 1953 may be considered very much as Bath engines, spending more time there than at any other subsequent location. Built at Crewe Works, No 41241 remained for ten years, with only the briefest of sojourns on loan to Highbridge or Barrow Road. In October 1959 she was reallocated to Wellington, Shropshire (84H) and taken out of service in 1966. Bought by the privately-owned Keighley & Worth Valley Railway, she may be seen running today, resplendent in the lined-out black

livery of early British Railways.

Sister engines 41242 and 41243 actually remained in the West Country for longer, both being transferred to Templecombe in 1962, so that they continued to give service to the S&D, albeit in new territory further south. In almost continuous use, it was inevitable that mechanical problems would arise – as with any piece of machinery – and after years of uneventful and reliable work No 41243 went through a troublesome phase which disrupted traffic and had men running about after her. This began in a minor way on 16th February 1960. Three weeks later, on 8th March, she was booked to work the 6.05pm stopping train to Binegar. Coming off shed at about 5.50, she was derailed on the main line crossover points, and thus effectively blocked workings to and from the station at a particularly busy time of day. Although the engine was re-railed at 6.40, the points had been damaged and it was necessary to institute single-line working

Having drawn the wagons out of the S&D yard at Bath Junction to allow the train-engine to couple to the head, 4F No 44146 prepares to give much-needed assistance up the bank to Combe Down Tunnel.   5.9.60   Colin G Maggs

between the station and Bath Junction. Trains were delayed: the all-important 7.03 to Bristol which carried mail for the Midlands and North could not leave until 7.50pm. Various other failures that year resulted in some strange replacements, such as 4F No 44557 hauling the Binegar local, and Standard class 5 No 73052 the 8.11am stopper to Temple Meads – unusual motive power indeed.

Apart from one failure in May, due to a problem with her rocking grate, 1961 was clear; indeed, she did quite a bit of substitution for No 41242 in February when that engine had persistent trouble with leaking tubes and was not allowed to go off shed on a number of occasions. In August 1962 41243 was transferred to Templecombe from where she worked services between there and Highbridge/Bournemouth, until being withdrawn in July 1965.

Banking and Shunting Link. This unnumbered link consisted of eight turns of duty: 3 banking, 3 shunting and 2 relief. Excluding the last named,

which has been dealt with earlier, the drivers and firemen in this link covered the Midland Bridge Road and S&D yards, private sidings and banking to Combe Down tunnel, as well as acting as station pilot at Green Park when required. Despite the perception of this as a light duty link, it was in reality extremely busy. Shunting went on virtually continuously from the early hours of Monday to the early hours of the following Sunday. Much of the considerable freight carried by both the Midland and S&D travelled through from one system to the other, although a break of journey was necessitated at Bath. Trains arriving in either of the yards would have to be broken up and shunted, and new trains formed. In order to deal with the enormous volume of traffic, the work of the shunting gangs was endless. It was essential that wagons were marshalled in exactly the right order for the train in question and that the trains were actually assembled in time for the scheduled departure. Men would be kept so busy that it was often difficult to find time to eat a

0-6-0 3F tank engine No 47506 halts shunting operations in the Midland Bridge Road goods yard to allow Stanier 8F No 48706 to depart with a freight over the Midland Line. Note the mechanical gong on the substantial post immediately to the left of the 8F.   24.1.66   J Blake

sandwich, and they would have to work right up to signing-off time. Occasional pauses in shunting would be necessary, however, for wagons to be transferred between the yards.

As a rough rule, the terms banking and shunting indicated in which yard the loco would be working. Thus the banking turns which began at midnight, 7.05am and 4.30pm involved shunting the S&D yard at Bath Junction, and assembling and assisting Dorset freights. A 4F was invariably allocated to this work until the early 1960s. The shunting turns began at 5.35am, 1.15pm and 9.45pm, and applied to the engine working the Midland Bridge Road yard, attending incoming S&D freights and shunting at the station. An 0-6-0 tank engine was generally given this work. Indeed, this type of loco had an almost exclusive preserve of the work described as shunting, between 1929 and 1959. Seven of these 3F tank engines built to the same Fowler design as for the LMS, were manufactured during 1928 specifically for allocation to Bath. They were delivered in January the following year, and carried the S&D numbers of 19–25. When the S&D stock passed into LMS ownership in 1930 they were renumbered 7150–7156, while in the general renumbering exercise of 1932 they became 7310–7316. Following nationalisation they were renumbered yet again, this time by the simple expedient of prefixing them with a number 4: 47310–47316. By this time, some of the original engines had drifted away and been replaced by other members of the same class. By

1950 only 47316 remained; she continued to give service until November 1962, and was generally to be found at Radstock.

It has become common practice to refer to these engines as Jinty tanks. However, at Bath m.p.d. men often referred to them as Bagnalls. The reason for this is to be found in the origin of the first batch to arrive in the city. With large numbers of these ubiquitous engines requiring to be built in a short time, contracts were farmed out amongst a number of manufacturers: 422 were built in just eight years. The seven which were destined for Bath were built by the firm of W G Bagnall Ltd at their Castle Engine Works, Stafford (at a cost of £3,500 each). One of the later arrivals and long-service 3Fs to arrive at Bath, 47465, was also a Bagnall and thus the use of the name was perpetuated – and indeed extended to all engines of this class.

Generally, only one or two of these locos actually worked in Bath itself, the others being sent to the small sub-shed at Radstock to cover shunting duties at the various collieries and quarry sidings between Braysdown/Writhlington and Binegar, as well as shunting at and banking from Radstock itself. Although any one of the Bagnalls spent much of their time at the sub-shed, they would return to the parent shed for servicing or repairs, at which time an exchange would take place. Thus while the allocation remained numerically constant, the actual engines rotated considerably.

The last few years saw the use of an ex-GW

pannier tank on shunting duties; it never looked quite right somehow, especially when banking trains to Combe Down tunnel bunker-first! By this time, 1962 onwards, the distinction between banking and shunting was no longer made and the pannier tanks were quite able to manage the task of assisting S&D freights.

Loco Shunt. This link was singular in every sense of the word. It consisted of just one turn: from 7.00am until 3.00pm and was therefore referred to as the seven o'clock loco shunt. For many years it was worked by the same driver: Lou Ricketts. No specific engine was allocated to the work because much of this duty entailed using a spare engine in steam to move others around the depot as required; move the ash trucks for the ash pit men; and move wagons on the coal stage as necessary. The loco shunt also had its own small cabin, situated in the angle of land between the coal road and the line leading out of the lower shed. In the busier summer periods another loco shunt turn might be provided in this link (2.10pm) when there was still much moving of engines to be done. A man on light duties would be assigned to this, Fridays and Saturdays being the main days when this work would be particularly necessary. A fireman was also paired up with the driver for this work.

PART 2: NON-FOOTPLATE GRADES

Each man on the footplate relied upon the endeavours and skills of a whole range of other men from labourers to craft specialists.

Shed Labourers. A team of men was employed to undertake a variety of manual tasks around the depot from shovelling smokebox ashes into the ash trucks and coal on the coal stage, to general sweeping and tidying up. Coming off duty, a fireman would open the smokebox of his engine and shovel the ashes out to the track side. A labourer would later have to dispose of them into a strategically-placed ash truck: at the lower shed this was kept on the short siding between the coal road and No 2 road, and would be moved as required by the loco gang. Another truck(s) was stationed on the siding between the turntable road and the Gas siding at the top shed. When the trucks were full, and a worthwhile number had been made up, they were taken to Gloucester for tipping, although the railway periodically sold off ash and clinker as a filler or to be used in the manufacture of breezeblocks.

In 1934 labourers earned 42/– (£2.10) a week, but could sometimes earn useful overtime money on a Sunday by shovelling coal from stock piles into the wagons which would later be transferred to the coaling stage in the coming week. They might well shift up to 16 tons of coal in one of these overtime stints, firemen also doing this work if they too wished to earn a little extra cash.

Ash Pit Men. A slightly higher grade of labourer, earning an additional 2/– a week, was the ash pit man. In addition to shovelling ash and cinders from the ash pits, these men were also responsible for lighting and extinguishing the gas lamps in and around the shed. Three ash pit men were employed on each of the three shifts to do this back-breaking work.

Tube Blowers. At 46/– a week came the tube blowers, who cleaned the steam and superheat tubes in an engine's boiler. The action of the blast of exhaust gases through the chimney of a locomotive resulted in ash and cinders being drawn through the boiler tubes from the firebox – even pieces of coal when the engine was being worked really hard – and it was necessary to clean out the tubes at regular intervals. Steam rather than water was used to clean the tubes, for the contrast in temperature that would exist between cold water on warm tubes could do damage. A steam lance was used, and because of its shape many men at Bath shed referred to it as a trombone. The engine's own steam would be used, providing there was about 100 psi showing on the pressure gauge. A flexible pipe was joined to the lance, and its free end was attached to a tap-valve located on the outside of the engine's boiler, immediately behind the smokebox. The nozzle-like end of the lance was inserted into one of the tubes, a valve opened, and steam blown through. The tube endings were all exposed in the tube plate, access to which was through the smokebox door, the operation being laboriously applied to each tube in turn. Sometimes the tube was completely blocked which caused the steam to blow back, so the men had to be careful. Each of the three shifts from Monday to Saturday employed three tube blowers.

The situation often arose where tubes became dirty even before the engine was due in for a service, and so crews would resort to a more immediate remedy. On a section of line with a steep rising gradient – of which the Bath Extension abounded – the engine would be working hard. With the powerful exhaust pounding from the chimney, the driver would

A 7F being 'disposed' over the ash pit on No 4 road. The problems created by the tender cab fitted to this engine in its first few years can be imagined, judging by the length of the fire-iron being used here! 22.7.58 R C Riley

increase the already tremendous draught from the firebox through the tubes to the smokebox by turning on the blower. The fireman would then take a shovelful of dry sand – kept in a bucket on the cab floor – and throw it as forcefully as possible onto the tube plate above the brick-arch. The draught was such that it drew the sand through the tubes and scoured them out, sending a great mass of black sooty smoke into the air. This action was very effective and was frequently employed on heavy northbound freights, the engines of which had been showing signs of poor steaming on the earlier trip south from Bath. With the steep and immediate climb from Evercreech Junction to Shepton Mallet the engine would be working flat out by the time it reached Evercreech New station, and so it was near here that the tubes were given a blast. About a mile and a half beyond this, the line in the vicinity of Prestleigh viaduct curved markedly, which gave the crew a good back view of their handy-work: a pall of sooty black smoke hanging over the track like a menacing cloud of locusts long after the train had passed.

Leaking tubes were another problem requiring the attention of the men in this grade. The problem was remedied by expanding the tubes into the tube plate, this being done by hammering a specially-designed wooden block into the tube endings.

Boiler Washers. Next up the scale at 48/– came the boiler washers, steam raisers and coalmen. The boiler washers divided their time between the two sheds, the larger engines being attended at the lower shed where a booster pump was available, and the smaller engines dealt with at the top shed. It was important to keep dirt or scale from accumulating on the crown and leading edge of the firebox, to maintain the effectiveness of the fire and prevent damage to the plates themselves caused by overheating.

Men would usually be able to wash out two locomotives in an eight-hour shift. A washed boiler would then be passed as clean by the boilersmith following a thorough check. There were two boilersmiths at Bath, one covering an early turn and the other a late turn; there was no need for a round-the-clock operation due to the nature of the work. When the sub-shed at Radstock ceased doing their own boiler washing, they sent their tank engines over to Bath for this to be done, receiving another engine in exchange.

Engines were often much the better following a

wash out. A good example of this was the Ivatt Mogul nicknamed the 'Flying Pig' or, at Bath, 'Doodlebug'. These locos made a brief appearance in the city around 1950. With their high, straight running plates they were distinctive engines, but had a reputation as poor steamers. After a wash-out, however, they steamed really well. Unfortunately, they quickly deteriorated when out on the road.

The boilersmith and his men were based in the former messroom situated at the back of the old Midland shed, which they shared with the tube blowers. Boiler tubes were also stored there, while a five or seven-plank wagon was generally on hand to hold the debris of dismantled brick-arches as well as smokebox ash.

Steam Raisers. Known also as lighters up, these men worked on cold engines, having to build up the fire from scratch. This task could take up to eight hours, requiring periodic rather than continuous attention, thereby allowing several engines to be dealt with during one shift. It was a particularly dirty job, and so new recruits tended to be put on this! Each shift employed three steam raisers, the men not only building up new fires but also keeping an eye on all locos in steam – in conjunction with the preparation gangs.

Coalmen. Work on the coal stage was hard, unremitting and back-breaking. Men worked three consecutive shifts on weekdays, with two men on duty at a time. Before Grouping, the Midland and S&D had their own coaling stages, but from 1934 a single structure was sufficient, (next to No 2 road of the S&D shed). Wagons of loco coal reached the stage via an incline on which a spare engine and coal wagons were stabled. The engine was needed to push the wagons into the stage as required by the coalmen. During the day, the engine used for this (usually a 2P or 4F) was off the 7.00am passenger from Templecombe. Arriving at Green Park at 8.42, the loco would stable its coaches, proceed to the m.p.d., turn on the table at the top shed, and then move to the coal road. The wagons had already been prepared in the sidings to the north of the loco road earlier in the morning and propelled to the coal road by one of the yard pilots. The engine now set back onto these wagons and was left there by the crew for the next six hours or so. When a wagon of coal required pushing into the stage for the coalmen to deal with at the shutes, the shed foreman would ask either the men on the loco shunt – or anyone to hand – to undertake the manoeuvre.

The coal stage was poorly designed because as the three shutes were so close together, only one loco could be coaled at a time. Even when a brick stage was built to replace the earlier wooden one in 1954, this design fault remained. Each coalman was required to shovel 20 tons of coal a day before he could earn a bonus. The nature of the work was such that it is not surprising that absenteeism amongst the coalmen was above the average for all other grades. At night, cleaners and passed cleaners could be required to help on the coal stage when no labourers were on duty. Theoretically, therefore, there was always someone on the stage, but just eight days before Christmas 1960 it happened that there was no-one at all there in the early hours. This presented the foreman with something of a problem, for although the engines for the 2.40am and 3.30am S&D departures had been coaled, the 5.00 goods had not. As a last resort the foreman himself, together with a volunteer driver and fireman, had to set to and fill the tender. The train left 25 minutes late as a result. The foreman was not amused and the missing coalmen had some questions to answer when next they reported for work!

Footplate men often complained about the quality of the coal, but that was obviously not the fault of the coalmen. All sorts of coal seemed to find its way onto the stage: some of the Welsh coal burned quite well, but at other times coal from the same source came in large, almost rock hard lumps which seemed reluctant to burn. Local Somerset coal was the worst of all; it dripped through the fire bars like treacle, caking them in a sticky clinker. On the few occasions when it was used, men would reckon that they would be lucky if they got as far as Radstock before the fire went out. The favourite coal was that from the North of England: it burned with such brightness that some men referred to it as 'snap, crackle and pop'. This was the type of coal frequently used at Barrow Road shed in Bristol, and consequently crews on local turns to that city sought to find any excuse for taking their engine on shed in order to 'cadge' some of it.

The sense of fun displayed by many of the men at Bath Loco combined with a sense of occasion on New Year's Eve. Over the weeks leading up to the close of the year, any detonators which were coming up to their end-of-life date (which was five years) were saved up in a couple of buckets at the store room in the lower shed. Late on in the evening of 31st December they were placed at close intervals along all four shed roads and the length of the boat road. Two engines would be got ready, and as midnight struck on the Abbey clock, one engine set off along the boat road and the other traversed to and fro over the shed lines. At the same moment, all the other crews of engines in and around the depot joined in by blowing their whistles. The noise was incredible, the cacophony being carried on the wind for a considerable distance: it could be clearly heard as far away as places like Southdown, for example, when the wind was in the right direction. What was literally a time-honoured custom came to an abrupt end, however, when a caucus of residents across the river in Norfolk Crescent complained, and that was that.

5. Goods Yards and Sidings

When the Midland Railway opened its line to Bath in 1869, the goods yard was still under construction. A substantial tract of land had been secured by the company in Sydenham Field to the north of the Lower Bristol Road. This allowed the construction of an extensive and spacious yard, although much preliminary work on preparing the site had first to be undertaken. The material used to build up the ground to a datum-level was brought from the cutting to the west of Weston station. The large stone goods shed and offices, loading dock and cattle pens could not be built until these earthworks had been completed, and it was not until Monday 2nd May 1870 that the yard opened for business. Known simply as Bath yard, it was administered in the early days by the Station Master from his office at the passenger station. The lack of any direct road access between the passenger and goods stations was a great inconvenience, as the river could only be crossed by the Victoria Suspension Bridge or the Old Bridge at the bottom of Southgate Street, both involving long detours. To remedy this, a new road bridge was planned parallel with the railway bridge and slightly to the south of it. This would connect the entrance to the goods yard with Green Park, the new road running at the back of Green Park Mews. To avoid constructing a central pier in the river, it was decided to build a steel truss-girder bridge, the framework of which was assembled on a flat site near the goods yard. A tramway, supported on piles, was then built across the river and the bridge run out along this until it was in position. The bridge was known as Midland Bridge and the road as Midland Bridge Road. In the 20th century the bridge proved to be too narrow and light-weight for the traffic using it, so it was replaced with the present trussed steel structure. The first bridge was relocated rather than scrapped, finding a use as the Destructor Bridge on Midland Road linking the Upper and Lower Bristol Roads.

If the number and layout of the sidings in Bath yard changed but little over the succeeding decades, the structural provision most certainly did. Traffic at the yard grew very rapidly. During the 1890s the main goods shed was more than doubled in length by the addition of a timber extension on the west end of the existing structure. This huge combined shed dominated the yard, and continued to do so even after closure when it was converted to other uses. The original shed, though massive, was well proportioned. It was built by Messrs Allport & Wilson (Engineers) and Saunders (Architect). It was constructed in local rough-hewn stone and had large recessed windows, with the two-storey offices for the goods agent and his staff at the eastern end. The plain timber extension was purely functional and offset the character possessed by the earlier building.

At the same time as the timber extension was being built, a second somewhat smaller shed was provided in the former timber yard siding to the south of the goods shed. The open loading dock in this vicinity was replaced by a large covered grain shed, the timber now being handled on the sidings near the cattle dock. The cattle dock was reached by a drove road, the gates of which were on the corner of Midland Bridge Road and Lower Bristol Road. In addition to handling animals to and from Bath itself, it also fulfilled a holding function. The important Gloucester Cattle Market was held on a Saturday, with animals being subsequently distributed over a wide area. Cattle trucks working into Bath for forwarding over the S&D arrived too late in the evening for a suitable freight to get them to their destinations at a reasonable hour, notably to Chilcompton, Wincanton and Templecombe. Sometimes the signalman at the former location was requested to stay on duty to enable the wagons to be sent out attached to the last down passenger train, but as a rule the cows were de-trained into the pens at Bath and fed and watered over the weekend until Monday morning.

The arrival of the S&D in 1874 enhanced the work of the yard and quickly put a strain on the capacity of the sidings, much of the new traffic transferring between the two companies rather than terminating or originating in Bath. A direct connection was laid in from the S&D at Bath Junction to the yard, running parallel with the Midland up main line. This line could be used for both S&D and Midland arrivals and departures. By this time another siding had been installed, running alongside the down main line which gave access to the Gas Works. Initially, there was no connection from the Gas Works siding to the main line at Bath Junction. The consequence of this was a tremendous bottle-neck at bridge 43 (over Victoria Bridge Road), this location giving access to the m.p.d., station and yard in one direction, and the main lines and goods lines in the other. To alleviate this pressure and accommodate the additional traffic, four sidings were installed at Bath Junction, to the north of the main line and running into the existing Gas Works line. Two sidings were also added to the north of the Gas Works line between bridges 42 and 43, while a connection was put in between the new yard and the down main line. The installation of these sidings necessitated the relocation of Bath Junction signalbox. Finally, a crossover with single slip was put in between the Gas Works line and up main line, allowing access from the former to the up Midland/down S&D lines. This now established a pattern of working which maximised the operating potential of the layout and at the same time facilitated shunting of through traffic without transferring between the yards to an undue extent. Midland freights departed from, and S&D freights arrived in, the Midland Bridge yard, whilst the reverse applied to the new yard.

The new yard at Bath Junction became known as the S&D yard although it only appeared as such in working timetables from the late 1950s (the whole layout at Bath was simply referred to as Bath yard before this). The original sidings and buildings were distinguished by the name Midland Bridge Road yard. The S&D sidings were numbered from the main line towards the Gas Works. Thus the longest, next to the main line, was No 1 and so on. Long freights had to be shunted back or assembled in two parts as the shorter sidings could only hold about 25 wagons. In 1944 an extra line was added (No 5) but even so the accommodation was often loaded to saturation point. At times when maximum capacity was reached, traffic would be diverted to the Midland Bridge Road yard, the staff there always trying to keep one of the long sidings by the signalbox clear for just such an eventuality.

Both yards were in continuous use from the early hours of Monday morning to the arrival of the last freights in the early hours of the following Sunday. To ensure the smooth running of the operation a number of people with clearly defined tasks were employed. The only people engaged wholly in a clerical capacity were to be found in the offices attached to the goods shed.

The **goods agent** was responsible for all matters pertaining to the freight side of the railway at Bath, including the payment of wages. He was responsible for supervising the work of the goods **clerks**, **goods porters** and **vanmen**. One of the best known goods agents in later years was Fred Marsh.

The goods clerks had to deal with the public and all the paperwork involved at the depot, and also operated the weighing machines. Goods porters dealt with the loading and unloading of traffic, either manhandling it or using one of the eleven 30-cwt cranes in the huge shed. They also had to arrange goods ready for collection or delivery by the railway van drivers, and attended a number of duties such as the retrieval and stowage of wagon tarpaulins. The security of the shed, wagons and their contents was the responsibility of the railway police. From the end of the 19th century to the early 1920s the yard possessed its own Police Office, situated near the Midland Bridge Road entrance. It was staffed by two uniformed officers and one detective constable. It was a sub-station of the Midland's main base at Bristol, and it was to St Philips that the men were eventually transferred and from which all police matters at Bath had then to be handled.

The day-to-day and vital routine of handling the traffic in the yards was the responsibility of an **inspector**, there being one such for each of the three eight-hour shifts. One of the most memorable inspectors was William Goodfield. He always wore boots and leggings which, taken together with his moustache and upright posture, gave him a military bearing and made him look the part to the full! He performed his duties with meticulous efficiency and placed a high premium on punctuality. If an incoming freight was late, he would require an explanation; and his constant reference to his watch earned him the nickname Ticker. He retired not long after the end of the last war.

The longest-serving inspector when the line closed was Bill Wiltshire, whose railway career had begun at Midford back in 1919. The yard inspector dealt with both Midland Bridge and S&D yards, but the nature of the work was such that he spent most of his time at the former. Under him came a **shunter** and **under shunter** on each shift and in both yards. These men supervised the breaking up and assembling of trains, walking many miles in the course of a week, changing points and coupling or

Some of the goods yard personnel; on the loco are under-shunters James Hippesley (left) and Reg Staddon; on the ground, left to right: Harry Shearn driver; Jack Pitt, fireman; Gustave Beeho, leading shunter; Jack Fratwell, guard; Frank Staddon, guard.   early March 1966   J Stamp

uncoupling wagons with their long shunting poles. A further two men were employed as **relief shunters** to cover gaps in the rosters caused by the absence of regular men on rest days, holiday or sick leave. Each yard also employed **checkers** who were above the basic goods porter grade. Their duties were many and varied. A major element was the checking of goods being forwarded with the relevant consignment notes made out by the customer, and inserting the weights where appropriate, ready for charging by the clerks. All received traffic was also checked against invoices (or recorded if it had arrived in advance of the paperwork). They also recorded dates on which wagons were unloaded, to enable the clerks to calculate demurrage and siding rent charges. Another job was to remove labels from incoming wagons or place them on outgoing ones (each truck was provided with a metal label-holder, a sprung metal clip keeping the card in place, the card itself showing the origin and

destination of the wagon and the type of traffic conveyed). Wagons originating in Bath had their labels made out in the Goods Office by one of the clerks, the inspector being responsible for co-ordinating the traffic with train availability. It was important for both he and the office staff to know which wagons went where, and exactly how many trucks were available. Latterly, the checkers would provide this information but in the days before nationalisation, when private-owner wagons and different railway company wagons proliferated, **wagon number takers** were employed to do this job. A clearing house existed in both yards.

Other people who found work in the yards were concerned with the wagons themselves, namely the **wagon examiner** who checked on the condition of the vehicles and attended to any problems with brakes, axles, handles and the like; and **greasers** who greased up the axle boxes to ensure free running. Both the wagon examiners' cabin and the grease store were situated side by side between the station signalbox and the river bridge.

Whereas the passenger guards booked on and off at the station, **goods guards** did so in the time office in the Midland Bridge Road yard (near the top of the steps leading up from the end of Victoria Bridge Road). The rosters for the goods guards were drawn up by the Station Master's clerk at Green Park station, and the men were paid at the booking office there from 2.00pm onwards on a Thursday afternoon. With the vast amount of freight traffic passing through the yards each day, a large number of guards were employed. Even after the drastic diminution in freight services in the early 1960s, 30 goods guards were still on the books in 1963.

The men booked on half an hour before the train was due to leave. If they were working an S&D freight they had to walk out to the yard at Bath Junction, from where the train started. The shunter would inform him on which siding his train was stabled, the guard then having to compute the loading of the train to ensure that it fell within the maximum loads set for the class of engine allocated and the nature of traffic carried. Details were entered in his journal. In order to codify the situation, the principle of working loads was used, and thus the number of wagons equivalent to loaded goods could be calculated – this excluded the brake van. Using the standard 12-ton goods wagon as base 1, a loaded mineral truck was twice the value, while an empty wagon was only two-thirds. In other words a train load of empties would contain more vehicles than a train load of goods, and that in turn double the number of mineral trucks. The guard would walk along the train looking at the labels on each truck, building up a cumulative weighting. If when he got to the maximum permitted for the train there were still other wagons in the formation, they had to be detached and taken on a later service.

If trains were to work out of Bath on the S&D unassisted, they were only permitted to carry a single load, that is the maximum laid down for each class of engine. When a freight was banked, the numbers could be increased, being equal to the combined total of the loads permitted for the two engines, plus one extra in lieu of a second brake van. Bath shed would always seek to roster a six-coupled class 4F to the banking turn, and even in the last few years of Western Region influence would allocate an ex-GW pannier tank (4MT) in preference to an ex-LMS Jinty (3F). Having completed this task, wagon destinations were obtained so that the guard knew how many wagons to put off, and where. He would then check the equipment in the brake van, this comprising one standard padlock (for the locker); one tail lamp and two side lamps; a hand brush; shovel; brakestick; shunting pole; bank engine uncoupling iron; and three sprags. Sprags were wheel stops made out of hard wood and shaped to fit between the rail surface and the leading edge of a wheel, and were slid into place by means of a long-handled attachment.

The skill with which engine men hauled heavy freight trains over the Mendips was a noteworthy fact, but less widely appreciated was the important role played by the guard. Hidden from view in his van the work he did went unseen. A few formal instructions were issued to men for certain sections of the line. On down trains, for example, they were instructed to gradually apply the brake once the whole train was in Combe Down tunnel (the gradient changing just inside the tunnel from level to 1:100 down), the effect of this being to stretch out the wagons and keep the couplings taut. Beyond the tunnel the gradient continued to fall towards Midford station, so the brake was kept on until the van passed the signalbox, at which point the guard eased the brake off and released it completely as the train passed by the up inner home signal just beyond the viaduct. On up trains rather more work had to be done. As the van passed beneath bridge 28 (600 yards or so to the east of Shoscombe and Single Hill halt) the guard had to apply the brake sufficiently to take the strain of the wagons right through to Wellow viaduct, when it could be released. Similarly, on passing Midford's up distant signal, the couplings were strained until the van passed the signalbox. No instructions were issued for the descent from Combe Down tunnel to Bath Junction, but guards would ease the brake on to assist the footplate crew who were applying the loco's steam brake and tender handbrake to prevent speed building up. There were places where a long freight train might be on two or even three gradients simultaneously, and the men on the footplate relied on the experience of the guard to assist them in keeping the train running smoothly. If couplings suddenly 'snatched' there was always the possibility of a train separating, i.e. wagons breaking away. No two jobs were the same, as the wagon number and loading varied

In charge of the 11am Bath to Evercreech Junction freight, 8F No 48737 exchanges the claustrophobic inferno of Devonshire tunnel for the open spaces and fresh air of Lyncombe Vale.....

.....followed moments later by ex-GW pannier tank No 3742 assisting vigorously in the rear on the 1:50 rising gradient to Combe Down tunnel.   13.5.64   M Mensing

Stanier 8F 2-8-0 No 48444 prepares to depart from the Midland Bridge Road goods yard with a Midland freight. The signal arm to the right of the picture still possesses scars obtained during the strafing of the yard during the last war. 25.10.65 J Blake

and the drivers' styles differed.

Before vacuum-braked wagons appeared, the difficulties of controlling trains on steep gradients were considerable. There was a tendency to load certain trains right up to the maximum permitted or even beyond, and many drivers would talk of 'losing it' on a bank – notably on the long steep descent from Masbury Summit, although runaways were of course very much the exception. On the very first time that a West Country Pacific was used on the 2.40am 'Mail' freight in 1951, things literally got a bit hot for the guard. On the descent towards Prestleigh viaduct it was apparent to the guard that the engine was not holding the train. Even though he had the van's brakes full on, the train was obviously running away. The wheels of the van became red hot, the heat actually so great that some of the wooden floorboards began to smoulder. As the train roared through Evercreech New, smoke was wafting from beneath the van, much to the discomfort of the guard – but at least they were almost at the Junction where what was now a small fire was quickly put out.

The northern descent from Masbury Summit was if anything even worse, as there was no midway camber to help the train crews. If the engine lost it coming down through Chilcompton and Midsomer Norton it had to be hoped that the continuous shriek of the loco's whistle would alert the signalman in Radstock Station Box to open the level crossing gates over the busy A367 – if he had not already done so.

On a heavy freight the situation was bad enough even with the guard working his brake. An incident where the guard failed in his duty serves to illustrate the necessity of his job. Soon after cresting Masbury Summit the driver began a cautious application of his brakes, but the train did not respond in the way he expected: the wagons seemed to be running too fast and the couplings were obviously not stretched. Speed began to increase even before Binegar was reached, and by Midsomer Norton the train was doing 60 mph. Racing through Radstock at a speed which must have surprised pedestrians and motorists waiting at the level crossing, the train only came to a stand near Shoscombe, almost two miles further on. Climbing down off his engine, the driver went back to the brake van and felt its blocks. They were cold. This confirmed what he already expected. In his van the guard was suffering from 'tiredness', possibly not unrelated to an earlier encounter with some cider at Evercreech! The driver was furious and remonstrated vigorously with the man, saying he would stop the train in Lyncombe Vale and pin down some of the wagon brakes as he obviously could not rely on the guard. By doing this, the train was overdue at Bath Junction, and on reaching the yard he was asked what had been the problem. Despite his anger, such was the *esprit de corps* on the railway that he simply replied that some of the wagon brakes seemed to be playing up and he thought it advisable to stop. He did not report the guard for dereliction of duty – the man had doubtless learned a sobering lesson in more ways than one! It is, of course, necessary to keep these incidents in perspective. Most freights ran without incident and most men were thoroughly professional; indeed, they took immense pride in a job of work well done.

In addition to the two goods yards, there were a number of sidings between Bath Junction and the River Avon which performed specific functions. With the exception of the coal sidings and boat road, these lines were technically known as private sidings. Whereas the railway agreed to install, and often periodically inspect, such sidings, the land on which they were laid was privately owned and thus legally separate, a gate often marking the boundary. Such sidings which existed in other parts of the city will be dealt with in the appropriate succeeding chapters.

Coal Sidings. The two lines running parallel with the loco road between bridge 43 and Bath Junction were generally to be seen occupied by coal wagons. Although the points at both ends were operated by hand, exit from the sidings at the east end was controlled by the same slender-posted upper quadrant signal which applied to the loco road. It was positioned at the top of the embankment at the end of the outer of the two coal lines and thus not only protected loco movements at the lower shed, but gave the engines ample room to manoeuvre over the points without fear of encountering conflicting train movements. At the west end, the sidings fed straight in to the Gas Works line and thus avoided conflicting with shunting movements in the S&D yard.

The two sidings served a number of purposes, all of which were concerned with coal traffic. In the main they were used for private siding traffic and for storing loco coal (several wagons being used for this purpose every day). The former consisted of wagons for the Co-op and Brickworks sidings on the S&D and coal and coke for Stothert & Pitt. Most of the work involving these wagons was done either overnight or early in the morning.

Boat Road. The name boat road was applied to the long siding which skirted the lower shed and ran down to and along the left bank of the River Avon to the wharves which were once served by barges. From the early days of the railway until well after the First World War, barges would regularly unload barley and timber at these wharves. Both of these commodities were then railed-out to destinations in the local area, although much of the timber remained on-site for seasoning or processing first.

The original sidings, quay, timber yard and saw mills of T Burgess & Son were joined around the turn of the century by H W Bladwell's stone and timber yard at Sydenham Wharf, and by Oscar Windebank & Son's Victoria Saw Mills (backing on to Stothert & Pitt). Even when the boat road was first installed it continued beneath and for 30 yards or so beyond the railway bridge at the station. The limited headroom here meant that engines were not permitted to work beyond a stop board positioned just before the bridge. In order to reach Bladwell's Yard – now the site of Hill, Leigh & Co's timber yard – the boat road was extended along the river bank to take it below Midland Bridge and into the yard; an extension of some 100 yards. The inability to work locomotives onto this long siding posed a problem in the method of shunting. To help the firm in dealing with this bulky traffic, the shunt was organised in a particular way. A large number of spare wagons were marshalled between the engine and the loaded trucks, the assemblage then being propelled down to the quay and along the siding. Even though the engine had to stop at bridge 44, the train extended well beyond, with the leading wagons conveniently at the entrance to the stone yard. It was an easy enough matter to manhandle empty wagons, and these were moved, singly, back to the vicinity of the stop board ready for collection.

In addition to the original commodities of grain, timber and stone, was added the considerable traffic generated by Stothert & Pitt. A line was put into their Victoria Works in 1898, the boat road serving as a head-shunt. By the outbreak of the First World War the amount of traffic using the boat road was such that it was deemed necessary to install a stop semaphore signal to cover access to, and subsequently protect, the riverside area. The signal was erected at the top of the footpath leading from Victoria Bridge Road, at the end of No 7 road. By virtue of its position, it was not practical to work it from the Station signalbox but rather from some distance down on the riverside. A detailed instruction was issued in connection with the working of the signal:

> The single-armed signal worked from near the riverside goods shed must be used to regulate the running of the engines to the riverside lines. It must always be kept exhibiting the Danger signal except when required to be taken off in accordance with the following instructions:–

> When an engine, with or without vehicles attached, requires to proceed to the riverside lines, a man appointed by the depot Master must walk over the line leading to and from the riverside lines, and after ascertaining that the lines upon which the engine requires to run are clear, he must take off the signal to allow the engine to approach, and at once proceed to the vehicular level crossing to protect the crossing, and no engine or vehicle must be moved over the crossing in either direction unless the man is in attendance at the crossing for its protection.

This instruction was quite a sentence, but it covered all eventualities! The signal worked by lifting a weighted, pivoted arm rather than by pulling a lever, the conventional signal wire running up to the post by No 7 road. No such arrangement was necessary in the reverse direction as the train's presence was warning in itself to vehicles and people in the vicinity. Coming back up the boat road past the m.p.d. offices, the engine would make the same cautious approach as any engine coming off shed. Sometimes the trains were so heavy that the engine had quite a struggle in hauling the load from the quayside. The shunter or one of the crew would need to use the telephone between Nos 3 & 4 shed roads to ask the signalman at the Station box to pull off the signal which permitted exit from the lower shed to the loco road.

The function of the boat road gradually changed over the years. When Bladwell's ended their private siding agreement in the early 1920s, the riverside siding was stopped-off immediately before the Midland Bridge, from where a crane and loading dock were still extant (and had direct access to the Midland Bridge Road yard). During the 1930s this latter facility was used less and less, and early in 1944 the siding was further shortened, buffers being installed a few yards north of bridge 44.

With all the original traffic gone by the outbreak of the Second World War, and with Stothert's shunting their considerable traffic internally, it became commonplace to use the boat road to hold prepared engines awaiting their turn of duty at busy times; and it also had to be used in order to reach No 7 road and from there the Fitting Shop. Even after the tracks in the rest of the m.p.d. had been lifted by February 1967, the boat road was retained for Stothert's traffic, and was actually one of the last lines to be lifted in Bath, in 1972.

Stothert & Pitt. At one time Bath's largest single employer, this firm had an extensive complex of private sidings. As a heavy engineering firm – specialising in cranes and dockside equipment – much of their traffic was sent by rail. To allow ease of working in a restricted environment, a series of wagon turntables were employed within the factory to allow abrupt right-angled turns not possible with conventional points.

The firm's original Newark Works site on the Lower Bristol Road became unable to handle all the work, and so a new factory was built to the east of Victoria Bridge Road. A rail link leading from the boat road was provided in 1898. As the firm continued to expand, more land was needed. They acquired a former cricket ground between Percy Terrace and the railway in the mid-1920s, and in order to service this site by rail, gained permission to knock down two of the railway houses in the middle of Albert Buildings. The rails were carried over that road by way of ungated level crossings.

The continual need to expand the factory area first saw the absorption of the Midland and Victoria Saw Mills into the complex, and then through the 1950s the tract of land north of Percy Terrace (which included Longmead and Cross Streets). Houses in Albert Buildings began to disappear as well; only 5 of the original 20 were left by 1954 (nearest the railway) and they too had gone just a handful of years later.

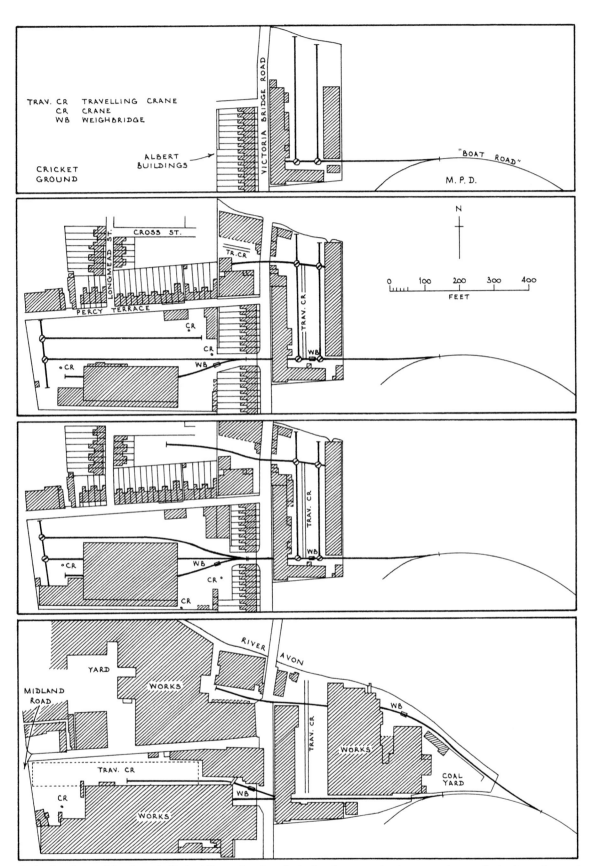

Scale drawings of Stothert & Pitt's sidings showing their development in the years (respectively, from the top) 1902, 1929, 1939 and 1965

With part of Stothert & Pitt's Victoria Works in the background, this huge aluminium lifting beam is being prepared for transport to Swan Hunter's shipyard in the North-East in early 1961.
Author's collection

The sidings were shunted by a tractor fitted with wooden buffer beams and coupling hooks, although the company also had a steam crane which could occasionally be pressed into service. In the main, this crane was used for lifting and moving heavy steel sections and is now seeing service on the Somerset & Dorset Railway Trust's site at Washford on the West Somerset Railway.

The works generated a considerable amount of rail traffic. Coal and coke went in for the foundries, while specials were made up to carry purpose-built loads which went all over the country. To cater for this traffic special wagons were brought in from far and wide to make up the required train, mainly well-wagons and low-loaders. The train would be assembled in the S&D yard and drawn down the boat road when required, before being propelled into the sidings. Getting the loaded wagons from the boat road back to the level of the main line could be quite hard work, and enginemen had frequently to resort to the sanding apparatus to enable their engine to keep her feet on the short but steep climb. The 9.15pm Midland freight was a popular train for loads going up country where a special working was not necessary.

Stothert's continued to provide traffic and thereby revenue to BR well beyond the withdrawal of passenger services, but the railway management did not seem interested in private siding traffic unless it was regular and yielded consistently high revenue. In this regard Stothert's was problematical due to the nature of the cargo handled, much of it too long, awkward or heavy for transportation by road, but by now only very occasional. A solution was found by reinstating a siding to the loading dock in the Westmoreland yard on the Western Region line in Oldfield Park. Crane sections were taken to the yard by road and stored on the platform prior to removal. This permitted the private siding agreement with Stothert's to be terminated, and the connection to the works, along with the boat road, were taken out of use towards the end of 1970.

Hopmead. The rank of ten terraced houses between the railway at Bath Junction and the Lower Bristol Road were known as Hopmead

The shunting-engine spur at Bath Junction is seen on the left of the picture. The extension for oil-tank wagons may be identified by the more sharply curved section of line beyond the tablet apparatus. Running past is the 9.05am stopping train from Templecombe.   1.6.63   Hugh Ballantyne

Buildings. This part of the Hopmead Estate was owned by the Midland Railway and the residents of the houses were all its employees and paid a weekly rent to the company (one of the clerks from Green Park station being despatched to collect the monies). A larger, detached house backing on to the railway embankment, and connected to the lineside by a path, was built by the company at the beginning of the 1890s and known as Hopmead House. It was used as the Station Master's residence for a few years on either side of the turn of the century. It was from this time that industrialisation began to affect the district, and though at first it was on a small scale, it quickly gained momentum. Having already witnessed the massive extension of Isaac Pitman's printing works (in 1913) on the opposite side of the Lower Bristol Road, the residents saw the vista on the other side of the railway blotted out by the construction of a second and gigantic gas holder at about the same time.

A few small commercial premises appeared over the next few years, but in 1930 the houses still possessed open ground on either side with allotment gardens at the rear and a pleasant green at the front. The residents were now faced with two proposals which would not only transform their immediate environment, but were potentially hazardous. The petroleum company BP wished to install a storage depot on the Lower Bristol Road, and required rail access. The ideal site was on the allotment gardens behind Hopmead Buildings, for not only would this open plot require the minimum of preparation but also had close proximity to the railway. The storage tanks did not have to be physically next to the rail tankers as the liquid could be pumped, and so rather than lay in a separate private siding, the simple expedient was adopted of extending the existing spur which paralleled the S&D down line at the Junction. The short spur was provided here for the yard shunting engine to await the arrival of incoming S&D freights. By extending the track by another 20 yards or so it was possible to fit three or four tankers as well as the shunting engine comfortably inside the protecting ground signal which allowed access to the goods line. The

One of the powerful 9Fs allocated to Bath m.p.d. for the summer of 1962, No 92001, passes the site of Hopmead siding on the approach to Bath Junction with a Bradford–Bournemouth express. The corrugated roof occupies the space where the coal hoppers had been located. The smoke deflector remains on the gantry above a non-existent siding, while that over the much-used goods road is missing! The hut beyond the bridge is for the use of fog-signalmen, the detonator lever being seen in front of it; the actual apparatus may be seen beneath the leading bogie wheels of the second coach.   14.7.62   Hugh Ballantyne

wagons were pushed to the back of the spur and had their brakes pinned down, while the leading vehicle additionally had its wheels spragged. As an extra precaution, scotch blocks were provided in the track. Hoses were connected to the valve gear on the wagons, and the contents pumped out when required. The facility was officially brought into use on 30th April 1931.

With the unsightly storage tanks and associated buildings now outside their back windows, the occupiers were soon dismayed to learn that the Bath & Twerton Co-operative Society was seeking to construct a warehouse and rail-served coal depot on land in front of their houses. Looking at a great blank end wall of the warehouse would be bad enough, but faced with the probability – even certainty – of a serious dust nuisance, they complained bitterly. However, living in tied houses and with their employer in favour of the project, their protestations went unheeded and planning permission was granted. The unusual feature of the scheme was to be the installation of coal hoppers beneath the siding (alongside the goods road). This was possible here as the siding was to be the same height as the existing embankment. Bottom-tipping wagons propelled into the siding would be positioned over the coal shutes and discharge their contents directly into the hoppers. This was the essence of the argument about containing coal dust.

The siding, about 80 yards long, was installed parallel with the goods road and connected to it just a few yards beyond the bridge over Midland Road. This necessitated the demolition of Hopmead House, which though no longer the Station Master's dwelling was still a company house. The points controlling access to the siding were worked by a ground frame situated by the toe of the point. The frame was provided with three levers, which could only be worked when released by the signalman at Bath Junction. The release mechanism, simply, was a rod like any normal point rod, linked to the signalbox's lever No 21. Known as Hopmead Siding, it opened in 1937.

Just as the residents had feared, the dust was indeed a problem, but as the Co-op's warehouse now suffered the menace as well there was perhaps some poetic justice! By the time the railways were nationalised in 1948, Hopmead siding was receiving little use; the Co-operative Society was tending to concentrate its coal traffic at its siding at Melcombe Road, on the S&D in Oldfield Park (opened in 1913). Soon afterwards in fact it was officially closed, although the track was not lifted for some time: the point rodding was simply disconnected and the points themselves padlocked. By 1953 the siding had

been removed and the coal hoppers were subsequently replaced by further warehousing. The terrace of houses survived for many years, albeit as a residential island in a sea of industry. The closure of the railway, however, was the *coup de grâce* and within a short time of that they had gone.

Gas Works. Built in 1818, Bath Gas Works is one of the oldest in the country, indeed, the main office building facing the Upper Bristol Road and inscribed Bath Gas Light and Coke Company is now a listed building. The washers, retorts, coke ovens and condensers were built on a site in Locksbrook between the north bank of the River Avon and the Upper Bristol Road. Road transport in the days of waggons and horses was slow, low-bulk and unpredictable, even from the relatively nearby North Somerset and South Gloucestershire Coalfields. Even coal brought to Bath by the Somersetshire Coal Canal and its associated tramways, and thence the Kennet &

The hoppers on the south side of the Gas Works complex viewed from the reception/dispatch sidings, c1971. The rail-mounted crane was engaged in demolition work.
R J Coles

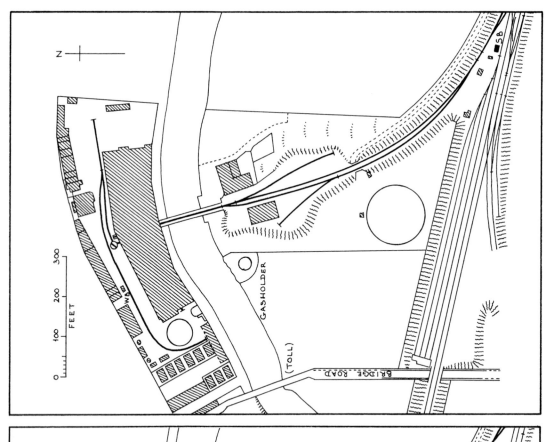

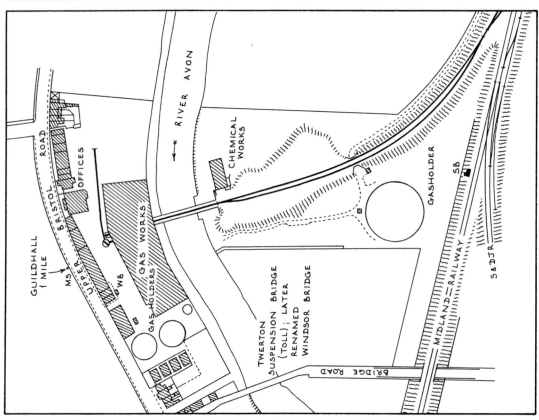

Scale drawings of the Gas Works sidings showing their development in the years (respectively, from the left) 1884 and 1902

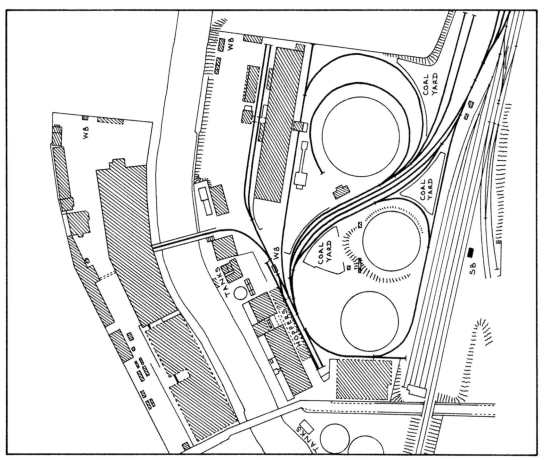

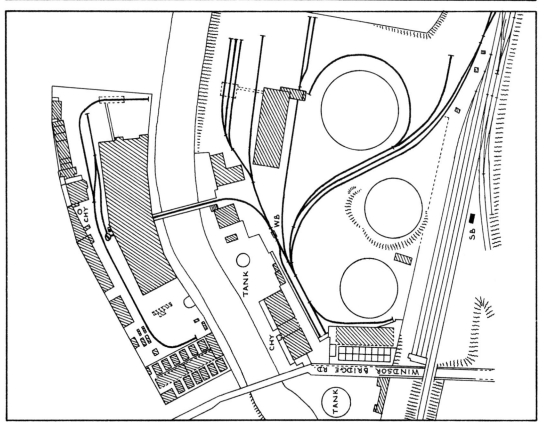

Scale drawings of the Gas Works sidings showing their development in the years (respectively, from the left) 1929 and 1950

89

Avon Canal, was transported but slowly: it could take three days for a consignment to reach the city from Radstock. Although this slowness did not matter providing there was continuity of supply, it was the question of bulk deliveries that posed the problem as the Gas Works began to expand. As the use of gas became more widespread, the need for coal correspondingly grew, and the arrival of the Midland Railway in 1869 was seen as a great benefit for not only would it permit bulk deliveries but would also open up the area of supply, notably to Midlands coal. With the Gas Works on the opposite side of the river to the railway, a bridge had to be built to allow access, and a 230-yard long siding was laid in. The opening of the S&D in 1874 provided more rapid access to North Somerset coal, although this was to be more significant later in the days of electricity power stations for which the coal was more suited.

The Gas Works complex began to expand rapidly, spilling over to the south side of the river. The site began to sprout more gas holders as the works was called upon to meet the ever-growing needs of both the city and the Bathforum Hundred (later Bathavon Rural District). The handful of railway sidings inside the grounds of the Gas Works in the early 1880s had reached five-eighths of a mile by 1900 and continued to grow steadily to reach almost a mile and a half by 1930. Substantial modifications were made to the layout later, but this rearranged rather than increased the mileage. To deal with all the shunting, the Gas Works acquired two 0-4-0 saddle tank engines. The first one to be delivered was built by Thomas Peckett & Sons at their Atlas Works in St George, Bristol, in 1912. As the workload grew, it was joined by a larger saddle tank, also Bristol-built, this time by the Avonside Engine Company of Fishponds in 1928.

Bath Gas Works engine No 1. This 0-4-0 saddle tank was built by Thomas Peckett and Sons in 1912, and carried the maker's plate No 1267. It was a most attractive little engine, painted in olive-green and lined-out in black and yellow, this livery being enhanced by its gleaming chrome steam dome.   21.3.59   P J Kelley

Gas Works engine No 2. The larger of the two locos, it was built in 1928 by the Avonside Engine Company and carried the maker's No 1978.
21.3.59   P J Kelley

The Gas Works would consume the equivalent of two full train-loads of gas coal each day, a full load on the Mangotsfield Branch being about 40 wagons. The wagons destined for Bath were assembled in Westerleigh yard and sent over on local 'trip workings' each weekday. Arriving at Bath Junction, the method of shunting would be determined by the nature of the train and the availability of the main line and S&D sidings. If all the wagons were of gas coal the brake van would be detached, the train drawn forwards to clear the double slip points leading both to the Gas Works and S&D yard, and then set back into the former on the command of the yard shunter. In the last few years before the sidings were taken out of use, the attractive saddle tanks were replaced by an austere if utilitarian 0-4-0 Ruston & Hornsby diesel mechanical shunter.

Any coal destined for the Gas Works from North Somerset arrived by way of S&D freights into the Midland Bridge Road yard. After the rest of the train had been shunted, these wagons had to be moved over to the works as a transfer trip. This particular transfer trip was done in the morning in a lull between passenger trains. Empty wagons had to be tripped over to the Midland Bridge Road yard before working back to the Midlands or to Westerleigh for other destinations as required. The majority of the empties were sent out on the 12.20am and 4.00am departures to Washwood Heath, Birmingham.

The volume of coal handled at the Gas Works was such that when the line closed to passenger traffic in March 1966, the ex-Midland line to Mangotsfield remained open for goods traffic, much of which was Gas Works coal. The works actually continued to expand, taking over the S&D yard site. The conversion from town gas to natural gas spelt the end for the coal trains, and the service was withdrawn on 28th May 1971.

For the last few years, the saddle tanks were replaced by class DS 306089 (Size 88) diesel-mechanical shunter No 23, built by Ruston & Hornsby. It is pictured here just a few weeks before the old Mangotsfield & Bath Branch closed completely.

24.4.71   Hugh Ballantyne

6. Signalling

When the Midland Railway opened its line from Mangotsfield in 1869, just two signalboxes were required to control the layout at the Bath end: one at Weston to cover the level crossing and sidings, and the other, known as Bath Station, to control movements to and between the station, yard and shed. The arrival of the S&D added a further two boxes: the Midland Railway's Bath Junction signalbox (1874) which controlled the double-track junction between the two companies' lines as well as the goods road to the yard (only the Midland Bridge yard existing at this time); and the S&D's Bath Single Line Junction signalbox (1876) controlling entry to and exit from the single line section to Midford. All four boxes were of wooden construction, with verandahs and steps on the east side, facing Green Park.

During the period of expansion in the 1890s the three Midland boxes were all rebuilt. They all incorporated the standard design of lever frame found all over the company's network. In the case of Weston and Bath Station, the new boxes were sited immediately next to the old ones; at the former location this was on the east side, hard against the level crossing, a move which involved relocating the steps to the opposite end. At Bath station the new box was also moved a few yards to the east, and was brought into use on 20th April 1892. At Bath Junction the renewal was brought about by the provision of four sidings joining the down main line, which became known later as the S&D yard. As the site of the original cabin was required for their construction, the new box was built over 100 yards to the east, much nearer the actual junction and still on the north side of the track.

In 1924 it was decided to combine the functions of the two junction boxes. The Single Line Junction box was situated immediately next to the skew bridge over the Lower Bristol Road and only controlled a single set of points, although it also dealt with the tablet and banking apparatus, of which more later. A new box was built in the angle made by the convergence of two lines, and was opened on 13th April 1924, after which the others were demolished. The pattern of signalling was now established until closure.

The Midland Line to Mangotsfield was double track throughout, being divided into a number of sections, each under the control of a signalbox. The sections were not of equal length, for the positioning of a signalbox depended upon the reason for its existence in any given place, such as a station, points requiring mechanical operation, a level crossing to protect, and so on. Thus the section between Bath Station and Bath Junction boxes was only 452 yards long and that from the Junction to Weston was 858 yards. However, between Weston and Bitton it was 5 miles 814 yards; and between Warmley and Mangotsfield South Junction 1 mile 572 yards.

In running a train between Bath and Mangotsfield, signalmen would be asked to accept it, in sequence, in the direction of travel. When the man in Bath Station box wished to send a train up from Green Park he would first call the attention of his colleague in the neighbouring Junction box. To facilitate this, electrically-connected devices called block instruments were used. Above the levers was an instrument shelf containing a large, framed and annotated diagram of the layout controlled by the box, along with the block instruments and their concomitant bells. By depressing a tab or ringing key on the instrument, a bell would sound in the next box. One beat on the bell would 'call attention', and had to be answered. When Bath Station received the answering bell, he would then offer the train to his colleague, i.e. ask him 'is line clear for...?', the actual bell code used depending on the type of train. Commonly used codes were:

4	express passenger train
3-1	ordinary passenger train
2-2-1	empty coaching stock
2-3	light engine
3-2	ordinary freight
1-3-1	parcels/perishables

Providing Bath Junction had no other train on line, or movement which might conflict with it, he would duly accept the train by returning the same bell code, and then turn the pegging handle on his up line block instrument. This changed its dial from 'normal' to 'line clear' and caused the repeating instrument at the Station box to correspond. The man here could now operate his signals by pulling the appropriate

Taken round about 1910, near the bottom of Brook Road, this picture shows the second Bath Junction Signalbox. The row of cottages was known as Parkhouse Buildings, and they survived until the Blitz of 1942. Bath Single Line Junction signalbox is hidden from view by the trees in the centre-left of the picture.

Bath Record Office

levers. As the train passed his signalbox, he would notify the Junction of the fact by sending a code of two beats: 'train entering section', having first called his attention as before.

The Junction acknowledged the bell code and turned his indicator to 'train on line' (this being repeated at the station). Where sections were of a moderate or considerable length, a signalman would now offer the approaching train to the man in the next box along the line, but in the case of Bath Junction to Weston the section was so short that the train would have arrived before this operation had been completed. Thus on his acknowledgement of the Station's request, Bath Junction immediately offered the train on to Weston – the man here in turn seeking 'line clear' from Bitton. In this way a train was offered all along the line to Bitton even before it left Green Park. The long section between Weston and Bitton allowed the latter to wait until he received the 'train entering section' bell before he needed to offer it on to Warmley. If Bath Station wished to send another train soon after the first, he would only be able to offer it after the preceding one had cleared the section; this being relayed to him by the Junction signalman by means of the bell code 2-1 – after the usual one beat call attention bell – and subsequent changing of the block instrument back to normal. When trains worked into Green Park, it was the station box signalman who was in the position to accept or refuse trains, and so he possessed the down line pegging instrument and the Junction repeater.

All the signalboxes mentioned above were known as block posts, in that they were able to accept or refuse trains, and thus divide the line into the distinct sections already outlined. At times of relative quiet the need for all the boxes did not really exist; a train could get all the way to Mangotsfield and beyond before another required occupation of the line. In such situations, signalboxes could be provided with a facility for switching out, the effect of which was to lengthen the section. When a box was switched out, all running signals had to be pulled to the all clear position. Only Bitton in fact was provided with a switch, working two daytime shifts Monday to Saturday (6.10am to 8.30pm) and switching out at night and Sundays. Bath Junction and the Mangotsfield Junction boxes were required by virtue of their junction status. The absence of freight activity between the early hours of Sunday and Monday mornings permitted the boxes at Bath Junction and Mangotsfield North Junction

to switch out, the points and signals being set for the main line. Thus Bath Junction box would close at about 5.50 on a Sunday morning and reopen at about 2.00 on Monday morning. In the summer months, however, a man would be required to work a short morning and evening turn in order to deal with traffic over the S&D.

The signalboxes at Weston and Warmley had to remain open continuously on weekdays to cover the public level crossings and they were not provided with a switching facility. Neither was Bath Station, and so these three boxes had to work a Sunday split-shift to deal with the two return journeys made by a passenger train all year round.

The long section between Weston and Bitton was not generally an inconvenience to the smooth flow of traffic except on summer Saturdays, when trains were more numerous and often not adhering to schedules due to late running and signal stops elsewhere. Another signalbox did in fact once exist at Kelston station, but it was not a block post, being able only to superintend the passage of trains through the section and not accept or refuse them. There was just one stop and one distant signal for each direction of travel, being of the old Midland Railway lower quadrant type. The small lever cabin was situated on the down platform just a few yards on the Bath side of the main station building. It was only opened as required, being operated on such occasions by one of the station staff. Visual display instruments, or repeaters, on a shelf above the four levers showed when a train was on line and distinguished between 'up' and 'down'. They responded to the settings of the block instruments in the signalboxes on either side. When the signalbox was not in use, the signals were kept in the all clear position, and did not have their lamps lit for the hours of darkness. The station closed on 1st January 1949, and the signalbox at the same time. The signal posts, devoid of their arms, were still in position in the summer of that year.

Signalling on the S&D line out of Bath was of necessity different from that employed on the Midland, as the section between Bath Junction and Midford was single track. Steps had to be taken to ensure that up and down trains could not be on the line at the same time. In 1886 a system of single line tablets was introduced. In order for a train to move over the single line, the driver had to be in possession of a tablet, a small metal disc with a hole in the centre. Although all

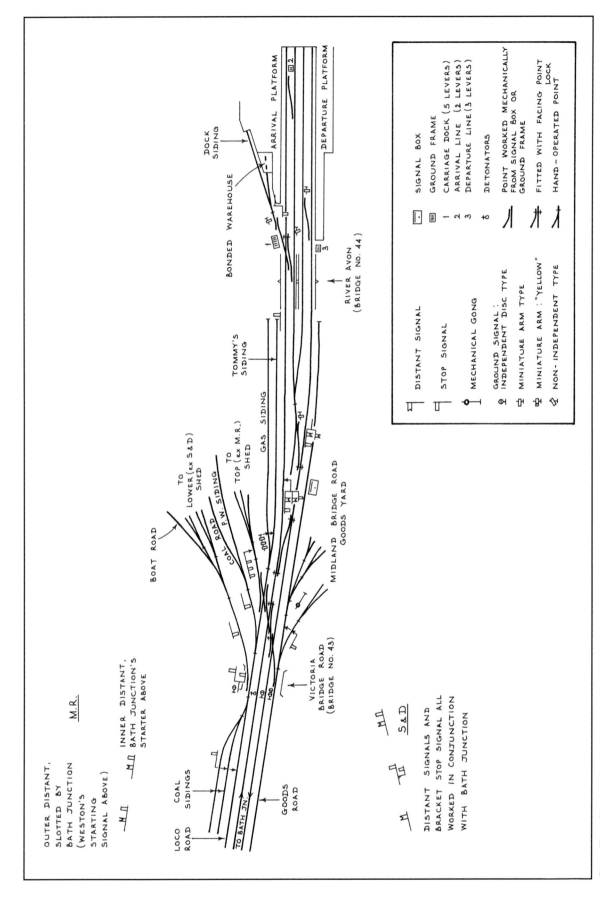

Signalling diagram for Bath Station in 1950

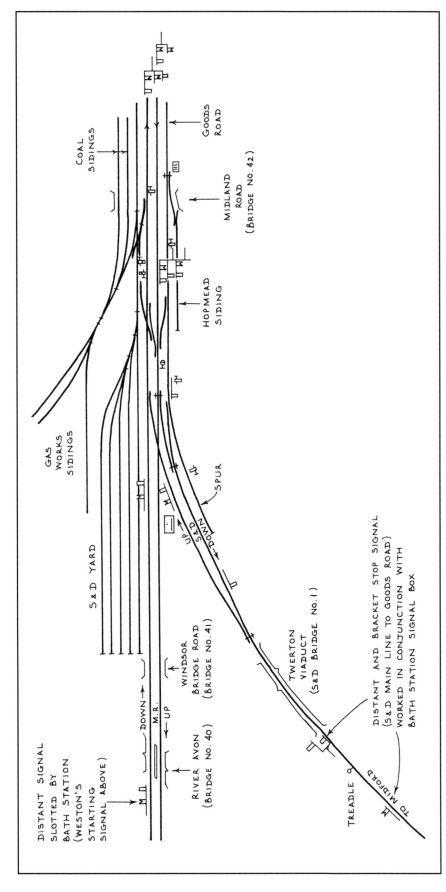

Signalling diagram for Bath Junction in 1950

the S&D tablets were round, section identity was more important on the single line Dorset section of the railway, the machined edge or drilled centre identifying the section to which they applied (thus Templecombe Junction to Stalbridge for example had three round notches cut in the edge of the tablet; while from Stalbridge to Sturminster Newton there was one square and one round notch cut in the circumference). The tablets were kept in a machine known as Tyer's No 6 Electric Tablet Apparatus, and could only be drawn when both signalmen followed a certain procedure. When Bath Junction wished to send a train to Midford, the signalman would depress the bell-plunger on his machine, one beat being the call attention code. This rang a bell on the instrument shelf in Midford box. Midford acknowledged this, whereupon Bath Junction tapped out the code of the train in question. If Midford was in a position to accept the train, he would hold in his bell-plunger on the last beat of the code for a few seconds. This action completed an electrical circuit, which allowed Bath Junction to draw a tablet. This was indicated to the signalman at Bath by an indicator (a centrally-pivoted vertical arrow-shaped needle) at the top of the instrument. When the bell-plunger was being used, the indicator would flick in sympathy; when the plunger was held in, the indicator lay obliquely. This enabled the signalman to turn his commutator – a dial behind the bell-plunger – to the left, the lowermost tablet in a stack dropping into a tray or slide, and changing the inscription on the lower of two dials to tablet OUT. He then pulled out the slide in order to extract the tablet, and the slide remained out until the tablet was put into the machine at Midford. This done, he sent a single beat on the bell-plunger, which changed the upper dial at Midford to tablet OUT. Midford then acknowledged this bell.

Taking the tablet out of the slide, the Bath man placed it in a leather pouch and secured the flap by a strap and stud. The pouch was then taken to the lineside apparatus on the left side of the direction of travel. This apparatus consisted of a pivoted arm at the top of a post, the height of the arm above rail level being such that it matched up exactly with the metal jaws of the tablet catching apparatus on the tenders of locomotives. Inserting the pouch into position, the arm was swung out to face the train. As the jaws of the apparatus on the engine engaged with the metal hoop of the pouch, the latter was snatched out of the holder, which then swung through a right angle clear of the train. The fireman was instructed to watch the exchange being made in case of a miss. At night he was supposed to shine a hand lamp or torch on the apparatus to ensure that the operation could be seen clearly. Before 1924 this apparatus was installed near Bath Single Line Junction signalbox. Due to the curvature of the track, this was not an easy location for picking up the tablet and crews kept a particularly sharp lookout. If the loco was not fitted with the requisite apparatus, the fireman had to catch the tablet by hand. In these cases a pouch with a larger hoop was used and Bath Control telephoned the instruction 'pouch' down the line, indicating that the larger version was to be used for this train.

Even at modest speeds it took practice for a fireman to catch the pouch confidently, the pouch being held aloft by the signalman standing between the tracks. It could impact against the shoulder with quite a blow, but at least it was not as potentially lethal as the unguarded metal staffs and token-holders used on many single lines. The regular S&D locos were all fitted with the tablet-exchanging apparatus, and the class 7 freight engines also had it fitted to the right-hand side of their tenders as well to allow for tender-first running on northbound trains. Visiting engines, or engines on extended loan, such as the West Country class, and later the 8Fs and 9Fs, could be fitted up with spare apparatus kept in the m.p.d.

Providing a tablet was picked up correctly the fireman had to retrieve it from the apparatus. This was usually done soon after the loco had obtained it, before crossing the Lower Bristol Road. This was easier said than done! It involved leaning right out of the cab, holding on to the cab rail with one hand and retrieving the catcher bar and pouch with the other. Passing through the fields below Midford Castle, the fireman had to put the pouch out again in readiness for the catcher opposite Midford signalbox. In the depths of winter with an icy slip-stream howling along the boiler of the loco, conditions for the fireman were unpleasant in the extreme.

Passing Midford, the lineside apparatus there retrieved the pouch. Once the train had passed, the signalman collected it . Taking the tablet out of the pouch, the slide on the Tyer's machine was pulled out and the tablet inserted. The slide was then pushed back in and the 'train out of section' bell was sent to Bath Junction, i.e. one bell to call attention and then 2-1. This was by no means

When engines were not fitted with the necessary tablet catcher, it was usual for Control to alert signalmen to give up the tablet by hand. However, on this occasion the fireman of 4F 44135 is somewhat precariously positioned to retrieve the small pouch from the extended arm of the apparatus. Note also the Falling Man dropped down in its housing between the up and down lines, for up freights, and the arm for all down trains. The fog-signalman's hut is situated in the angle of the tracks, as are the lay-by tracks for the Permanent Way trolley and trailer (until recently there had been just one set of tracks, with a substantial wooden shelter for the trolley).   28.3.59   Colin G Maggs

the end of the story! When the Junction acknowledged the above code, Midford held in his bell-plunger to allow his colleague to turn his commutator from left to right and push back his empty slide. This done, he sent a single beat on the instrument, which changed Midford's upper tablet dial to IN. Midford then lifted a lever on the left-hand side of his instrument, which emptied the slide. This was now pulled out to be checked, and straight away replaced, whereupon a single beat was sent to Bath Junction to change his bottom dial also to IN. With the dial indication changing, the Junction sent a single beat back to Midford, who acknowledged this. The operation was now complete.

Theoretically, the system was fool-proof. There was no way that a tablet could be drawn without the co-operation of both signalmen, and no way that more than one tablet could be drawn out at

a time. A chance event at Midford, however, showed that reality could be otherwise. When the old S&D Single Line Junction and Midland Junction signalboxes at Bath were replaced by a new single structure, the tablet machine had to be moved to the new location. It was duly installed and tested. There were no problems. Some time after this a relief signalman at Midford decided to dust around the box during a lull between trains. Flicking the duster over the face of the Tyer's machine, it caught the commutator and moved it over. To the man's surprise a tablet dropped down into the tray. Pulling the tray out, he removed the tablet and put it to one side before contacting his opposite number at the Junction and also the signal lineman. The latter was somewhat incredulous, but soon arrived on the scene. The machine was examined and seemed in perfect order, failing to repeat the trick. Somehow the impossible had happened, and the cause of the fault had to be traced. Even the makers of the machine were called in to investigate, having expressed disbelief that this could happen. The errant machine was stripped down and thoroughly examined, but no fault could be found.

The unsolicited tablet became something of a talking point amongst the regular signalmen. Sitting in his box one day soon afterwards, one of the Bath Junction men happened to be looking towards the Lower Bristol Road. From the box it was possible to see the tops of the trams as they clattered on their way between the city centre and Twerton. Because of the limited clearance beneath the iron bridge by the *Royal Oak* pub, the overhead wires were lower than they were along the open road, and were attached to the underside of the bridge. The signalman watched the familiar sight of the sprung arm of the tram dip down as the wires lowered to pass beneath the bridge. As the telegraph wires on the S&D were carried across both the bridge and Twerton viaduct by being attached to the actual structures and not carried on the usual poles, it occurred to him that perhaps the live tram wires were not properly earthed and were interfering with the railway's communications when a tram's arm pressed the wires upwards beneath the bridge. When another tram came along he was waiting, and turned the commutator on the machine: sure enough, a tablet dropped down! He reported his discovery and the fault was quickly rectified.

The automatic tablet-exchanging apparatus described above was designed by Alfred Whitaker, the S&D's Bath-based Locomotive Superintendent, and was installed in 1904. It allowed trains to pass exchanging points at speeds much higher than would be permitted for manual exchange: 40mph at Midford, but only 20mph at Bath Junction due to the curvature of the track. Up S&D passenger trains running into Bath gave up the tablet at the apparatus near the Junction signalbox. So that the signalman did not have to leave the box to set the collecting arm in the correct position, he had a specially-designed handle near the floor in the corner nearest the apparatus. By pulling this, the attached wire drew the arm through a right angle into position. Freight trains, however, ran into the Midland Bridge Road yard. Coming off the single line at the Lower Bristol Road bridge they were directed on to the down main line before taking the goods line at the junction proper. As tablets were exchanged on the left-hand side of the direction of travel, the catching apparatus had to be installed within the six-foot way between the running lines. Due to the limited clearance here, the apparatus was of a different design. A bottom-weighted, pivoted post surmounted by the usual metal catching jaws was contained in a sub-triangular housing at ground level. When not in use, the apparatus was tilted backwards, the jaws resting in a high-sided protective casing on the ground behind the main structure. When its use was required, the signalman turned a large wheel on the side of the housing which raised the catcher into the vertical position. As the loco ran past and the pouch-hoop was engaged by the jaws, the forward momentum of the impact caused the catcher to fall back to the ground, from which position the signalman later collected the pouch. Men called this the Falling Man.

The successful operation of the equipment depended upon an exact alignment of the apparatus on the locomotive's tender and that at the track side. While most exchanges were accomplished without a hitch, there were bound to be exceptions. Sometimes, on a down train, the catcher had not been inserted absolutely square or perhaps the engine rolled slightly just at the point of collection, so that a clean snatch was not made, and the pouch was knocked to the ground. A miss was a source of annoyance to drivers, as they had to hurriedly stop the train in order to let the fireman walk back and retrieve it. A cold start then had to be made on the 1:50 gradient which began even before the single line section had been entered. A sudden and unexpected halt generally caused passengers' heads to appear out of the carriage ventilator and door windows to see why they had stopped. On one occasion when this happened, the fireman overheard a woman say in answer to a fellow passenger in the compartment: 'he's picked up a handbag someone's dropped'!

Mishaps at Midford on down trains could be particularly inconvenient as the ground fell away steeply from the track side to the Bath-Hinton Charterhouse road below. On several occasions the pouch containing the tablet was sent flying onto the roof of the *Hope & Anchor*, thus delaying trains until it could be retrieved. Until the tablet was replaced in the machine, the section to Bath remained effectively blocked, so Control was notified of an inevitable delay to trains. When the miss happened during the hours of darkness, its retrieval was a more protracted affair. Once, just before the outbreak of the last war, a tablet seemed to disappear into thin air! Soon after leaving Combe Down tunnel the fireman put out the pouch as usual. Passing through Midford, he heard the metallic click as the jaws of the apparatus hit the hoop of the pouch, and he assumed all was well. When the signalman left his box to retrieve the tablet, there was nothing there. He could not stop the train as it had already passed his advanced starting signal, and so he had to phone ahead to Radstock Station signalbox – the three intermediate boxes all being switched out at night. Bringing the train to a stand by his signalbox, the Radstock man told the crew that they had forgotten to put the tablet out at Midford. This information came as a surprise to the men, and so the Midford man was duly informed that there had obviously been a miss. After a long search, no sign of the pouch was to be found: it seemed simply to have vanished. In order to keep trains running, a pilotman was used on the line in the meantime, the man acting in effect as a human tablet. Exhaustive searches of roof-tops, gardens, lineside vegetation and the road next morning all drew blanks, and so the tablet was officially declared lost. Some years later, signalman Harry Wiltshire was surprised when the man who lived in the house by the viaduct came up to his box and presented him with a soggy pouch which obviously looked very much the worse for wear, but which still contained its tablet. He had decided to clean out the water butt at the back of his house and had found the pouch lying on the bottom!

Bath Banking Engine Staff. Because of the steep climb between Bath Junction and Combe Down tunnel, most freight trains required assistance, i.e. banking. As the banking engine only assisted to the mouth of the tunnel and then returned to the Junction, authorisation was necessary for two simultaneous if opposing train movements on the single line to take place. This was achieved by means of the Bath Banking Engine Staff. This was a metal staff about 12 inches long with a keyed attachment at one end, known as the Annett's Key. This attachment was inserted in a correspondingly-machined device on the side of the tablet machine and was turned in the same fashion as a door key. The legend Bath Bank Engine was inscribed on one side of the staff. When the Junction signalmen offered the train to Midford, and had it accepted, the tablet would be drawn from the Tyer's machine in the way described earlier. This action unlocked the banking staff – there was only the one – and allowed the signalman to withdraw it. The action of turning and withdrawing the staff locked the tablet machines at both the Junction and Midford and so prevented another train entering the section until it had been returned. Once the staff had been withdrawn, it was placed in a large leather pouch and secured by a flap and stud. As the freight set off from the S&D yard, the signalman would leave his box, stand between the tracks facing the train, and hold the staff aloft. As the wagons passed him, the fireman on the banker leaned out of the cab in readiness to grab the staff. This achieved, the signalman returned to his box and sent 'train entering section' to Midford.

With the single line junction points safely negotiated both engines would have to work hard to move the freight up the bank to Combe Down tunnel. On the way to the summit the train had to pass through Devonshire tunnel; in fact the banker had to pass through this tunnel twice, once on the outward journey and again on the return light engine trip back to the Junction. The unpleasantness this entailed has been detailed elsewhere. Fourteen minutes were allowed for the bank engine to assist and arrive back at the Junction, while the train itself was scheduled to reach Midford in 15 minutes. In order to allow the banker to return to the S&D yard, the Junction signalman would tap out the code 3-3-2 (shunt into forward section) on the block instrument to Bath Station signalbox. This permitted the engine to run onto the down main line to clear the points leading out of the yard. The points would be changed, the ground signal pulled off, and the light engine would duly set back to resume shunting duties in the sidings.

If the freight that the banker had been assisting was running fast, or the banker was only ambling back – the crew perhaps enjoying the weather on a nice day – the freight would be out of section before the latter's return, which often brought forth a tongue-in-cheek sarcastic comment from the signalman like 'been picking the daisies then?' He always knew when the engine was approaching because 50 yards in advance of the bracket signal at the south end of Twerton viaduct it ran over a treadle which activated a buzzer in the signalbox. This would continue to sound until the signalman cancelled it by pressing a button on the instrument shelf. A telephone was provided on the opposite side of the track to this signal post to enable loco men to contact the signalman if they were brought to more than a momentary stand here. Arriving back at the Junction, the fireman would give up the banking staff which was then duly replaced in its machine. Even if Midford had already put back the tablet, it would be impossible to draw another while the banking staff was still out of the machine at Bath. In this way the engine was completely protected on the single line, Bath Junction not acknowledging Midford's 'train out of section' until the staff had been restored.

The Signalboxes. The tall wooden Station signalbox controlled movements to, from and between the station, motive power depot and goods yards, being sited to have view of all three. The 38-lever box was manned continuously on weekdays and only closed for a few hours on Sundays. The amount of work to be done warranted the classification of the box as a class 2. Always a busy box, life on summer Saturdays was distinctly frenetic, requiring double-manning over the peak eight-hour period of holiday expresses. To effect this, it meant that two signalmen had to work 12-hour shifts. The early turn man took over from his colleague on the night shift at 6.00am and worked through until 6.00 that evening. At 10.00am the late turn man booked on to begin his 12-hour stint, thus providing double manning between 10.00am and 6.00pm. With engines changing over on through services, and other engines requiring to move between the upper and lower sheds, use the turntable, coal up and be marshalled in the correct order for return workings, congestion was almost unavoidable. It was bad enough if everything ran to time, but with inevitable late running the signalmen had to make constant snap judgements about which movement to allow next – sometimes to the annoyance of Control, for whom loco movements and the marshalling of local stock took second place to plotting paths for the expresses. The Station and Junction signalboxes, together with the Control office, had to work closely together in order to keep things moving, but at times life became so hectic that it was difficult to remember which engines were where: there was no track circulating and not always a tell-tale column of steam from a lifting safety valve of an engine perhaps up to 400 yards away in the station. To remind themselves that an engine was still down in the station, men would sometimes put a clip on the protecting home signal lever, but if they forgot to do this, they would have to ring up the station and ask one of the staff there to tell them if there was an engine in either of the platform lines! The absence of freight trains and local transfer workings from about 8.15am until 5.15pm on summer Saturdays removed further potential chaos, although it was freight that made up a sizeable portion of the work done by the signalmen on other weekdays. When the signalbox closed, albeit for only brief periods on a Sunday, it obviously had to be locked. Each signalman possessed a key to the box to which he was attached. When a relief man had to cover for one of the regulars, a spare key would be concealed somewhere, such as under a particular fire bucket or some such other agreed location.

The box opened for two half shifts to deal with the out-and-back passenger service for the Midland line to Bristol on winter Sundays, and for slightly longer in the summer when a limited service also ran over the S&D. This split shift was understandably unpopular when worked by one of the regular men, especially as they were only paid for the basic four-hour period, unlike the footplatemen who saw the morning turn in particular as a chance to earn a bit of overtime. The signalman opened the box soon after 7.00am in order to give sufficient time for the tank engine to come off shed and perform any necessary manoeuvres at the station. The two coaches had been berthed in the Departure platform overnight, the loco coupling up to them at about 7.30, with departure half an hour later. The generous waiting time at the station allowed for the engine's steam heating to take effect in the cold carriages, and also permit any shunting movements (notably the attaching of vans from the dock siding when theatre traffic required to be taken up country after a run in Bath's Theatre Royal – the vans were attached to the main line express at Mangotsfield).

The train did not return until 10.30am, working into the Arrival platform to enable the engine to run round its train and push the coaches back to the buffer stops in readiness for the evening departure. This simple operation could be drawn out to take 20 minutes or more, the engine eventually dawdling back past the signalbox with the crew grinning knowingly at the signalman. Although the engine would be kept in steam for the evening at the top shed, the crew would sometimes find a compelling reason to visit the lower shed: a manoeuvre which required the signalman's participation. Drawing up to the

Bath Station signalbox. The wooden signalbox and lower quadrant bracket signals are of typical Midland Railway design. Notice the fog-signalman's hut in front of the signal post and the ganger's trolley parked on the short spur. 2P 40568 pilots Black 5 44917 towards Green Park with the northbound 'Pines'.   2.4.56   the late Ivo Peters

water column at the top shed, the crew let the water into the tanks at what seemed like a trickle. With this task completed, they then whistled for access to the loco road. Crawling out onto bridge 43, the signalman changed the points for the lower shed. He was now completely at their mercy, for as one man put it, 'Once they were down there, they could do what they wanted'. Eventually, after what seemed like an age to the seething signalman, the engine whistled-up for the signal, and made its way slowly back to the top shed. As locomen were paid time and three-quarters for this Sunday work, it was in their interests to draw out the job for as long as possible! Consequently, the signalman regularly booked off well after his prescribed 4 hours, and on one occasion did not get away until 1.30 – doubtless getting home to a spoiled lunch!

The evening train left Bath at 7.05 and returned at 9.24pm, connecting with main line services at Mangotsfield. The boxes at Weston and Warmley also had to open to facilitate this Sunday traffic – as they controlled public level crossings – while the station had to be staffed. This expensive mode of operation – for there was rarely more than a handful of passengers – continued right down to the economies instituted in March 1962.

Bath Junction signalbox was also a busy place at all times of the day and night, most of its modest allocation of 31 levers getting plenty of use. On a weekday in 1953 for example up to 110 trains passed the box in 24 hours, with a further 10 light engine movements, together with an unspecified number of transfer and shunting movements. As at the Station, summer Saturdays were particularly hectic. Bath station's two platforms were inadequate to deal with the influx of Midlands and North of England expresses and their reliefs, while the single line to Midford was a serious bottleneck. Decisions had to be made

This was the third signalbox to control the layout at Bath Junction, and consisted of 31 working and 7 spare levers for most of its life. Note the single line tablet apparatus arrayed along the boardwalk: on the left, in front of the telegraph pole, the arm to collect the tablet from up passenger trains; and the wagons on the sidings of the S&D yard. R E Toop

quickly as to which train the Junction should accept or forward in order to prevent late-running. Trains might well be queuing up on both the S&D and Midland to get into Bath, while both the station platforms would also be occupied. Some signalmen always liked to have something on the single line in an effort to keep late-running on the S&D to a minimum. If a man cleared back a train which had just arrived from the Dorset and Midford offered him another train, he accepted it straight away even if he knew that Bath Station was about to offer him a Bournemouth train. The latter could always wait at the gantry signal in advance of the junction and thereby release one platform road at the station. Although he did not have to worry about freight movements, the signalman at the Junction would literally be kept on his toes, sometimes not even having time to stop and eat his sandwiches. In addition to answering the constant ringing of the bells and attending to the pulling of levers,

he was in and out of the box with the single line tablet, constantly on the phone to Control and neighbouring boxes, and also attempting to keep an accurate record of all train movements in the Train Register. Very occasionally it was necessary to work a 12 hour shift due perhaps to short-notice illness or some other unforeseen circumstance. This would be exhausting. If it was difficult to find time to eat, it was even more inconvenient (literally!) to answer the call of nature as the signalbox did not possess a lavatory. The nearest one was a public convenience on the Lower Bristol Road at the foot of a path which led down from the railway opposite the bottom of Brook Road. If things got desperate, men would dash down there! The signalbox was also without a supply of water, so this was brought out in cans from the yard. The favourite working for this purpose was the Midland Bridge Road shunting engine, which would carry the cans on its buffer beam and stop almost opposite the signalbox on

One of Bath's Standard class 5s runs in over the junction points with the noon stopping train from Templecombe. The distant signals in the background were controlled by Bath Station box and informed the driver that he had a clear run to the buffer-stops at Green Park. The huge gas holders continue to dominate this location – but minus the smell! 11.3.64 Hugh Ballantyne

the shunting spur.

One feature at the Junction which surprised many people used to signalling practice on the GWR, was the use of working distant signals for trains running into Green Park, even though that station was a terminus. These signals were mounted on the posts right by the signalbox and functioned as Bath Station's inner distants. Indeed, when the Western Region of BR took over the management of the lines in 1958, their S&T Department was horrified by this practice, and urged that it be discontinued forthwith. The railwaymen at Bath argued strongly in their support, probably as much out of loyalty to the old firm as their belief in their efficacy. With only a short distance between the Junction and the Station's bracket home signal, it was useful for a driver to know whether he had a clear run right through to the stop blocks, or might have to make a hasty stop. With the distant 'off' he could have a controlled deceleration into the station. Despite all the official protestations, the signals remained in use until the railway closed! Because of the height of the signal posts and their nearness to the box, the Junction signalman could not see the signal arms unless he went to the window and looked up. To avoid this

inconvenience, repeating instruments were provided, displaying the words ON or OFF in a window below the appropriate inscription. He would need to know this because his own distant signals would only work in conjunction with those of the Station. Through an arrangement known as 'slotting', the Junction's distant signals for trains working into Bath would only show 'clear' when both signalmen had pulled the appropriate levers. Due to an interaction between counterweights at the base of the signal post, the arm would only show 'clear' when the last man pulled his lever, but would go back to 'caution' whichever man put his lever back first. A similar arrangement existed at Weston signalbox.

When trains left Bath they had to move over the facing point at the Junction. To ensure that the point blade did not move as the train passed over it, it had to be bolted in whichever direction it was switched. The point rodding and bolt were worked by the same lever (No 15). This arrangement involved an ingenious and meticulous piece of engineering: as the signalman pulled the lever, a square-sectioned bolt was withdrawn from a matching groove in the point tie-bar, which moved laterally as the point changed, thereby presenting another

Congestion at Green Park and its approaches was a feature of any Summer Saturday. Here, a BR Standard loco waits at the old Midland Railway lower quadrant bracket home signal for the 4-4-0 compound No 41144 with a Bournemouth to Sheffield train to clear the Departure platform.   17.8.57   Hugh Ballantyne

groove into which the bolt now fitted tightly. This held the blade firmly against the inside face of the rail. Such a bolt was necessary in case the passage of a train over the points caused the blade to move or in case the blade had not quite firmly closed up in the first place. Lever No 15 could be troublesome, the bolt occasionally being unwilling to register correctly in its groove. This was most likely to happen in hot weather. If the bolt had not gone in properly the signalman would find that the lever clasp would not drop into the frame, so the lever was moved again – usually with more vigour. If the point had not registered properly, the signalman would be unable to pull the appropriate signals, this interaction between points and signals being known as detection. This was achieved by precisely-machined grooved metal plates set at right angles to the point concerned, being connected both to the point rodding and signal wire. As one

signalman said of No 15 when it was in one of its moods: 'you would really have to work at it!' If after several attempts to change the points it would still not register correctly, it would be necessary to call a shunter over from the S&D yard opposite to push the point blade hard over with his foot, or ease the bolt in with his shunting pole. That usually did the trick, but if not the ganger could usually be relied upon to sort it out.

Signalbox Administration. In order to reflect changes in traffic patterns, a review of signalbox classification was carried out soon after the last war. The most important boxes were graded as class 1, the scale going down to class 5. In order to gain a more objective view of the work-load undertaken at various locations, signalboxes were now to be classified according to the number of point lever movements performed and bell codes dealt with in a given time. A signalbox which simply passed trains all day, with only perhaps one daily freight which required any shunting, used signal levers almost exclusively, and would thus be placed at the bottom of the scale. A busy junction or location involving considerable train and/or engine movements would do well out of this system. Thus, in 1946, the most highly graded box in the area was Bath Station as a class 2, the wages being 65/– a week (£3.25p). Bath Junction was a class 3 box (60/–; £3.00); Weston a class 4 (55/–; £2.75); and Midford and Wellow class 5 (50/–; £2.50p). In addition to these classes, the Midland also had intermediate grades for signalboxes off main running lines but in charge of freight/shed movements; for example class 4G, Barrow Lane, Bristol (which paid 52/6; £2.62½).

As a result of this exercise Midford went from one of the top boxes on the S&D to one of the lowest. It had always been regarded as one of the key boxes on the line, because of its role in controlling the single line junction and the more complicated safety devices that this entailed. This demotion not only lost the signalmen money – about which they were most displeased to say the least – but also much self-esteem. Bath Junction, in comparison, fared rather better. The post-war recovery in regular services was boosted by a massive growth in summer excursion traffic at weekends. Shunting locos were hard at work in both yards, necessitating several transfer trips between them; whilst light engine and banking engine movements were also numerous. As a consequence of this the box went up to class 2.

The signalmen were paid their wages on a Thursday. The men at the two Bath boxes had to go to the station booking office to claim their pay packets, while at the out-of-town boxes like Weston, Midford and Wellow men received their money from the Station Master. The men came under the jurisdiction of a District Inspector, whose office was situated in the suite of rooms in the north wing of the forebuilding at Green Park station. Occasionally, men had to report to Bath for lectures on various aspects of signalbox working, rules, regulations and the like.

Signal & Telegraph Linemen. As the name implies, these men were responsible for attending to matters relating to signalling and telecommunications along a stretch of track. Two men covered this work. The signal lineman dealt with the mechanical side, including such things as signal wires and point rodding, together with associated features like slide-bars and facing point locks. The telegraph lineman had responsibility for telegraph equipment and signalbox instruments, including the single line tablet machines. The demarcation between former Midland and Somerset & Dorset Companies persisted even after the Grouping of 1923. The Midland line to, and including, Bath was covered from the S&T Department at Mangotsfield, while the S&D as far as Cole was covered from Bath. The S&D linemen's hut was near the short siding leading from the turntable in the motive power depot. They made regular visits within their territory, either travelling to specific jobs or attending to routine matters. One of the best-known faces on the S&D over the years was Fred Mitchell who could always be recognised by his cloth cap. When a signalman wished the lineman to call he would place a lineman's board in a prominent place on the outside of his box; or, more usually in later days, contact Green Park direct.

Much of the work was occasional, as circumstances dictated. Other tasks however had to be attended to at regular intervals, such as the greasing of point mechanisms and inspection of facing point locks. When the Co-op siding in Oldfield Park required a visit, the lineman would generally ride out and back on the engine of the 7.25am 'Co-op shunt' in order to avoid a long walk. He would attend the points while the shunt was being performed.

Because of the nature of the flow of traffic over the single line section between Bath Junction and Midford, the lineman had very occasionally to sort out an imbalance in the tablets. The Tyer's No 6 machine at each signalbox could hold about 20 tablets, but the number actually present depended upon traffic patterns. By the end of a summer Friday night rather more would be at Midford than the Junction because of the larger number of southbound freights. In the early hours of Saturday there was a procession of southbound passenger trains full of sleepy holiday makers travelling down from the North and Midlands (as one of the Station signalmen put it: 'you saw some sights on those trains, mind!'). The four regulars from Sheffield, Derby, Bradford and Manchester were often supplemented by two or three relief trains in the high season and also a special excursion or two during Wakes Holidays from factory and mill towns up-country. Add to this the 'Down Mail', which ran with vans only on summer Saturdays, and the signalman at Bath Junction could in very exceptional circumstances be left with no tablets

In 1956 the wooden lower-quadrant ex-Midland Railway bracket signal was replaced by an upper-quadrant London Midland Region steel version. The structure was assembled on the ground and then lifted into position, as seen here. The work was done on a Sunday morning, when there would be little traffic about. The distant signals were worked by Bath Junction signalbox, while the small arm signalled access to the goods road.   3.6.56   the late Ivo Peters

at all in his machine by 4.30am and yet the 6.55 and 8.15 down stopping trains had to clear Midford before any train returned northwards. When this happened, the lineman had to be contacted. He would travel out to Midford by taxi, unlock the Tyer's machine there and remove a few tablets – but not too many because there would be a heavier south-north flow later. This done, he returned to Bath Junction.

Once a year, each signalbox was visited by a locking fitter and his mate, who checked the equipment in the locking room below the lever frame. They could also, of course, be called on additionally in case of emergency. If one of the linemen was not available for more minor matters, the ganger would often oblige providing it was a fairly straightforward mechanical matter.

The Signals. Signalling on the Branch from Mangotsfield was installed by the Midland Railway Company, and although the signalling on the S&D came to be the province of the London & South Western Railway, all the signals in Bath were of the Midland type. The square-sectioned timber signal posts were slightly tapered and capped by a pointed wooden finial. From about 1930, finials on stop signals were painted red and those on distants yellow. Although their design was undoubtedly decorative, their existence was functional, to protect the wooden post from rain damage. When tubular metal posts came to be used later, the finial was no longer incorporated, the post simply ending in a flattened cap. One exception to this was the bracket signal installed opposite the Station box in 1956 – sentiment obviously still outweighed finance in this particular case!

The signal arms were also originally made of wood, although thin pressed steel versions superseded these if and when the need arose to replace them. The metal spectacle plate containing the coloured lenses for the lamps at night looked rather ungainly, almost as if they had been added as an afterthought! All the early signals were of the lower quadrant type. Upper quadrant replacements encroached evermore on the scene in the years after nationalisation, but never completely ousted the older type, notably Bath Station's superb bracket home signal by the bridge over Victoria Bridge Road, and also the S&D starting and up distant signals at Bath Junction, and Weston's down distant.

While these post-mounted signal arms were used on running lines, many of the movements between those lines and sidings were controlled by ground signals. At Bath, as elsewhere in the West of England, ground signals were generally referred to as dummies. The original ones installed by the Midland Railway were of the miniature-arm type. Mounted on a post about two feet above the ground, they were as their name suggests miniature versions of the full-size semaphore signal arms – complete with spectacle plate – and backed by a white semicircular plate, the topmost arc of which extended above the upper edge of the arm. This last detail means that, technically, they were not disc signals. The signal arms were painted red, with a white vertical stripe after a fashion of ordinary stop signals and as such could not be passed in the 'on' position (arm horizontal). At Bath Junction there was a variation on this theme. As S&D yard shunting and banking manoeuvres meant that the engine was constantly moving to and fro over the points leading from the sidings in its never-ending task of marshalling freight trains, it would be a great imposition to expect the signalman to operate the two ground signals concerned for each manoeuvre. In this sort of situation, the usual red miniature arm was replaced by a yellow one, with black vertical stripe. Trains were permitted to pass them in the 'on' position providing they were running straight ahead, i.e. in a direction which did not involve the switching of tracks. Only when a train wished to leave the yard and join the main line would the ground signal be pulled (the arm tilting to the left to lie obliquely). The two examples of this type of ground signal at Bath Junction were arranged more or less back to back near the double slip point, and remained in use until the line closed.

Just as the L&SWR's and MR's conventional signals possessed different designs, so too did the ground signals. Those used by the former company, to the south of Bath, were of the Stevens flap type. The only flap-type signal used at Bath was actually a repeating fog signal employed to cover the Station's bracket home signal. The years following the grouping of the railway companies saw a greater standardisation in signal patterns. As miniature-arm type signals came to be replaced for various reasons, the LMS disc-type ground signal was substituted. This consisted of a large white disc with a painted red bar running horizontally across the centre. The red and green lamp lenses were incorporated in the face of the disc. Aesthetically far less attractive than the ones they replaced, they were clearer by day and eminently functional. A handful of these crept into Bath over the years, including the partly overlapping double disc at the entrance to the Midland Bridge yard. Following the Western Region takeover of 1958, their smaller diameter signals appeared on the scene, replacing many of the MR and LMS types; but by the end of the line's life in 1966 all three types could still be seen.

As a round the clock operation, all semaphore and ground signals required to have their lamps lit. At the two Bath signalboxes the signalmen were far too busy to attend to their own lamps, so that this work was done by lampmen, who were actually porters at Green Park station with an extra job description. The signalmen at Weston, however, had to prepare their own lamps, that is, clean, fill and trim them, a job which was done once a week. A porter from the station there actually put the lamps out, as it was not possible for the signalman to leave his box for the length of time that this would require. When the station closed to passengers, a man was sent over from Bath to do this work. It certainly entailed much walking about with the large, heavy lamps used by the LMS. This included the long walk out to the down distant signal just beyond the bridge over

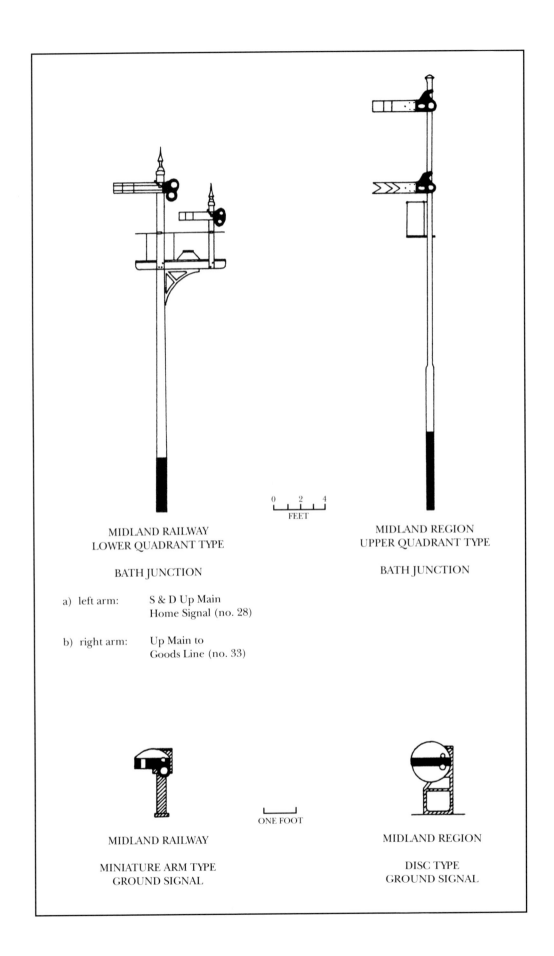

MIDLAND RAILWAY
LOWER QUADRANT TYPE

BATH JUNCTION

a) left arm: S & D Up Main
                 Home Signal (no. 28)

b) right arm: Up Main to
                 Goods Line (no. 33)

MIDLAND REGION
UPPER QUADRANT TYPE

BATH JUNCTION

MIDLAND RAILWAY

MINIATURE ARM TYPE
GROUND SIGNAL

MIDLAND REGION

DISC TYPE
GROUND SIGNAL

0   2   4
FEET

ONE FOOT

110

Brassmill Lane. Climbing the ladder, the lamp had to be carefully lowered into position in the lamp case. In such an exposed location, high on an embankment, the lamp would sometimes blow out as it was being lowered in, and the porter would then have to try to relight it without taking the whole thing out and have it happen again.

Permanent Way Gangs. The maintenance of the track and the land forming railway property was a vital job, if relatively little known to the travelling public. A constant eye had to be kept on the track itself, the ballast, boundary fences and the state of all the ground within those boundaries. Both the Midland line and the S&D were divided into relatively short lengths, each under the supervision of a gang. Each gang consisted of a ganger, sub-ganger and packers (later called lengthmen) whose number depended on the length of the section. As the parent line, the Midland had responsibility for the length between the buffer stops at Green Park station and Bath Junction, including the yards and motive power depot. The shortness of this length is explained by the enormous amount of trackwork to be covered. This Bath gang, like all the gangs on the Bath Branch, possessed nothing more than a small four-wheeled wooden trolley for carrying materials from place to place. This had to be pushed along by hand: no pump-action handle or petrol-engine trolley here! Their trolley would often be seen up against the buffers on the loco spur at Bath Junction when work was being done there or in the S&D yard. It was light enough to be manhandled off the track when not in use. One of the best-known gangers before the war was Emmanuel Gunning, whose three sons – Bill, Tom and Archie – and grandson Reg all became drivers at Bath. His latter-day successors had relatively brief tenures of office: Joe Selman, Jack Taylor, Ron Moore and, finally, Percy Smith. Jack Taylor, incidentally, moved on to head the Midford gang.

At Bath Junction the Weston gang took over. Their trolley was generally kept on the short spur at the Locksbrook Road end of Weston yard, and when they required heavy materials to be brought out from Bath – such as metal chairs or even sleepers – these came out on the afternoon goods and were unloaded in the coal yard. The longest part of their length lay to the west of the station out to Newton Meadows and Kelston Park, where the Kelston gang took over. There was no yard at Kelston station and no official base for the men. However, at regular intervals along the line were packers' huts (also known as platelayers' huts). These were simple wooden cabins, commonly made out of old sleepers, with a brick-built fireplace and chimney and a single shuttered window. They were used to store materials like spare wooden track keys, key-hammers, spanners, scythes and the like. They also contained a simple wooden bench and thus afforded a modicum of comfort for meal breaks in cold weather. As the men were not provided with any fuel for the fire, they had to use anything that came to hand: from old keys and bits of crates and damaged fencing, to lumps of coal kindly thrown down by a passing train crew. The ganger would arrange to meet his men each morning at a particular location where work needed to be done; they would not necessarily travel out from Kelston.

The Kelston gang was succeeded by the Bitton gang and that in turn by the Warmley gang who covered the line out to Mangotsfield South Junction. Over the years the men got to know every inch of their length, for not only did the line have to be walked every day but prolonged periods would be spent in one place thereby giving time for the local environment to impinge thoroughly on the consciousness! Towards the end of the line's life, the gangs were rationalised. The Weston and Kelston gangs were amalgamated with Bath; Bitton was extended in length; while the section including and beyond the level crossing at Warmley was covered by the men from Mangotsfield.

On the S&D, similar short lengths existed for most of the line's history. Thus, the Bath Junction gang covered the length from the junction with the Midland up the bank through Oldfield Park to the footbridge just short of Devonshire tunnel. These men were forbidden to work their trolley over the Midland line to Bath yard or station unless it was absolutely necessary, and then only when accompanied by a member of the Midland's Bath gang. Company demarcations were strictly adhered to! The Tunnel gang took over from the Junction gang and was responsible for the two tunnels and Lyncombe Vale in between. These men had a particularly unpleasant job, working in the damp and smoky interior of the tunnels. Each man carried a lamp and key-hammer which they used to tap the metal chairs of the rails in the event of their lamp going out. This enabled them to grope their way through the tunnel until daylight could be seen. Recesses were provided at regular intervals in the tunnel walls to provide a refuge when trains passed through, the light from the man's lamp serving as an indication to the driver that he was there. On no account was the gang allowed to take a trolley through the tunnels as there was insufficient clearance to lift it off and stow it safely. Consequently, all materials had to be carried. Any heavy work was done on Sundays when there were no trains, and materials could be conveyed from Bath by a special working if necessary. The routine inspection of the track and everything pertaining to it went on during weekdays, but useful overtime could be earned sometimes on a Sunday by cleaning out the tunnels. In a fairly short period of time they would accumulate a distinctive slush, comprising water, stone fragments from the walls, pieces of ballast, cinders, soot and chunks of coal. Ballasting would also be done on a Sunday, with special trains occupying the single line for several hours. This work required the attendance of the gang.

On the Combe Down side of Tucking Mill viaduct, the Midford gang took over, covering the line out to Twinhoe where the Wellow gang succeeded. They were followed in turn by gangs based at Shoscombe, Writhlington, Radstock and so on along the line. In the early days, the S&D gangs like their Midland counterparts, possessed only a small non-powered trolley. However, in more recent times the use of a petrol-driven, four-wheeled machine allowed a gang to cover a much longer section and thus permitted a degree of rationalisation. Thus it was that the Midford gang absorbed the lengths formerly undertaken by the Tunnel and Junction gangs, thereby giving them a five mile length. A lengthman still had to walk the section each day noting anything which required attention and reporting it to the full gang which would be working somewhere in the length. The ganger made the decisions on the schedule of work to be undertaken, unless of course something required urgent attention. There were no intermediate places between Midford and Bath Junction where the trolley could be parked, so that it had to travel right through the entire length. This meant that it would be treated as a train, i.e. the signalman drawing the single line tablet in the usual way. There was no need for a separate ganger's occupation key. The general practice at Midford was for the lengthman to catch the first train of the day to Bath and then walk back, checking all the features in his remit. He carried a lamp, a few spare keys and a key hammer with which any

loose keys would be knocked back securely between rail and chair.

In post-nationalisation days a larger, covered petrol-driven trolley was used to convey the men and a small quantity of tools, while a low-sided four-wheeled trailer was provided for carrying bulkier materials and equipment, this being towed behind the trolley. Two sets of rails at right angles to the running line were provided as lay-bys for these vehicles near the Junction signalbox, a wooden shelter on one of the lines housing the trolley while the other open set was used to stable the trailer.

The maintenance of the track around Bath was exemplary. The chamfered edge of the ballast was kept trim and the walkways clear. If for some reason ballast had moved, perhaps after heavy rain, loco crews would detect an unaccustomed rough ride on the footplate and often make a note of the exact location on a piece of paper and in the case of the S&D between Midford and Bath put it in the pouch with the tablet. The signalman would then ensure that the message was passed on to the gang.

One duty which fell to the gang was to act as **fog-signalmen**. In poor visibility it was up to the signalman to decide if fogging was necessary. Each box had its own visibility markers, perhaps a particular signal lamp or telegraph pole. When this could not be seen the man would contact Control who in turn would arrange for the fogmen to be called out. Each member of the gang had a fog hut allocated to him. It was vital for the driver of a train approaching Weston, Bath Junction and Green Park station in fog to know if he had a signal check, for to overrun in any of these locations could have serious consequences. The distant signals would require covering: Weston's down distant was at Rudmore Park while Bath Junction's distant was between Claude Bridge and the Co-op siding. The fogmen were required to place one detonator on the rail right by the signal when it was 'on' (i.e. at caution) and only remove it when he could see that the arm had been lowered and was showing a green light. Passing the signal at caution the driver would be alerted by a single loud explosion beneath his engine's wheels and would prepare to stop at the impending home signal. If the signal was 'off' (i.e. showing all clear) the fogman was instructed to show a green light on his hand lamp as the train approached. On the single line out of Bath the detonator would only apply to up trains. Thus when the man heard a train pounding up the bank on a southbound working he had to remove the detonator until the train had passed.

Important home signals were also protected by detonators. These were covered by three detonators, which gave off three quickly succeeding reports when a train ran over them, meaning in effect 'emergency stop'. The signalbox at Bath Junction did not possess detonator levers and so they had to be placed by hand at the home signals as for the distant. In the case of Weston's up distant signal for trains on the main line – situated on the gantry by Midland Road – it was not convenient let alone safe for the fogman to have to keep walking to and fro over the goods line. In this location therefore the detonator was placed mechanically by the fogman. By the road bridge was a small fog hut outside which was a lever, normally kept padlocked. This was connected by a rod to lineside apparatus. By pulling the lever, the slide containing the detonator was propelled from its metal protective housing and onto the surface of the rail.

Although the Station signalbox had a lever (No 32) to place detonators for its home signal, a fogman was still required here to replace them in case they were exploded (his hut was by the abutment of the bridge over Victoria Bridge Road). The problem at this location was that the signal was offset someway from the line to which it related. It was also a particularly fog-prone location due to its proximity both to the river and the motive power depot. If a train had to stop – whether or not it had exploded the detonators – the driver needed to know when he had the 'all clear'. To overcome this problem, a flap-type ground signal was provided to repeat the movements of the signal arms. It was set between the down main line and the loco road, in line with the signal. Its rectangular lamp case was supported by a short, narrow pedestal similar to that employed on the miniature-arm ground signals. Near the top of its face was a hole, covered by clear glass which would thus emit a white light. A hinged flap with a red spectacle plate incorporated in it was arranged so that when the home signal was 'on', the flap covered the upper part of the repeater in such a way that the two lenses were in line and thus showed a red light. When either of the arms dropped to 'clear', the flap moved down to reveal a white light. A more modern colour light repeater replaced this in later years.

Another fog hut, resembling a sentry box, was situated opposite the Station signalbox. From here the fogman could cover Bath Junction's up LMS/down S&D distant signals which were mounted beneath the station's starting arms on both arrival and departure lines. The ganger had to make periodic checks of the detonators stored in the fog huts, and after five years from the date marked on them see that they were replaced.

Fog-signalmen had to remain at their posts until either told to leave or relieved by another man. In locations away from signalboxes, field telephones attached to telegraph poles allowed the fogmen to keep in touch with signalmen. In the days before smokeless zones and central heating, fog could sometimes last for days on end, especially in the Avon Valley to the west of Newbridge. All in all it was a pretty miserable job on a freezing winter's day, but at least the men were given time off their normal duties in compensation.

An annual task undertaken by the Permanent Way gang was the handling of signalbox coal. The boxes received their year's supply of fuel in the autumn. As all three Bath boxes were manned virtually continuously, they had an equal allocation.

Breakdown Gang. Until relatively recent times a breakdown train was kept on permanent standby in Bath. Consisting of a crane, open wagons and mess coach, it was generally to be found in the long siding next to the coal stage. Its use was only occasional and would be manned by the Bath gang and the shed foreman fitter when it was required.

Although the crane was taken away from Bath in the early 1950s, a breakdown gang was retained, if only in name, for it was severely limited in the sort of work that it could do, minor derailments in the main.

One of the attractive small Johnson 4-4-0s, No 18, is crossing S&D bridge 2, the pedestrian subway linking Bellotts Road with Inverness Road, and is about to cross the GWR on its journey south. Built in May 1891, the loco is seen here circa 1904, and remained in service until September 1931, although with three reboilerings her appearance was drastically altered.

L&GRP, courtesy of David and Charles

The 6.05pm stopping train to Binegar, hauled by a grimy Standard class 3 2-6-2 tank engine, No 82041, with a GWR Hawksworth coach, passes the former siding connection into the brickworks. This can clearly be seen in the foreground.

9.9.65   Hugh Ballantyne

7. Oldfield Park

Leaving the Midland main line at Bath Junction, the S&D crossed the Lower Bristol Road by the *Royal Oak* public house and proceeded to curve and climb through the densely built-up suburb of Oldfield Park. This name is used more in a generic sense than a geographical one, for in reality it passed through or formed the boundary between the districts of East Twerton, South Twerton, Moorfields and Bloomfield, as well as fringing Oldfield Park itself. As the last named is currently in wide, if unofficial, use by residents on both sides of the line it has been taken here to apply to the section between the old Bath Single Line Junction signalbox and the western portal of Devonshire tunnel.

In traversing this district the line climbed through a vertical distance of about 150 feet in 1.4 miles. With the exception of the short level section by the Co-op siding at Melcombe Road, the climb was at an almost constant gradient of 1:50. Whereas at Bath Junction a down S&D train was travelling in a west, north-westerly direction, the line through Oldfield Park was so sharply curved that within three-quarters of a mile this had changed to south-easterly. Once over the ex-GW line at Bellotts Road, much of the line was carried on embankments, although between Claude Vale and the Co-op siding it passed through a shallow cutting in soft but sticky lias marl and clay (these heavy clays being the bane of many a gardener hereabouts!). Lying on top of these was a thin capping of geologically recent gravel, and it was in this material that mammoth tusks dating from the last Ice Age were found during the construction of the line. The significance of the geology in this district also found expression in the rail-served Brickworks at the end of Dartmouth Avenue and Millmead Road.

Perhaps because of the ease with which passengers could leave Green Park station without surrendering tickets, it was considered necessary to collect tickets before arriving in Bath. On the Midland Line, ticket collectors boarded down trains at Weston for this purpose. The absence of such a convenient station on the S&D led that company to build a ticket platform 1.4 miles from the terminus, near the later site of the Co-op siding. Known as **Bath Ticket Platform** it was on the up (south) side of the track, and was

about 200 feet long, but had no public access. A signalbox was also provided a few yards to the east, a substantial affair with balcony and steps. The platform had staff allocated to it, consisting of signalmen, telegraph clerks and ticket collectors, but details of its construction and the function of the signalbox are lacking. An article in the *Bath and Wilts Chronicle and Herald* on 7th May 1934, however, in referring to the ticket platform, states: 'The situation of this platform is clearly indicated by the long-disused brick signalbox, which is now utilised by the Permanent Way Department'. On 5th November 1876 the platform was taken out of use, when a new one was built on the double track section between Bath Single Line Junction signalbox and the junction with the Midland Railway. This location was operationally more convenient, in that a southbound train could pass while the up train was waiting at the platform. It was also better for the staff who were nearer the centre of operations. The signalbox connected with the old ticket platform remained in position, though disused, for some years after its function became redundant. Indeed, it was still shown as such on the First Series Ordnance Survey maps for 1885.

High density and extensive housing development in Oldfield Park and South Twerton between 1890 and 1910 transformed the railway's physical setting in this district from rural and semi-rural to urban. Between the wars there was occasional talk in railway circles of reinstating the platform as a halt, providing access to St Kilda's Road and Claude Avenue. Despite the building of a halt for the scattered communities in and around Shoscombe and Single Hill in 1929 and for the growing developments at Oldland Common in 1935, any plans for the populous Oldfield Park district came to nought.

May's Siding. In the early 1880s Thomas Hughes Delabere May moved to Bath, and took up residence in Montpelier House, Springfield Place, on the slopes of Lansdown. Being something of an entrepreneur, he quickly realised that the tract of meadows, orchards and farm land between Oldfield Park and Twerton Village were poised on the edge of urban development, due to a quickening of industrial and commercial expansion on the western margins of the city. As land values were still

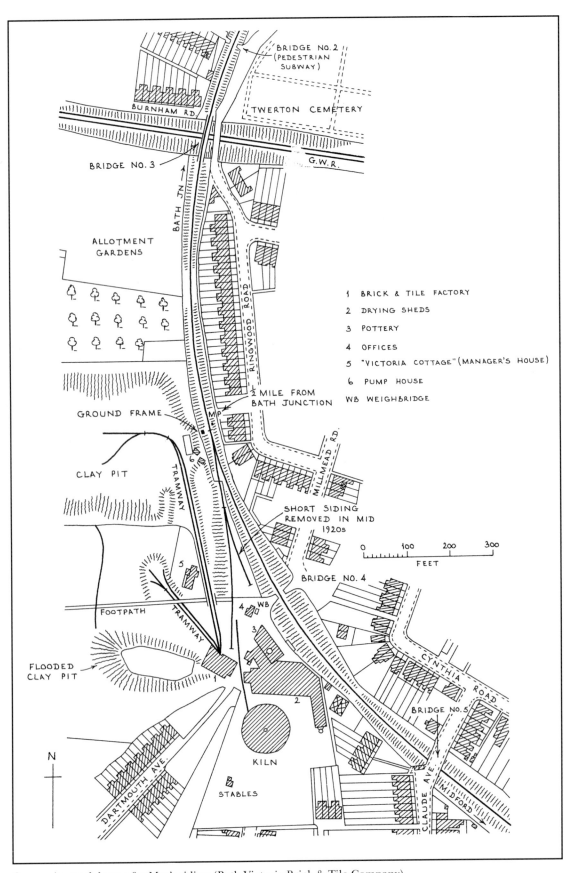

Composite track layout for May's siding (Bath Victoria Brick & Tile Company)

'483' class 4-4-0 No 71 in charge of a down train (with 'foreign' stock?) passes over the connection between the main line and May's Siding. The ground frame hut may be seen opposite the tender. This loco was built April 1914 and arrived in Bath the following month. In 1928 it was renumbered, becoming No 40. The houses behind the engine are in Ringwood Road.

L&GRP, courtesy of David and Charles

relatively low, he began to acquire pieces of real-estate as and when the opportunity arose, in December 1885, July 1886, January 1887 and September 1889. Individually, the parcels of land were quite small, but as they were contiguous amounted collectively to a substantial area, bounded on the east by the S&D in the vicinity of bridge 4. On discovering the quality of the clays and marls of his acquisitions, he considered that he might obtain more revenue from the manufacture of bricks, tiles, field drains and the like, and consequently abandoned his original plan for speculative housing (there were already two brickworks in the district, one in Lower Oldfield Park and another on Monksdale Road).

The need to provide coal for the kilns at the proposed brickworks caused May to make an initial approach to the Joint Committee of the S&D in July 1888 with a view to the provision of a private siding. The private siding agreement was concluded on 11th November 1889, while the company itself was incorporated on 19th May the following year as the Victoria Brick & Tile Co Ltd (in 1894 the prefix 'Bath' was added to the title, and so it remained until closure). Work began on installing the siding, which was to be connected to the main line half a mile from Bath Junction, and it was formally brought into use on 8th April 1890. Having set up the business, May promptly sold it to the directors of the company for £3,000 just two months later. Despite his early departure from the scene, the name of May stuck firmly to the works, and railwaymen were still referring to May's siding 60 years later. There is also the popular belief in the area that the nearby Maybrick Road took its name from his works, although the neighbouring Mayfield Road is more likely to have been so called after the may trees which were once a feature of the district (and still are if you know where to look). It is interesting that two of the place-names of the fields bought by May continue to find expression in present-day locations in the district: Mill Mead and Shophouse Field. Soon after the turn of the century, a pottery was added to the complex, located next to the railway bridge. If railwaymen

117

Bath Victoria Brick and Tile Works c.1905. In the foreground one of the narrow gauge tramways picks its way through a desolate landscape of old quarry workings, which back right on to the gardens of the houses at the bottom of Dartmouth Avenue. Above the three Midland Railway trucks is the embanked S&D climbing towards Claude Bridge; a bottle-shaped kiln belonging to the pottery can be seen against the embankment above the right-hand wagon.   Bath Record Office

referred to the siding as May's, locals simply called the site the Brickyard – a term which remains in use to this day, even though houses and playing fields occupy the area.

The works possessed its own internal narrow gauge tramway system, linking the clay pits with the storage and processing sheds and waste tips. In two places, double-track self-acting inclines crossed the lane leading to The Hollow, one of them on a wooden trestle overbridge – to the entertainment of pupils on their way to or from West Central School (more recently Culverhay Lower School), for which premises the company sold 1¼ acres of land to Bath City Council in April 1910. Watching the tub-like trucks rumble overhead was innocent enough, but every now and again some of the local lads would sneak up to the top of the incline in the evening, unhitch a wagon from the endless steel winding rope and give it a push to send it on its way down to see what would happen. The answer was usually

nothing or a disappointing collision, but even so it was a dangerous playground – more so in later years when the large clay pit nearest the works had become exhausted and was occupied by deep water.

Although referred to as a siding, singular, two lines were initially laid in, one curving and sloping steeply down to the yard between the kibbling shed and the weighbridge house (which, incidentally, still remains as part of the sheltered workshop which now occupies the site). The other, shorter siding more or less ran in straight from the main line and maintained a more level grade. Where these two sidings met, a gate was provided across the line denoting the point of demarcation between railway and private property. The connection to the main line, which faced down trains, was controlled by levers housed in a covered ground frame. It was obviously essential that the points from the running line could not be changed when the siding was not in use, and also that the point blade did not move as a train passed over it. To ensure safety, a series of locking devices were employed.

The traffic using the siding consisted of wagons of coal in and empties out. The bricks and tiles produced in the works generally went out by road unless there was a particularly large order. The coal was needed for the enormous Hoffmann kiln which dominated the site, and the siding was generally shunted about three times a week in the years between the wars. This task was performed by one of Bath's shunting engines propelling the wagons from the junction, and if possible was done in association with work at the Co-op siding further along the line. The difficulty of getting occupation of the single line section between Bath Junction and Midford for long enough periods to enable shunting to take place, severely limited the times of day when this job could be done. By the end of the 1920s the shorter of the two sidings had been removed.

By 1946 the natural resources of the area were nearing exhaustion, and some of the clay pits had already been worked out; indeed, the tramway nearest the S&D was out of use. In 1949 the company sold off the plant and machinery, and on 25th March the following year the disused works were purchased by Bath City Council (although the company was not officially wound up until 1952). In order to save the annual rental on the private siding, the council immediately negotiated with the railway to terminate the siding agreement, from 21st April 1950. Arrangements were then made to demolish the 120-foot high kiln chimney (in July) after which the derelict circular kiln base made an excellent platform for train watching – indeed, the whole site became something of a playground well into the 1960s.

Co-op Siding. Until 1922 the Bath and Twerton Co-operative Societies maintained an independent existence. The latter had coal offices in St Peter's Terrace on the Lower Bristol Road and in the

The Co-op siding pictured three months after it had closed to rail traffic. The wooden ground-frame hut is seen in line with the gate, while the roof in the foreground belongs to a Permanent Way hut. Colin G Maggs

Midland Bridge Road yard, into which the coal was brought by rail. At the end of the first decade of the present century the society sought to establish a bakery and domestic coal yard on a new site in Oldfield Park. Having bought a large rectangular piece of land between the railway and Melcombe Road – which until 1912 was devoid of houses – an approach was made to the railway to arrange for a private siding (in April 1911). Later that year the foundation stone of the bakery was laid, the private siding agreement having been finalised on 25th August. Known as Twerton siding, the facility opened in July 1913, and a few months after the two societies merged to form the Bath & Twerton Co-operative Society, became the sole coal depot for that organisation (except for the short-lived venture on the Lower Bristol Road mentioned in an earlier chapter). From 23rd March 1939 its formal name in railway timetables was changed to Bath Co-op siding, but railwaymen continued to refer to it simply as the Co-op siding.

The siding, i.e. that part of the line inside the boundary gate, was only about 70 yards long and occupied the short but only level stretch of track between Bath Junction and Combe Down tunnel – just over a quarter of a mile further along the line from May's siding. As with the last-named siding, the points were controlled from a ground frame, the levers housed in a wooden cabin. The traffic was of the loaded in/empty out nature, the former consisting of domestic coal, together with coal, flour and salt for the bakery.

Up to ten wagons could be accommodated in the siding, but the usual number conveyed on any given day was nearer four or five. Providing the number did not exceed four, there was no need for the train to have a brake van, the shunter riding on the footplate with the locomen. If the number for the Co-op alone, or Co-op and May's combined, exceeded four vehicles a 20-ton guards van had to be attached to the leading wagon from Bath in order to give the necessary braking power when wagons were left unattended on the main line. A very generous half an hour was allowed for this shunt. The formal inclusion of this job in working timetables was a recognition of its regular nature. Although the train ran as required this was commonly four or five times a week. The only time when the single line section was clear of trains for any length of time was between the clearing back from Midford of the 6.55am Bath–Bournemouth passenger and the occupation of the line by the

8.15am Bath to Templecombe stopping train. For years, the Co-op shunt was booked to leave Bath at 7.25 and return at 8.10. If the Co-op wanted an urgent delivery which had not arrived in Bath in time for the 7.25, or for some reason not all the work had been done on this shunt, a second trip had to be made. In this event the work would be done on the return from banking the 12.35pm Bath to Evercreech freight to Combe Down tunnel, as the line would be available for half an hour – the next train requiring occupation being the 1.10pm Bath to Templecombe passenger. This mode of working was not popular with the shunters as it meant going through the foul, smoky Devonshire tunnel. Indeed, some men hoped that the train would be travelling sufficiently slowly as they approached the siding to enable them to jump off and wait for the train to return! In most cases, however, they just had to endure it as did the footplate crew several times each day! When this special trip was run, the number of vehicles was limited to four, although in more recent times it was very rarely necessary.

The siding was well-used. In its hey-day, before the end of the 1940s, up to four wagons of flour and six of coal would go in in just one working and, indeed, it continued to do a brisk trade in domestic coal right into the mid 1960s, even though the bakery side had diminished. The volume of traffic was sufficient to merit retention of the siding after the closure of the S&D in March 1966. The main line was officially taken out of use from a point six chains (132 yards) beyond the ground frame, and coal trains continued to serve the siding until the end of November 1967. The closed track beyond the siding was not physically blocked as access was required for demolition trains to the south. The track through Oldfield Park was lifted just a few months after the demise of the siding. The Bakery closed in June 1971, and although flats occupy the site of the siding (Melcombe Court), the Bakery building remains in use today as a CRS milk depot.

Claude Bridge. Between the Co-op siding and May's siding came Claude Bridge (S&D bridge 5). When the S&D line was put through the district in 1874 the landscape was largely one of open fields with just a few scattered cottages and occasional nurseries, orchards and market gardens. A narrow bridge was built over the line to allow little more than a lane to link Bridge Road with fields between there and the present Ascension Church. The housing development in

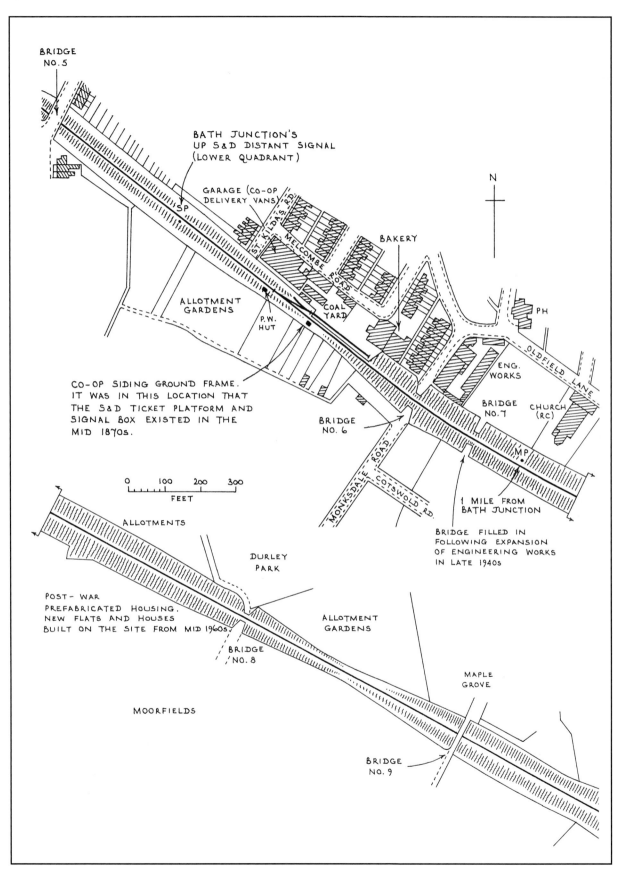

Track layout for the Co-op siding and the Moorfields Section

Stanier 8F No 48309 struggles up the bank near Claude Bridge with an enthusiasts' excursion in April 1965. The signal in the foreground is Bath Junction's up S&D distant. Being ¾ of a mile from the box, with most of the line on a curve, the signalman had to give the lever a hefty pull to lower the arm to 'clear'. R E Toop

the area around the turn of the century necessitated widening the bridge on the east side. Some drivers who lived within ear shot of the bridge had their own personalised whistle code on northbound trains, letting their family know that they would soon be home! On a personal note, great was the sense of relief on numerous occasions during seemingly interminable arithmetic lessons at South Twerton School when the up 'Pines' whistled on its approach to the bridge – we knew that it was coming up to twelve o'clock and the end of morning school!

Claude Bridge featured in one bizarre incident in 1936, namely, the Writhlington Runaway. Tank engine No 7620 was on shunting duties at the Writhlington and Braysdown Colliery sidings near Radstock on the morning of Wednesday 29th July. At a few minutes before ten, the engine was standing on the up main line facing Radstock, with eight empty wooden coal wagons behind it. Although the line was blocked beyond his home signal, the Writhlington signalman had

accepted the 8.10am ex-Evercreech freight from his colleague at Radstock. The shunter was protected by the aforementioned signal, but unfortunately the 37-wagon freight was running too fast after its descent of the Mendips and, although slowing, was obviously going to overrun the signal. As the gap between the two engines narrowed, the crew of the 7F jumped from their footplate. Putting his locomotive into reverse and opening the regulator wide, the tank engine's driver sought to outrun the freight, or at least minimise the force of the collision. By this time the two engines were almost buffer to buffer, and as the 2-8-0 was now travelling slowly driver Charlie Rawlings on the 0-6-0 thought he could stop her. Jumping from his own footplate he duly climbed aboard 13803 and brought her to a quick stand. Unfortunately he had not told his fireman of his intention, and not unnaturally he followed suit, jumping from the other side of the cab. Neither man had closed the regulator and so the tank engine and eight wagons continued

Derailed 3F 0-6-0 tank engine No 7620 seen, below, beneath Claude Bridge, after her 8¼-mile crew-less and chaotic journey from Writhlington. While the line remained blocked, a bus shuttle service operated between Bath and Wellow. Once the 3F was rerailed, she was hauled away by a 4F 0-6-0, the pair seen, above, near Bath Junction, having just crossed the Lower Bristol Road.   29.7.36   Bath & Wilts Chronicle and Herald

merrily on their way towards Shoscombe.

At Midford the train had to pass through the trailing junction, where the double line became single; fortunately there was no down train on line. The coal wagons were already riding roughly due to the unaccustomed speed and nature of propulsion, and the wheels of the leading truck became derailed on the points. Serious damage was done to the signalbox by this vehicle, while the next six hit the station platform, showering debris everywhere before glancing off and crashing down the embankment towards the old Somersetshire Coal Canal. The buildings here had a narrow escape from serious damage as fragments of wood and masonry showered down. A piece of metal went through the roof of the house behind the *Hope & Anchor*, narrowly missing the owner's pet parrot. Normally a garrulous bird, she was so unnerved by the disturbance that she did not recover her speech until an hour later! Out in the garden, the family dog also had a close call. The trucks meanwhile came to rest at an appropriately drunken angle in the pub garden. Back at the top of the embankment the track was twisted but not broken, allowing the engine to hold the rails and

continue towards Bath with a shattered remnant of the last wagon.

Negotiating the uphill gradient through Combe Down tunnel, the runaway progressed through Lyncombe Vale and Devonshire Tunnel, now on a falling gradient. However, by this time her fire was failing and steam pressure falling. The severe lateral movement of the truck, or what was left of

9F 92204 hauls the 7.35am Saturdays only Nottingham to Bournemouth up the embankment between Hillside Road (left) and Durley Park, and enters the shallow cutting leading to bridge 9. Work on constructing the Bath Extension had begun early in 1872, the engineers being faced with several challenges in Bath alone. The half-mile long embankment at Moorfields, together with the earthworks on either side of bridge 4 took almost 12 months to complete. This location today marks the southern end of the Linear Park, as Devonshire tunnel is well and truly sealed.   September 1960   R E Toop

it, caused by its only having one pair of wheels, made the heavy hinged end door flap vigorously to and fro, until as it approached Claude Bridge the door fell off. Lodging beneath the engine's wheels, she came off the track right inside the restricted bore of the bridge, which in fact enabled her to stay upright, leaning against the Bridge Road side of the bridge wall.

As the wagons had left the track at Midford they brought down telegraph poles and broke communication between there and Bath. However, the runaway had already been notified, and its shambolic departure from Midford had been passed on by public telephone. When the train did not arrive at Bath Junction – it had been expected just after 10.15 – there was an urgent need to find out where it was: had it come off or lodged in either of the tunnels, then the authorities would have had a real problem on their hands. The crash at Claude Bridge quickly attracted a crowd of sightseers who hurried from nearby houses and peered over the bridge parapets. The news quickly spread, and soon reached the officials at Green Park. The breakdown gang was sent out to the bridge and discussions took place as to how to rerail the 0-6-0 tank engine. It was decided to attach a steel hawser between No 7630 and the 4F which was in attendance, and ease the derailed engine back onto the track. By this time, quite a crowd had gathered and fortunately they were high up on the bridge away from the track side, for as the wire took the strain, it suddenly snapped, a violent whiplash sending it swishing into the embankment. The railmen were standing well clear when this happened, a very wise precaution as it turned out. A later attempt proved successful, however, and by about 2.00 the engine was back on the line, although she could not be towed away until all the wreckage had been

124

One of the Somerset & Dorset's old faithful 4Fs, 44561, approaches Devonshire tunnel, having passed beneath bridge 9 – a footbridge connecting Maple Grove with Egerton Road. Built in April 1922 by Armstrong Whitworth & Co of Newcastle, the 0-6-0 gave 40 years of service to the line.

July 1953   R E Toop

cleared from beneath her wheels. The track and bridge were then inspected. The sleepers on the down side of the bridge had been scored by the flanges of the derailed engine's driving wheels, but were not so seriously damaged as to hold up the reopening of the line at round about 7.00 that evening (the permanent way repairs at Midford being the main concern).

Moorfields. The long embanked section of the S&D beyond Monksdale Road gave particularly fine viewing, especially of heavy southbound trains where both train engines and either their pilots or bankers were working hard. Before the building of the prefabs after the war, the line here ran across open ground until it reached the short cutting crossed by the three-arched bridge from Maple Gardens and was then swallowed up by Devonshire tunnel. From their chosen vantage point, children in the district waved enthusiastically at the troop trains which were a

regular feature of the line during the last war. They hoped the trains would be carrying American servicemen as their efforts would be rewarded with packets of chewing gum and sometimes even chocolate thrown from the carriage windows, to be followed by the inevitable free-for-all scramble to retrieve the booty. One could always tell when an American troop train had passed over the line as there would be an abundance of rubbish which the men had thrown from the windows. On a long journey, such as from Liverpool, the troops had been issued with food parcels and once the contents had been consumed containers, wrappers and tins were discarded. On arrival at their destination, there could be rich pickings for the carriage cleaners – and the loco crew who usually got in on the act. Tins of spam, bread, chocolate and a few cigarettes could usually be gleaned from amongst the rubbish, a real windfall in times of national

Standard class 4 2-6-0 No 76013 climbs past the back gardens of Ringwood Road with the 5.55pm Bristol to Bournemouth stopping train (7.05 off Bath).
30.8.65   M Mensing

stringency! The poor old British soldier fared much less well when it came to the quantity and variety of food parcels!

In spells of dry weather residents living near the line were always mindful of the possible hazard of fire on the embankment caused by sparks. After the terrible damage and loss of life in the district during the Blitz on Bath in April 1942, a grass fire at night brought people running from their houses to beat out the flames.

Ringwood Road. As in the Moorfields district, Ringwood Road was also very close to the S&D. To an enthusiast, a railway at the end of the garden might seem like paradise. Others were less enamoured. On the west side of Ringwood Road, the S&D passed just yards from the backs of the houses, although the people who lived there were used to the passing of the trains, even the heavy freights pounding past at night. The problem was not so much the noise, as the

vibration. Householders had to remember every now and again to push loose ornaments and the like to the back of shelves and mantelpieces as, with the periodic vibrations, they gradually worked their way forwards. If this task was overlooked, the mini-earthquake caused by the 'Pines' saw the items wobble to the front and fall to the floor! Interestingly enough, many of the people today look back on 'the old Dorset' with nostalgic affection.

At the north end of Ringwood Road was S&D bridge 3, over the Great Western main line. Just a few feet from this was a road overbridge which joined Ringwood Road and Lyndhurst Road with Bellotts Road. This was the location *par excellence* for the railway enthusiast. One could lean on the parapet and watch trains hauled by Midland, S&D, Western and occasionally Southern engines – with never more than a few minutes in between them on summer Saturdays!

8. The Tunnels

The secluded, rustic charm of Lyncombe Vale stood in marked contrast to the loathsome tunnels which bordered it: the 440-yard long Devonshire tunnel to the west and the 1,829 yard long Combe Down tunnel to the east. Both were damp, unventilated, steeply graded and of very limited clearance all round. As feats of engineering they were a tribute to the men who built them, especially the long curved Combe Down tunnel which had been largely rough-hewn through massively-bedded Bath freestone – the local limestone which had been exploited by quarrymen right back to the days of Ralph Allen. To footplate crews, however, they stood as a challenge, with the intervening Lyncombe Vale providing a welcome breather in between.

There had been considerable opposition to the railway from residents in the area, as was evidenced during the second Quarterly Meeting of Bath City Council on Tuesday 7th February 1871. In its haste to expedite matters in Parliament, the S&D had made a few errors in describing certain properties along the line of the survey, notably at Wellow and Radstock, and although this did not materially affect the general route it failed to satisfy standing orders. The company set about requesting interested parties to petition Parliament to abolish the standing orders in this case. At the meeting there was a lengthy and heated debate on this request. The residents of Devonshire Buildings and South Lyncombe were opposed to the Bath Extension Railway because they feared the effects on their homes and environment, complaining that the company had not made available sufficiently detailed plans of the route. Their spokesman, Councillor Bright, voiced the view that the 'proposed railway would break up and destroy one of our most beautiful suburbs, and considerably reduce the value of the land as building sites'. He continued by saying that Bath's allegiance was due to the Great Western 'who will before long lay down the narrow gauge in the districts which have been referred to, opening up the Somersetshire coalfield. After all, it is only the Midland backing up the Somerset and Dorset; as far as the latter Company is concerned, they are perfectly incompetent to carry out the work.' Heated arguments followed about the merits of the GWR, and where the

city's allegiance should lie. Opinion was greatly divided, but eventually the Council decided that they would petition Parliament – but only to suspend the standing orders, refusing actually to promote the railway (this getting through by a vote of 15 to 12).

In seeking to take the S&D south of the city, the engineers were confronted by the 500-foot high plateau of Combe Down. As the Midland Railway's line at Bath was only about 70 feet above sea level, a tunnel would be the only practical way to take the new line through without excessive gradients. Even so, much of the two mile climb from Bath would have to be at 1:50, at which gradient another tunnel would have to be driven beneath an intervening ridge at Bloomfield. In mid-May 1872 the Somerset & Dorset Railway Extension Company (from their office in Shapwick House, Bath) served notice on the owners of land at Culverhouse Close – off Greenway Lane – that they were to begin tunnelling operations here in the near future. The rising costs of the Bath Extension, together with great difficulties encountered in digging Devonshire tunnel, caused many residents in Bloomfield to express concern in case the S&D decided to open out the works at this location and make a deep cutting instead. In the event, their fears were not realised. Combe Down tunnel was an even greater project, taking about 18 months to complete. Built without air shafts, it was to become the longest unventilated tunnel in the country. The absence of shafts meant that men could only work on the tunnel from the two ends; there could not be any intermediate excavations, as at Box for example.

The presence of the navvies certainly disturbed the peace and tranquillity of Lyncombe Vale while the work was in progress, and when it was finished one of the residents – Mr Moger of Lyncombe House – did his best to landscape that part of the raw earthworks he could see from his house (between bridge 14 and Combe Down tunnel). Referring to his endeavours at the bridge, the *Bath Chronicle* reported on 23rd July 1874: 'This arch, by the aid of turf, plants, and other garden accessories, has been made as pleasing an object from the house as a railway bridge, perhaps, could possibly be under the circumstances'.

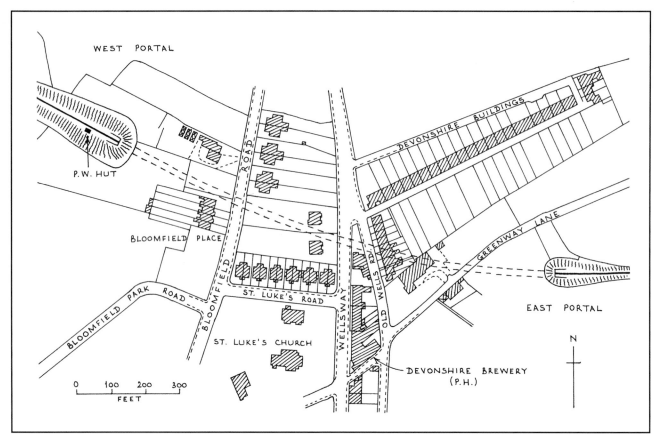

Track layout diagram for the Devonshire tunnel in 1902

At 1 mile 32 chains – just under a mile and a half – from Bath Junction, the line entered the slightly curved Devonshire tunnel, which ran beneath the spur of ground between Bloomfield Park and Lyncombe Vale, mid-way between Devonshire Buildings and Devonshire Brewery. In the early days it was known as Bloomfield tunnel.

The sequence of rocks in this area, as in other parts of Bath, encourages the occurrence of springs, i.e. the juxtaposition of impervious clays and marls with porous sands and limestones. When the tunnel was being dug severe problems were encountered with water; indeed, for years natural springs in the area had provided an abundant and free supply of fresh water to the residents of Bloomfield Park. Unfortunately for the railway engineers the downward percolation of ground water was arrested by an impervious band of clay at the very level at which the tunnel was being driven through, forming a spring-line. The tunnel engineers tapped off the water as the work extended, but because the rocks undulated slightly, as soon as one spring was dealt with another was encountered further in. Such was the problem that they found it necessary to line

the bore with not just one but two courses of masonry in an effort to make it water-tight. In the short term they succeeded, although their endeavours caused much annoyance in the locality as the springs people had been accustomed to using dried up.

The solution employed by the engineers had a practical application for the railway. The sheer volume of water in the tunnel was such that it was put to good use as the main supply for the motive power depot. In the down side (north) tunnel wall a large alcove was excavated, access to which was through a door. Other, smaller recesses were provided along the tunnel wall as refuges for permanent way staff walking through or working in the tunnel. Inside, the alcove steps led down to a sump, dug below the spring-line mentioned earlier. The sump measured about 15 feet by 10 feet deep. Water dripped copiously from the rocks at this point, the walls of the sump being lined with a green algae. About half way down the west wall of the sump a 6" diameter pipe lead off towards the tunnel entrance, from which it emerged below track level. The base of the sump became clogged with debris after a while and so the pipe was situated sufficiently high above this

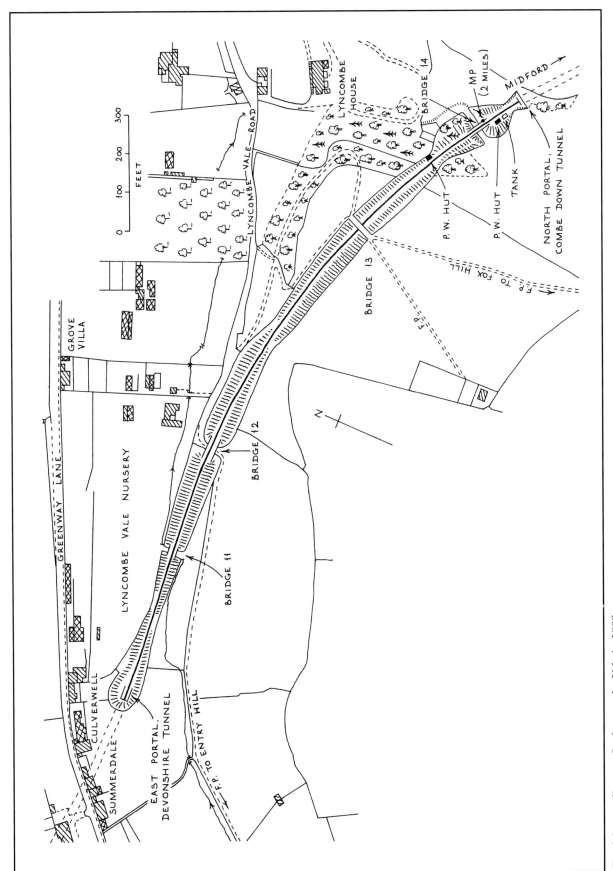

Track layout diagram for Lyncombe Vale in 1902

to avoid becoming blocked itself, but not so high as to be above the water level in dry weather. The sump was cleaned out about once a year, this task falling to the Midford ganger and his men, and was done on a Sunday – this being the only time when an engineer's train could occupy the section for the required length of time.

At times, the amount of water percolating from above was particularly great and despite the double lining of the tunnel, the water had a way of finding points of weakness, and another spring actually formed inside the tunnel. Although this was usually little more than a trickle it could develop into a definite flow after prolonged wet weather. From time to time it would wash out the ballast margin nearest to it, leaving the end of one or two sleepers unsupported. The ganger in his daily inspection would have to get his men to pack the ballast back, and also direct the water away. On one occasion back in the early 1920s the water washed out the ballast from beneath the edges of several sleepers, the deep indent thus produced causing ballast from beneath the rail itself to slip down into the cavity. Walking through the tunnel that morning on his routine inspection, the ganger noticed the damage and as a makeshift repair wedged a large piece of loose masonry that was lying nearby beneath the unsupported sleepers. He did not report either the situation or his action to the signalman at Bath Single Line Junction or Midford, or contact Control. The vibration of passing trains slowly worked the block back out, so that when the Bournemouth to Manchester dining-car express roared through the tunnel, the engine lurched to one side, the crew fearing that they were about to hit the wall of the tunnel – with what would have been unthinkable consequences. The incident was reported on arrival at Green Park and the tunnel hurriedly investigated. The cause was found, and train services temporarily suspended while remedial work was carried out. The ganger was dismissed.

The summit of the two-mile climb from Bath Junction was reached at the entrance to Combe Down tunnel. The next few yards were on the level to be followed by a mile-long descent at 1:100 to the portal at the Midford end. The long central part of the bore was straight, while the end sections were curved in order to allow an alignment between Lyncombe and Horsecombe Vales. As with Devonshire tunnel, water was also harnessed for use at the engine sheds. This time, the spring emerged near the Lyncombe Vale

portal rather than actually inside the tunnel itself. At its point of issue a sump was dug and the water piped off in a 9" diameter pipe which ran the 2¼ miles to the motive power depot accompanying the 6" pipe from Devonshire tunnel. The pipes were arranged one above the other, with the smaller of the two on top. They were boxed in with sand and gravel as a protection against the frost, and ran entirely underground except where they passed over the GWR on bridge 3 (Bellotts Road) and the Lower Bristol Road on bridge 1. The premier supply was that from Devonshire tunnel, with Combe Down being used as a supplementary feed. At Bath Junction, valve gear was installed which could shut off the supply should any maintenance be necessary. Even after the line closed, water continued to flow through the pipes, though now running to waste in the River Avon. When the overbridge at Millmead Road was being demolished, a mechanical excavator employed in preliminary work on the embankment above the abutments severed the upper pipe, its presence and the sheer volume of water issuing from it surprising both workmen and residents.

The tunnels made quite an impression on long-distance passengers who did not know the line. On a hot, sultry summer Saturday afternoon people would generally have the carriage window ventilators wide open as well as the compartment doors and corridor windows. The unsuspecting holiday makers got a nasty shock when the train pounded its way into one of the tunnels, thick sulphurous smoke instantly pouring into the compartments. The ventilators were hurriedly slammed shut and the compartment door closed as the corridor filled with the swirling exhaust. Bursting out into Lyncombe Vale the ventilators were promptly opened to let fresh air back in, only to be slammed shut again moments later when the second tunnel was entered. The footplate crews had no such protection, and knew only too well what to expect.

Southbound trains from Bath would be on a rising gradient through Devonshire tunnel, and northbound ones likewise in Combe Down tunnel. The tunnels were built to take a single track only and then to a very restricted bore: there was barely 12 inches clearance between a loco's chimney and the roof. The towering blast from a hardworking engine on a rising gradient – especially on a slow moving heavy freight – was suddenly confined on entering the tunnel, and

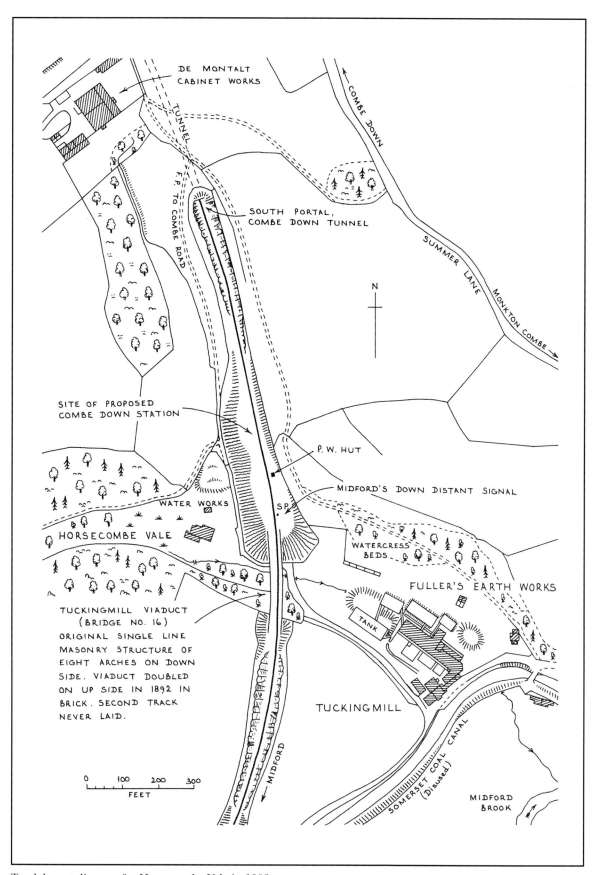

Track layout diagram for Horsecombe Vale in 1902

In its lined-out black livery, 2P No 40569 coasts out of Devonshire tunnel's west portal with a 3-set of ex-L&SWR coaches. An impression may be gained from this picture of the extremely tight fit between trains and the tunnel walls and roof.

September 1952   R E Toop

was deflected straight back with tremendous force, swirling onto the footplate. If the smoke was not too thick the driver and fireman would put a handkerchief over their nose and mouth, but if they found the tunnel hot, smoky and airless they would dip a cloth or rag in a bucket of water and cover their face, or sometimes drape it right over their head. On double-headed expresses the conditions for the crew on the train-engine were particularly unpleasant, as they were also for the crew on the Bath banking engine in Devonshire tunnel – which they had to go through twice when performing a banking duty. Sometimes men would crouch on the floor of the cab as the choking smoke got lower and lower, and on occasions were forced down onto the cab steps as the thick smoke enveloped the footplate. Looking along the boiler a red glare would be seen between the loco's chimney and the roof of the tunnel as the engine worked flat out to haul its train through. The noise was deafening and the heat tremendous. The cab hand-rails would sometimes get too hot to hold and breathing could become difficult.

To make matters worse, although the limestone through which Combe Down tunnel was cut was massively bedded and structurally coherent, it was porous. Consequently, the tunnel was always wet. The tunnel builders had only considered it necessary to line the end portions of the work, and left most of it rough hewn. In fact, the tunnel possessed its own micro-climate. With both ends being curved, smoke tended to linger in the central portion: even the portals took 20 or 30 minutes to clear. If the wind was blowing from either a northerly or southerly direction the tunnel would clear more quickly, as a through-draught was set up. With water constantly dripping onto the floor and ballast, humidity was high and on many occasions a white mist about three feet thick hung miasmically over the track. The rails were frequently greasy and drivers had to manipulate their sanding apparatus in order to prevent slipping. Slipping in fact was one of the great dreads of footplate crews. With such a restricted, unventilated bore the effect can be imagined. Smoke glanced down off the roof together with cinders, ash and lumps of burning

The powerful exhaust pounding from the 9F's chimney immediately explodes upwards as the loco bursts out of Devonshire tunnel and into Lyncombe Vale at the head of the 9.03am Bristol to Bournemouth. With less than 12" between the rim of the chimney and the tunnel roof, conditions on the footplate were extremely unpleasant.   11.8.62   R C Riley

coal. Unless the loco could quickly find her feet the crew were in for a really bad time. The light-footed West Country Pacifics were notorious for slipping, and did so on a number of occasions in the tunnels. Devonshire tunnel, unlike Combe Down, was lined. However, as was explained earlier, this tunnel was also damp. If the problems outlined would seem to be on a lesser scale for this much shorter tunnel, this was partly offset by the fact that it was built on a gradient of 1:50 compared with Combe Down's 1:100.

Priming in the tunnels was another worry. If a fireman set off from Bath with too much water in the boiler or with dirty water – as when the m.p.d. was using river water – problems could arise. The engine would be working hard with the firemen using the injectors before reaching the summit. Soon after entering Combe Down tunnel the gradient began to fall and water overflowed the dome and ran to the front of the boiler. Boiling

water thus entered the cylinders in addition to steam, sending scalding water cascading out of the funnel and over the locomotive, putting the crew at risk of injury. One particularly horrific incident involving priming in Devonshire Tunnel, happened to the Bath banker. Banking engines before the last war were coupled to the brake van of the train they were assisting – very fortunately as it happened in this case. Soon after entering the tunnel the banker started priming badly. Boiling water came raining down out of the swirling smoke. The driver felt a terrible burning sensation round his head. Instinctively he clasped his hands to his head and sank to the floor of the cab in extreme pain. Not only were his hands scalded but, worse still the boiling water injured his head so badly that he lost his hair and even scalp tissue. Fortunately, the train-engine was able to drag the incapacitated loco through.

(left, upper) Resplendent in the S&DJR's Prussian blue livery, one of that line's 4-4-0s (No 67) traverses the Vale with a southbound train in the early 1920s. The bridge beneath the leading coach carried the line over a farm track and the tiny Lyn Brook. Until comparatively recently the south-facing slope of the Vale was noted for its nursery gardens, complete with extensive greenhouses and neatly regimented rows of plants.   L&GRP, courtesy of David and Charles

(left, lower) In this 1936 view, large-boilered 7F 13807 (ex-S&D No 87) heads through the Vale with a down freight, an 0-6-0 4F giving rear-end assistance. Built in 1925, the 7F was given a smaller boiler in June 1954, and was the last member of the class to remain in service, being withdrawn in October 1964 (although actually working her last train on 5th September).   L&GRP, courtesy of David and Charles

(above) One of Bath shed's long-stay ex-LMS 4Fs, No 44422, with a stopping train to Templecombe in July 1964, by which date this part of the Vale had a more urban look. Built at Derby in 1927, the loco has been preserved by the North Staffordshire Railway Society (near Leek).   R E Toop

Poor steaming was another of the problems made infinitely worse when it happened in one of the tunnels. Many freights, indeed most, were banked out of Bath and so at least a poorly-steaming train-engine had assistance and could usually limp through. Having a banker did not always guarantee that all would be well. It has been known for the train-engine to go forging ahead and leave a poorly steaming banker behind, while a tank engine was not always powerful enough to usefully assist a heavy train – for this reason a 4F was usually rostered on the banking turns. Before the last war one of the heaviest freights from Bath was the one minute past midnight, the 'Ghost Train' as railwaymen called it. The banker was assisting vigorously in the rear when, on one night entering Devonshire tunnel, steam pressure suddenly dropped like a stone and the engine lost all power. There followed a severe jolt as the coupling tightened, causing the tail lamp on the brake van to go out. The train-engine just managed to keep the whole formation moving on the steeply rising gradient when the banker suddenly and unaccountably started up again, running into the back of the van with a hefty bump. The guard was shaken but there was no damage and mercifully the van was not derailed in the foul confines of the tunnel.

Banking engines assisted freight trains almost to the tunnel entrance, and on seeing the brake van disappear into the portal returned light engine to Bath Junction. Note the lineside telephone, bottom right. On the 4F's footplate is driver Oscar Pitt.

5.9.60   Colin G Maggs

Banking engines would assist right up to the entrance to Combe Down tunnel, by which time the train-engine would be over the summit and on a down grade. Having seen the guards van into the tunnel, the banker returned light engine to Bath Junction. Northbound freights, however, were not assisted and they had the hard uphill slog of over a mile through Combe Down tunnel. If on the approach to Midford the crew saw the distant signal showing 'clear' they knew they could get a good run at the tunnel – the Whitaker tablet apparatus fitted to the tender allowing trains to run past the signalbox at speed, not that a heavy freight would be travelling fast! Quite often, however, the distant would be 'on' i.e. showing caution. This frequently meant that the train would have to stop at the outer home signal to await the clearance of a southbound train from the single line section. A stop at Midford was not a problem under normal circumstances, but if an engine was steaming badly the driver might not wish to risk the tunnel.

When boiler pressure fell to about 100 psi, the engine's steam brake would start to drag on and thereby further slow down an already labouring train. Some drivers in this situation of poor steaming would stop outside Wellow signalbox and ask the signalman whether or not they would have a clear run into Bath. If not, they might put off a number of wagons in the small yard at the station in order to lighten the load – arrangements then having to be made by Control for another train to collect them later. Alternatively, they might continue to Midford and wait there for steam pressure to build up. Depending upon the train movements and the seriousness of the steaming problem, the freight might have to set back wrong road onto the down line if another up train needed to pass. This facility was in fact properly signalled, with setting back signals positioned at each end of the station, and a ground signal to bring the train back out from the down main line to the single line. If steam pressure could still not be raised

The Lyncombe Vale, or north, end of Combe Down tunnel viewed from the footplate of a down freight train. The picture was taken early in 1963, not long after the blizzards which had wreaked havoc with train services at the beginning of the year. The railings between the loco and the permanent way hut belong to bridge 14.   Driver John Stamp

Two of the S&D's original 4Fs – 44559 piloting 44560 – with the 10.38 Saturdays only Manchester to Bournemouth service, passing the site put aside by the company for a station for Combe Down Village. The station, like the double track planned between here and Midford, never materialised. 19.6.54 R E Toop

sufficiently in a reasonable time, a request for assistance would be telephoned to Bath and an engine sent out to pilot them home. An unassisted train that got into difficulty beyond Midford might be brought to a stand in Lyncombe Vale for a blow up, that is, to build up steam pressure. A telephone was provided at each end of the tunnels, attached to the nearest telegraph pole to the entrance.

The propensity of an engine to steam depended on a number of factors such as the condition of the fire, the state of the boiler tubes, the length and weight of the train, and the skill of the driver and fireman. Even so, some locos could vary from day to day even with the same crew.

While the tunnels were unpleasant at best and downright evil at worst, they brought out, indeed demanded, the best performance of footplate crews. In a way, this was acknowledged by one of Bath's veteran drivers on the very last day of public service, Saturday 5th March 1966.

Although a couple of specials ran over the line on the Sunday, the last service passenger train was due into Green Park at 9.50pm on the Saturday night – an up stopping train from Bournemouth. As was usual with 'last trains' it was running late, due to people taking their farewells at all the stations along the route, reaching Bath at about 10.35. Twenty minutes or so behind this train came Standard class 3 tank engine No 80037, running light to Bath shed. As the fireman collected the single line tablet at Midford the crew realised that an era was coming to an end; very little was spoken on the footplate as it was an emotional occasion. Entering Combe Down tunnel, the driver suddenly stopped the engine, walked to the cab doorway, leant out and touched the wall of the tunnel saying 'I've always wanted to do that!' The loco then set off again, bringing to an end the association between a remarkable feat of engineering and a remarkable driver. Literally a touching story!

During the Baedeker raids on Bath in April 1942 the recesses in the tunnel walls, especially Devonshire, were used by a few residents as refuges for a while after the terrible Blitz on the City on 25th and 26th. When the sirens sounded – especially at night – they trooped from their homes into the tunnel until the 'All Clear'. Train crews would sometimes see the faces of the people momentarily illuminated by the glare from the ash pan or firebox as they passed by just inches away. The noise, smoke and danger of the tunnels was evidently considered a better risk than enemy bombers.

The Wreck of No 89. Mention has already been made of the problem of poor steaming in locomotives. The extreme consequences of this happening in Combe Down tunnel may be graphically highlighted by the events of a winter's evening in 1929. On Wednesday 20th November the engine rostered to bring the 1.25pm freight from Evercreech Junction to Bath was 7F No 89 – 53809 of later years. The driver was Harry Jennings of Lymore Avenue; his fireman Maurice Pearce of Midsomer Norton; and the guard Christopher Wagner of Belvoir Road. The engine had already worked down from Bath that morning on another train, and would have to travel back tender first as the turntables at Bath and Evercreech were not long enough to accommodate the class 7s. The first hint of a possible problem came whilst they were waiting in the yard at Evercreech. Driver Jennings in conversation with the guard happened to mention that the engine 'was not working up to scratch'. At 1.25 the train left the up sidings, the formation consisting of loco, three loaded wagons, 33 empty coal trucks and a brake van. Without any banking assistance, the steep and immediate climb out of Evercreech was a laboured affair, the train losing time. Soon after leaving Shepton Mallet the situation began to deteriorate seriously and despite all his efforts with the fire, Maurice Pearce was growing increasingly concerned at the drop in steam pressure. With the climb through Winsor Hill to the summit at Masbury still to come, this was bad news, although the men managed to keep the train moving. With the engine steaming badly by now, the train crawled over the summit 23 minutes late. Back in his van, guard Wagner realised that the driver was having difficulty, but at least the falling gradient north of the summit would bring a respite and perhaps allow the situation to improve. On arrival at Midsomer

Norton the train had to stop to put off the coal empties for Norton Hill Colliery and pick up a few trucks from the station yard. Whilst No 89 was waiting in the up platform during the shunting operations, the 3.00 passenger train from Bath arrived in the down platform; the two locomotives ending up alongside each other. The drivers had a brief chat and, knowing that 57-year old Harry Jennings had been ill with bronchial catarrh until the previous weekend, driver Boucher on the passenger enquired as to his health. Jennings said that he was better and stated that his concern at the moment was the difficulty he was having in getting No 89 to steam; and that he had only just managed to get over Masbury Summit. With shunting completed, the northbound freight set off down the bank to Radstock, where a number of loaded wagons from the collieries in the area were to be attached. The train was now heavily laden, with 30 loaded ten-ton wooden private owner coal wagons, one empty coal truck, an empty oil tank wagon and a 20-ton brake van. Before leaving Radstock yard, the guard expressed his concern at the prospect of attempting to take the train through Combe Down tunnel. He suggested to the driver that they stop at Wellow and ask the signalman the state of the road to Bath in the hope of getting a good run at the tunnel. However, with the single line between Midford and Bath Junction in heavy use at this time of day, a stop at Midford seemed inevitable.

Leaving Radstock, the train lumbered on its way north, passing Wellow at 4.53pm and coming to a halt at Midford's outer home signal at 5.02. There would be a long enforced wait here as the single line ahead was occupied by two succeeding southbound trains, the first a passenger and the second a freight. The fireman resolved to use the time to good effect in an effort to improve the engine's performance. He set about cleaning the clinker from the fire bars and attending to the fire itself. In spite of his efforts, however, the driver was not at all happy. When the signal eventually came off he was not prepared to risk going through the tunnel with the engine in its present state, and so he drew forwards to the signalbox to ask signalman Larcombe to let a Templecombe–Bath passenger train precede him. This would entail setting the freight back onto the down line, a facility allowed for at Midford as has been mentioned earlier. This would give more time still to get the steam pressure up. In addition, the driver asked that when the line was clear for his train he be allowed to carry the single line tablet with him back to his engine, as he wanted to make full use of the length between Midford and Tucking Mill viaducts to get a good run at Combe Down tunnel (in 1929 the single line junction was right outside the signalbox and so it was not possible to use the Whitaker apparatus when running 'wrong line').

At 6.13pm, after a wait of 71 minutes, the freight set off, the Midford signalman sending the 'train entering section' bell code to Bath Junction, the guard entering the time in his journal. Guard Wagner was, however, becoming more concerned as the train passed through Midford station at only about 10 mph and seemed to be losing speed even then. Labouring through the still, damp November evening blackness below Midford Castle and the countryside near Horsecombe Vale, the train was indeed slowing down and approached the dreaded tunnel at walking pace. Once inside the restricted bore of the tunnel, smoke swirled around his van. In order to see whether or not the train was actually moving, he opened a window and shone his handlamp onto the tunnel wall. Although he could see in the beam that they were still moving, it was painfully slow: a mere crawl. With smoke pouring into his van, conditions for Christopher Wagner were unpleasant, the worst he had experienced in 32 years on the S&D, and he wondered what conditions must be like on the footplate.

Working hard with his fire on the approach to the tunnel, Maurice Pearce left off firing as they entered. Very soon afterwards he found the air inside the tunnel unusually thick, and began to cough. Despite the fact that they were travelling tender first, the atmosphere was hot and choking. Pearce began to feel extreme discomfort, so sat down on his box by the fire hole and wrapped his coat round his head. Driver Jennings took no such action and continued to coax his engine up the 1:100 gradient.

Back in his van the guard realised that they would be in the tunnel for longer than usual, perhaps ten minutes or more, but at least they were still moving and the locomotive was not slipping. Anticipating the wagons would begin to close up once the train crested the summit near the Bath end of the tunnel, he prepared to apply his hand brake. After what seemed like an age, the wagons indeed began to close up, but the train was also evidently gaining speed even before it left the tunnel. The guard began to screw on

his brake gradually and carefully, expecting the driver to apply the steam brake and the fireman the tender handbrake at any moment. However, as they traversed Lyncombe Vale, this did not happen. He turned his brake harder and harder, being careful not to snatch the couplings. Continuing on the down grade through Devonshire tunnel the train gathered speed, and it became obvious now that something was seriously wrong. Looking out of his van he would see lumps of coal flying back from the top of the tender while sparks showered from the wheels of his van. He listened for a whistle from the driver but none came (when an engine could no longer hold its train, the driver would keep the whistle open as a warning). Coming down the bank at Moorfields the train was travelling at 45 to 50 mph instead of the customary 20 mph. By the time they reached Claude Avenue bridge the guard had his brake full on. With sparks cascading from the squealing wheels, he realised that there was nothing more he could do as the train continued to gather speed.

Standing in the back doorway of his house in Ringwood Road, a mere 20 yards from the line, off-duty signalman Gardiner was horrified to see the freight race past him. The wagons were rocking, thereby causing sparks to fly as the wheel flanges dug into the rails. The time was 6.30. Fourteen minutes were allowed for a freight to travel between Midford and Bath Junction, and so the signalman at the latter place was keeping a look out for the train as it was now overdue. It was signalled into the goods line which gave direct access to the Midland Bridge Road yard. Standing in the spur by the Junction box was the yard pilot tank engine, while shunter Hill and Day together with checker Richards stood on the bridge over Victoria Bridge Road waiting to deal with the train when it arrived. Anticipating the impending arrival of the freight, 58-year old goods inspector John Norman of West Avenue came out of his yard cabin and looked along the line.

Peering over the Lower Bristol Road bridge, signalman Walter Cook suddenly spotted the lights on the tender of No 89; the train was obviously running very fast. Driver Frank Porter and fireman Shipp on the pilot loco looked in amazement as the train roared past them, swaying over the two sets of facing points but holding the road. They could not see anyone on the footplate as the train lurched and clattered past them. The noise of the train attracted the attention of men in the S&D yard cabin and soon afterwards in the shed area and yards also. Signalman Cook could only send a bell code to the Station signalbox and was powerless to do anything else. Running on the straight goods line, Christopher Wagner decided to jump; the train was about to be wrecked and at least there was a grass embankment here to break his fall. As he jumped, inspector Norman realised that the approaching train was a runaway and yelled to the three men on the bridge 'Clear out. Look at that engine!' The men scattered, but before Mr Norman could decide which way to move the locomotive hit the points at the entrance to the yard at about 60 mph. The tight radius of the curve leading into the sidings derailed the engine, which careered on for a few more yards and then overturned crushing the inspector against the wall of the wooden cabin, which it all but demolished. The following coal wagons piled into each other, tearing up the track and sending their contents flying.

Minutes before the ill-fated freight appeared, a passenger train had arrived from Bristol. One of the people on board was 23-year old Jack Loder, a railway relief clerk who lived in Canterbury Road. Rather than walk home via Midland Bridge Road he and a colleague decided to take a short cut to the bottom of Brougham Hayes by walking through the yard. He was just approaching the yard cabin when inspector Norman shouted his warning. At the very moment he stopped, the engine turned onto its side, crashing into a cast-iron yard lamp post which toppled over and struck Mr Loder, killing him outright. As the buffers of the tender ploughed into the ground, the gas pipe which supplied the cabin and yard lamps was broken. The lamps all went out and gas began to escape from the shattered pipe. The stove in the cabin was knocked over as the building crumpled and burning coals spilled out, setting fire to the splintered timbers of the building, which in turn ignited the gas.

The tremendous force with which the engine ploughed into the ground flung burning coals across the tracks towards Albert Buildings, a terrace of houses which ended right up against the north side of the embankment. Coals were hurled through the windows of Mr & Mrs Jones' house, next to the bridge, and a small fire started, although this was soon put out. Four doors up the street a piece of burning coal went through an upstairs window and landed on the bed of three-year old Joan Carpenter. Her mother rushed into the room and grabbed her to safety as the bed clothes and curtains caught fire: these too were quickly extinguished. The noise of the crash brought railwaymen running from all directions, while members of the public rushed up the embankments to see if they could help in any way. The tender was lying in a huge depression gouged out by the force of the impact, while steam was escaping from the engine. Flames from the gas leak made rescue attempts difficult. The fire brigade arrived very quickly and put out the fire, the gas supply then being turned off. An eyewitness summed up the scene thus: 'It was pitch dark, and the only lights available were from hand lamps and small flickering flares. These illuminated a scene of chaos and devastation. The great engine lay over on its side, one end being in the goods yard cabins with coal wagons piled up on ends, a mass of splintered wood, and twisted and broken steel. Coal from the wagons lay strewn in all directions.....Railwaymen with tears in their eyes worked hard to recover the dead and injured men.'

Driver William Bowles of West Avenue had brought in the passenger train from Templecombe which had passed the doomed freight at Midford. He was one of the first on the scene and managed to get into the cab by crawling through the tender coal-hole. He found driver Jennings trapped and with his clothes on fire; and fireman Pearce beneath a pile of coal, his head wrapped in a jacket. Beating out the flames on the one man and getting the coal off the other, both men were extricated from the debris and carefully taken out through the tender and rushed to hospital. The guard was found badly hurt on the line side, while the bodies of the other two men were discovered by the track.

The driver died very soon after being brought out of the cab, while his fireman was also thought to be dead, a message to that effect being sent to his wife in Midsomer Norton. In fact, although badly scalded, cut and bruised, Maurice Pearce was only unconscious, and his wife's grief disappeared when she arrived at the Royal United Hospital. The guard had broken both his legs in the leap from the brake van, and ironically although much of the train had been wrecked, his van had remained upright on the track. Both injured men were to be in hospital – in the same ward – for several weeks. After a prolonged period of convalescence, Mr Wagner took up duties on the railway once again, but this time as a porter at

Green Park station.

The crash came as a terrible shock to railwaymen in Bath and indeed to the city as a whole, the funerals of the three victims at Twerton Cemetery being attended by large numbers of men from the LMS, S&D and GWR. Even today it remains a vivid memory for many retired railwaymen. The subsequent inquest was to highlight the vile conditions which occasionally prevailed in Combe Down tunnel, although it was never completely explained how the train came to run away.

The tragedy brought home to the people of Bath the foul and capricious nature of Combe Down tunnel, (and to a lesser extent Devonshire tunnel) which footplate crews had to endure day in and day out. Although, mercifully, such an accident never happened again, all drivers and firemen who worked on the line have their horror stories to tell; and there were some very close calls.

At the time of the accident, No 89 was only four years old. Following extensive repairs she returned to Bath to give valued and uneventful service. In 1930 she was given the new number of 9679 and in 1932 became 13809, a number which she retained until nationalisation in 1948. As 53809 she remained at Bath until June 1964, when she was taken out of service. After languishing in a scrap yard at Barry for several years, she was rescued by the Midland Railway Trust, based at Butterley near Derby. She made an emotional return home in 1987 whilst on the way to Basingstoke to work a special on the Southern Region. Slowing down as she ran through Oldfield Park station just before 7.00pm on Wednesday 16th September, she loudly whistled a salutation to her home city and to the crowds who had turned out to see her. Thirteen days later she passed through again, this time on her way to the Severn Valley Railway, but as this was at 3.00am few witnessed the event!

9. Weston

The station at Weston, just under a mile from Green Park, opened on the same day as its larger neighbour, Wednesday 4th August 1869. The main station building was on the down (Bath) platform. It was designed by the Midland Railway's own civil engineering department at Derby, the members to whom the work was assigned showing an admirable appreciation of local building materials. For the walls of the main building they used the attractive light blue-grey Pennant stone with sills, lintels and corner-blocks fashioned from the honey-coloured Bath stone. The roof was of grey slate, while decorated wooden barge-boards adorned the gable ends. This part of Lower Weston was still very largely open countryside: there was no Ashley Avenue or Shaftesbury Avenue. Orchards occupied the land between the Upper Bristol Road and the railway, with the damp water meadows of the Avon floodplain taking over beyond Locksbrook Road. Initially, road access to the station was by means of a long curved driveway, which began in the angle made by the junction of the Upper Bristol and Locksbrook Roads. Foot passengers could additionally reach the down platform by means of the path leading from the level crossing, next to the Station Master's house.

The platforms were not of equal length, due to the provision of a siding behind the up platform. To begin with, the siding was connected to the running lines at each end of the station, which thus made the up platform an island and restricted its length to 380 feet (including ramps). Considering the lengths of the trains using the Midland's Bath Branch, the 690 feet allowed for the down platform seemed generous to say the least, but this may partly be explained by Weston's function as a 'ticket station' for Green Park. As the station at Bath was, to use modern parlance, an open station, all down trains originally stopped at Weston for the ticket collectors to board and collect or inspect tickets. The coaches in use in those days were short, non-corridor stock and if a long train overhung the platform the collectors would not be able to gain access unless the train drew forwards. Regular trains would be no problem, but longer excursions had to be provided for. Both platforms were lit by oil lamps, while the facilities on the up side consisted merely of a simple open-fronted wooden waiting shelter.

In the mid-1890s a number of significant changes occurred at Weston. The original signalbox by the level crossing was replaced by a new structure of standard Midland design; the yard points at the level crossing end of the station were removed and the down platform was altered. With the removal of the yard points an opportunity now existed to lengthen the up platform but this was not done. Instead, the down platform was cut back by about 150 feet at the Bath end, to bring the two ramps in line and thereby allow the provision of a board walk across the tracks, which greatly reduced the previous long detour from the booking office to the up platform via the level crossing. In partial compensation for this truncation, the opposite end of the down platform was extended by some 100 feet. The construction of Ashley Avenue at about this time also created a major change in road access to the forecourt. A new entrance was made at the right-angled bend in the Avenue, while a gate was installed in the wall by the station building to allow direct access to the existing drive without having to pass through the booking hall. Whilst people from the Locksbrook district might still continue to use the old station approach road, patrons from Lower Weston and Weston Village tended to use the new entrance. This shift of emphasis, together with the addition of a new rank of houses between the level crossing and Locksbrook Road, saw the name Station Road transferred from the former to the latter. Until 1950 Weston village was separate from the city of Bath, being in the old Bathforum Hundred (later renamed Bathavon Rural District). On 1st October 1934 the station itself underwent a renaming, being known thereafter as Weston Bath instead of simply Weston as previously. The platform nameboards were altered accordingly – although most of the people who used the station did not feel in need of this elucidation!

The daily routine of the station was superintended by the Station Master. Although an administrator, he had to have a thorough grounding in many aspects of railway operation, having come up through the ranks. At Weston his staff consisted of two porters, three signalmen and the permanent way gang: a ganger, sub-

The main station building on Weston's down platform, c1900. Note the ornate barge-boards and decorative ridge tiles. The floral borders on the platform were a noteworthy feature throughout the life of the station.   M J Tozer collection

ganger and two lengthmen. Much of his time was used in a clerical capacity: from the completion of weekly and monthly ticket-sale returns and the handling of paperwork associated with private siding goods traffic, to the drafting of staff rosters and requisitions and the dissemination of a plethora of notices and bulletins from regional headquarters. One of the weekly rituals at the station was pay day. On a Thursday morning the wages for the staff arrived in a leather pouch conveyed from Bristol in a stout travelling safe in the guard's compartment. The Station Master took delivery of the pouch from the guard, signed for it, and subsequently paid his staff, generally at the changeover in shifts for porters and signalmen. The permanent way gang would report to the station for their money at some time during the day, while the night-shift signalman had to make his own arrangements to collect his pay packet. Other visits would periodically be made to the signalbox to sign the Train Register, one of these always being on a Friday when the men's forthcoming roster sheets were delivered. With such a small staff there was little need to supervise routine as everyone knew what to do!

Weston's last Station Master, Thomas Hall, was a strict rules and regulations man whose hobby was

bee-keeping (the hives adorned the garden of Station House). This was virtually his sole talking point beyond railway matters, and he would wax lyrical on the subject at any opportunity! He also kept a dog, which startled many a passenger as they walked along the footpath to the down platform alongside his garden. His reign lasted for 18 years, and following closure of the station he continued to live in 16 Station Road until the early 1960s. The property then became empty for a short while until the railway sold it as a private residence. Incidentally, the house had not always been the residence of the Station Master, nor always referred to as Station House. It had been designed for the first Station Master to live in, but had also been used by other employees of the Midland Railway (when it was known as The Gatehouse). For a good part of the 1880s and early 90s it was the home of a signalman, and then from 1894 until 1908 that of a porter and ticket collector. Only in the latter year, with the appointment of a new Station Master (Edwin Redman) did it return to its intended function and gradually come to be known as Station House.

Right from the outset, Weston station had been provided with floral borders on the down

M J Tozer collection

platform. These were always well kept and not more so than during the long attachment of Walt Morgan to the station as porter. He was a keen gardener and in between his official duties expended much expertise and affection on the flower borders. His colourful displays won a number of prizes over the years, and when Walt was transferred to Green Park as a parcels porter following the closure of Weston, he continued his interest there. Weston certainly had its characters. During the last war, a lady porter, May Foreman, was attached to the station. She was by all accounts something of a live wire, always having a cheery word for servicemen beginning or finishing leave, and a practical joke for unsuspecting colleagues. Just after the war one of the signalmen, an ex-naval man, would turn up for duty with wool and needles to do a bit of knitting in between trains.

One event which passed into local railway folk-lore also involved signalmen. One of the regular men during the war years lived out in the country to the south of the city. He would sometimes bring a couple of rabbits into work, one for each of his colleagues – a gesture much appreciated at a time of meat shortage. The man covering the night shift the week before Christmas had been unable to buy a chicken for the traditional seasonal dinner, but his butcher had offered him a goose instead. Not knowing how to pluck the bird properly, he asked his country colleague for advice – the man he felt sure must be well versed in matters relating to wildlife. The man expressed his willingness to pluck the bird for him, and next morning duly arrived for work armed with a cleaver. He took the goose down to the locking room beneath the lever frame, while his grateful colleague worked the box in his place. Without a proper worktop, the would-be butcher experienced some difficulty in cutting the head off the bird, but with this eventually accomplished, he set about the task of plucking it with great verve – so much so that small pieces of down and feather began to float up through the slots in the lever frame. This continued for some time, until the man appeared, covered from head to toe in feathers but triumphantly holding one plucked goose! In the locking room there was down everywhere; in fact it was so bad that the signalman was rather concerned to leave it in that state. It would hardly be politic to call out the signal lineman all the way from Mangotsfield to clean up the bars and rodding frames, so he cautiously enquired whether the ganger would be prepared to do it – strictly on the quiet. The man graciously obliged. Word inevitably got round and references to geese seemed to find their way into conversations for a long time afterwards!

Elevation drawings of Weston Station: top – north (Ashley Avenue); centre – south (platform); bottom left – west end; bottom right – east end

One feature of note at Weston was its possession of Bath's one and only level crossing. To control this, as well as work the sidings, a signalbox was provided immediately next to the crossing on the west side. The 18-lever signalbox was manned continuously on weekdays, because as long as trains required to use the line, the box had to be open to work the crossing gates. At the time it was built, the comfort of the signalman was not a major concern of the Midland Railway Company. No water was available in the box and the lavatory consisted of an earth closet housed in a wooden shed between the box and the end wall

of the adjacent house: it remained on site if rarely in use until the box closed in 1968, as men did not like having to use it!

Through the 1930s and 40s the signalmen obtained their supply of water by courtesy of the Misses Jobbins. Each morning the early turn signalman would leave a large enamelled pitcher outside their house (8 Station Road) to collect it again shortly afterwards when one of the ladies had obligingly filled it. The grounds behind No 8 contained a number of apple trees and at the end of each summer the ladies would always make a gift of apples to the regulars in the box. Neither

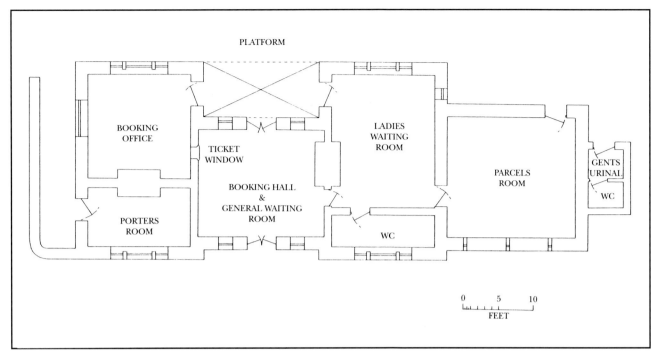

Scale drawing of Weston station interior showing its uses in 1950

did their beneficence stop there, for every Christmas the men received a Christmas Box of half a crown (12½p). It is not surprising therefore that the ladies were always welcome, if unauthorised, visitors to the box and it was not uncommon to see the younger sister turning the wheel which worked the level crossing gates.

Operating the gates required the signalman to know the running times of various classes of trains, especially of those working into Bath. The section to Bitton was over five miles long and if the Weston man closed the gates as soon as his colleague sent 'train entering section' on the block instrument, road traffic might have to wait for several minutes. There was no track circuiting, so in order to inform the signalman of the impending approach of a down train, the distant signal was provided with a buzzer. This signal was situated just to the west of the bridge over Brassmill Lane at Rudmore Park, and about 600 yards or so in advance of the signal was a treadle. This was a metal plate fixed by means of a pivot to the inside of the rail. As the wheels of a train passed over it, the plate was depressed, the action of which tripped a short-interval buzzer in the signalbox which sounded for 10 or 12 seconds. If the signalman had not already closed the gates, he still had time to do this, and lock the wicket or side gates to prevent pedestrians crossing. One lever locked the road gate bolts in both the 'open' and 'closed' positions, while the

wickets had one lever each.

When the gates were closed across the tracks, the lever which released them stood in the 'normal' position, i.e. at the back of the frame. When the signalman wished to open the gates, he first pulled the lever half way over in the frame. This action lowered the locking bolts in the metal plate between the tracks and thereby freed the gates. The wheel was now worked and the gates swung through a right angle, closing over the road. The lever was now pulled the rest of the way, which raised the bolts in the road plates and thus locked the gates in that position. The reverse procedure was followed after the train had passed, the lever being so well balanced that a slight knock with a hand sent it sliding back unassisted to the half-way position. The three levers connected with the crossing were painted brown.

Up trains were more problematical. The sections between Bath Station, Bath Junction and Weston boxes were short, and so bell codes were passed straight up the line. Once Bath Junction sent the 'train entering section' bell to Weston the train would be almost at the station, so the signalman had to use his judgement as to when to open the gates. There was not much traffic on Station Road before the end of the 1950s, so there was no great problem except for the passing of the up 'Pines'. This express came through a few minutes after midday, which co-

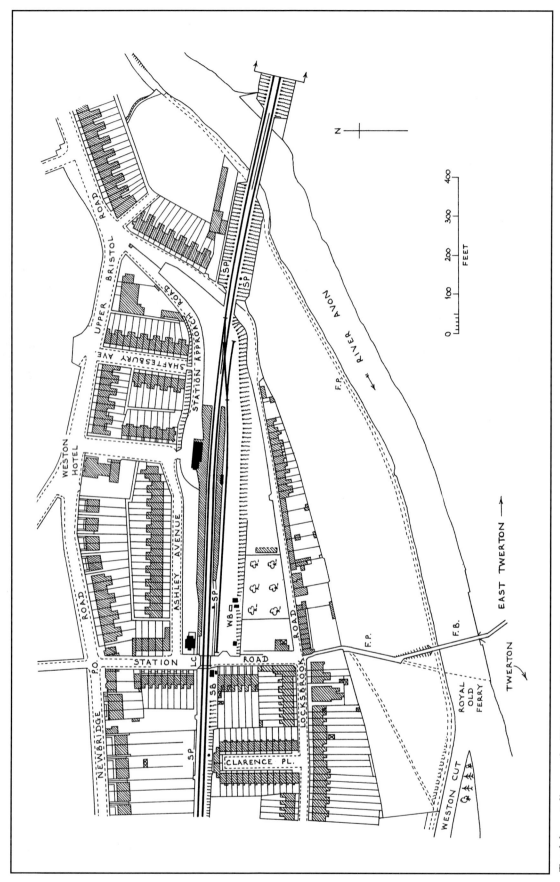

Track layout diagram for Weston station in 1902

The signalman's view of the station and coal yard, c1912. This picture clearly shows the markedly different platform lengths, with much of the down side backed with the archetypal Midland Railway slanted fencing. The houses in that part of Ashley Avenue running parallel with the railway were built between 1894 and 1898. The west-end crossover, beyond the signal, was installed in 1905.   M J Tozer collection

incided with the arrival of employees from Horstmann's Engineering Works on Newbridge Road. Men came streaming down Station Road on their bicycles on their way home for dinner, and some would dodge through the narrowing gap as the gates closed. The signalman had to be very quick off the mark, turning the gate wheel as rapidly as possible and at the same time ensuring that no-one was trapped between the gates.

One of the workers learned to his cost just how forcefully the gates could be closed. The base of the wicket gate was attached to a metal bar, which was pushed through an arc when the lever was worked. The wicket would close up with quite a clatter against the wooden stanchion. Determined to cross the line, even though the train was approaching, the man lodged the front wheel of his bicycle in the gateway, seeking to thwart the signalman's attempt to close it. Giving the lever a hearty pull, the wicket slammed into the post and in so doing bent the bicycle wheel completely out of shape!

One signalman had an experience which quite unnerved him. He had closed the gates across the road and pulled off the signals for a train from Bath. With the train now on line he checked that the crossing was clear – which it was – and locked the wickets. As the train thundered past his box and he looked out after it to check that it possessed a tail lamp, he was horrified to see two small children suddenly appear on the steps leading to the balcony. They had gone through the up-side wicket a couple of minutes earlier, but instead of crossing the line they had walked quietly and unsighted to the front of the signalbox, against the wall of which they were standing as the train passed, just inches away. The signalman experienced quite a gamut of emotions in the following few minutes!

The proximity of Weston to Bath Junction meant that in order to prevent the possibility of over-running the Junction's home signal at danger, Weston's down distant signal was slotted; that is to say it worked in conjunction with the Junction's distant signal which was situated on the same post as, and a little below, Weston's down starting signal. This particular operation was not as simple as might have been thought, because Bath Junction's down distant was also slotted by Bath Station's outer distant!

Only when both the Bath men had pulled their respective levers would the signal arm move into

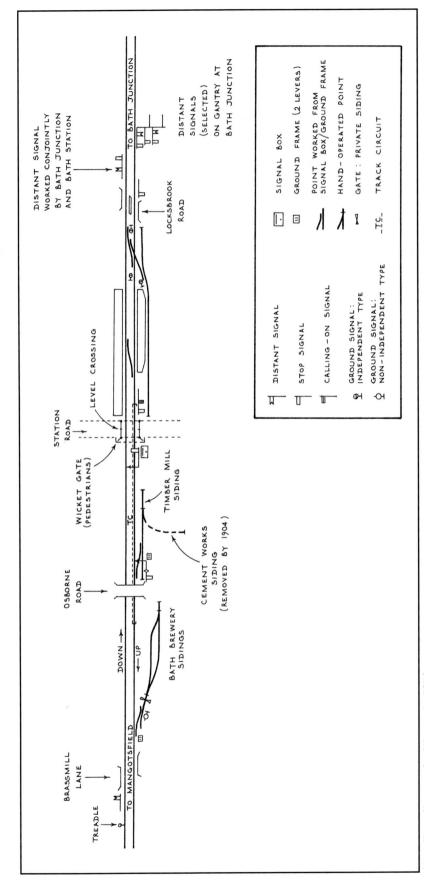

Signalling diagram for Weston in 1950

Weston's timber-built signalbox, seen here in the early years of this century. It contained a standard Midland raised frame, installed in May 1905, with 18 levers. These were grouped according to function: west end points; down and up running signals; east end points and related ground signals; level crossing gate levers.

M J Tozer collection

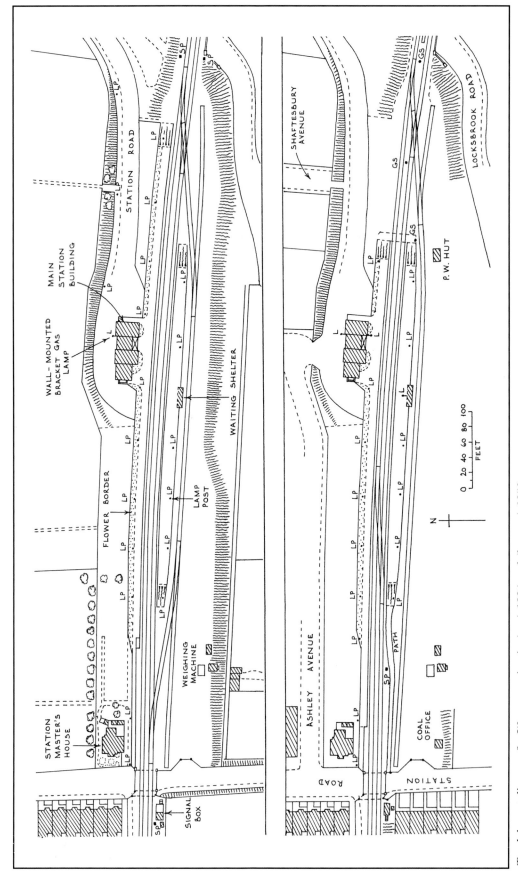

Track layout diagram for Weston station in (top) 1884 and (bottom) 1950

the all clear or 'off' position, and thereby enable the Weston man to pull his own distant. A mechanical indicator was provided to inform the man of the position of the slotted signal, and so relieve him of the inconvenience of a lengthy observation of the far-removed signal. When the signal was at caution, the word ON showed in a window in the face of the instrument. As soon as the arm moved to clear, the tab in the indicator changed to OFF, this being accompanied by a distinctly audible sound so alerting the signalman. The Weston distant would then be pulled. As this was out of sight of the box, it was provided with a repeating instrument: a dial fixed to the front of the instrument shelf above the yellow distant signal lever (the up distants were similarly covered).

One driver regularly rostered to work the 'Pines' between Gloucester and Bath before the last war seemed not to appreciate this arrangement. He set himself the target of an average speed of a mile a minute point to point of a tightly-timed schedule, and would fear that his plan would be thwarted when he saw the Weston distant showing caution. What had happened was that Bath Station was in the process of dealing with the coupled pilot and train engines which would take the train onto Bournemouth. Until they had crossed the down main line from the m.p.d. to the up main, the station could not signal the train in. Consequently Bath Junction's distant remained at caution, as did Weston's in turn. As the 'Pines' ran past the latter's box at greatly reduced speed, the driver would shake his fist at the signalman!

If great care was taken to avoid over-running at the Junction, a similar possibility for down trains approaching the level crossing was not so catered for. The crossing was only protected by the distant and home signals and even then the latter had to be wrong sided in order to give a better view to crews on the long curve past the Timber Yard siding near Clarence Place. If the distant was showing caution, there was no outer home signal to act as an extra check to this one stop signal, a facility which would have been more useful at night. Running on the level embankment across Newton Meadows, a passenger train would generally get up to a good speed – 60 mph was the official maximum on the line. As it rumbled over the Avon girder bridge at Newbridge and the distant signal came into view showing caution, the driver had to bring the speed down in case he was required to stop at the home

signal. The usual reason for the signal being 'on' was not due to any event at Weston, but to the line being occupied at Bath Junction or the station approach. When it was not possible to send a train on, the signals at Weston would not be pulled, but the level crossing gates were closed across the road as a precaution against over-running.

The wisdom of this precaution is illustrated by the following event in the mid 1930s. A heavy freight was being worked into Bath at night and was manned by a crew from another m.p.d. who were unfamiliar with the route. They were not travelling very fast as they crossed the river bridge and saw the distant showing an orange caution light. Knowing there was a level crossing ahead, the driver brought the speed of the train down further as it lumbered on. Having passed beneath the Osborne Road bridge the men were keeping a look out for the home signal, and as they continued round the curve they saw a green light where they knew the signal to be and so continued without applying the brakes further. Up in his box the signalman was not a little surprised to see the train go rolling past and on over the crossing. With the starting signal by Locksbrook Road bridge showing a red light, the driver realised something was wrong – he should have been checked by the home – and brought his train to a stand. On reaching the shed later, the driver reported the incident at the office. As can be imagined it brought forth some comments from local men in the messroom! A short time later, however, the errant signal performance was repeated.

Working back to Bath on the heavily-laden Avonmouth freight just before one o'clock in the morning, the driver was keeping his usual sharp lookout for the home signal. Passing Long's timber siding, a green light came into view and the driver eased off on the brakes. However, as the train drew closer to Clarence Place, where the signal was situated, something did not seem right. Peering into the blackness of the night, he noticed just below the green light a much dimmer circle of red light. Realising the latter actually belonged to the signal, he promptly brought the slowly-moving train to a stand. A semaphore signal arm which is clearly visible by day is more difficult to distance at night. Although the spectacle plates on the signals were regularly cleaned, the light they emitted was nothing like as powerful as the present day colour-light signals. In those days there were few bright coloured lights to confuse train crews, and even most of the city's street lights were switched off at midnight. So, whence the green light?

It so happened that the driver of the Avonmouth train lived in Oak Street, opposite the factory of the foundation garment manufacturer Charles Bayer. At home a few days later he noticed an unaccustomed green glow in the mirror on the bedroom dresser, and on investigation found it was a reflection from a newly erected illuminated sign on the roof of the factory (the name of the firm had been edged with a fluorescent strip). Although the sign faced the Great Western's line across the Lower Bristol Road, the aspect of the roof was such that the leading edge of the sign was visible at right angles to the face. Weston level crossing was a mile and a quarter away, but being such a high building it occurred to the driver that this end-light might be the culprit. When next he was rostered on a night-time run over the LMS he kept a special look out on his return. Rounding the curve into Weston there again was a small but clear green light glowing in the darkness where he perceived the signal to be. As it might actually be the signal the crew kept a sharp lookout, and as they got closer saw a second fainter green light below the first. Staring intently at the apparent double signal, the true situation revealed itself as the train came closer: the fainter of the two belonged to the home signal.

As the driver knew one of the employees at Bayer's, he asked him if it could be arranged for the sign not to be illuminated on the next night. This was agreed. Approaching the level crossing later that night the home signal's lamp glowed out of the darkness in splendid isolation. This seemed conclusive, and so the driver mentioned his exploits to the District Inspector at Green Park station. The latter thought the whole thing sounded improbable, but as there was obviously a problem at Weston he agreed to look into it. He asked the driver if he could get Bayer's to oblige again on a pre-arranged night, to enable him to view the scene with the sign both illuminated and switched off. This was duly done, and it was agreed that the sign was the cause of the problem. The two lights had an almost exact alignment, while the green of the sign was far more dominant than either the red or green of the signal. The factory management agreed to mask the leading edge of the sign, which neither affected the sign itself nor caused problems for locomen thereafter!

The level crossing was always well used by pedestrians, for a path led from the bottom of Station Road across the Avon floodplain to a footbridge over the river. It was an excellent short cut to Bath Cabinet Makers factory and the textile mills in Twerton. Vehicular traffic came to use the crossing in greater volume as car ownership increased in the early 1960s, so that when the Bath Branch closed to passenger trains in March 1966, the signalbox was retained to cover the crossing for the passage of the freight workings which still used the line. The same situation existed at Warmley. Although Bitton box had been closed the previous July, both the Bath boxes remained and so block-signalling continued as before. With such a limited service, and modifications to the junction, the need for signalboxes was confined to the two locations with level crossings: the Bath boxes were closed on 12th September 1966. The closure of Weston box was inevitable, however, although it was not until 4th May 1968 that the signalman closed for the last time. Trains continued to use the crossing – on the up line only from that date – but the gates had been modified. Instead of being worked from the signal box, the rodding and bolt-locks were removed and the gates simply padlocked across the tracks, the second man or guard on the diesel-operated freight trains having to unlock and operate them. The red targets on the gates themselves were supplemented by Stop Boards on either side of the crossing in the place of the signals, and for another three years a single daily freight continued to make an appearance on weekdays. The down line was lifted between Weston and Mangotsfield so that the whole 14¾ mile length from Yate South Junction was worked in effect as a long siding.

When the line finally closed and the tracks were lifted – on 8th May 1972 at Weston station – the level crossing gates remained as padlocked and increasingly battered and shabby guardians of a once busy crossing. They too disappeared in time to be replaced by fencing, but the gap in the houses and the shelf on an otherwise sloping road, both bear witness to the fact that a railway once passed through here!

Passenger Services. In the first few years of existence of the Midland Railway's Bath Branch, all trains called at Weston, the service being spread throughout the day on Mondays to Saturdays, and with a limited service on Sundays. Following the opening of the S&D and the institution of through expresses between the

This 1932 view, looking west, shows the station in its characteristically well-maintained and neat order. The signal at the end of the up platform is of the old MR/LMS lower quadrant variety. The slightly shorter lower arm is a calling-on signal, used in conjunction with shunting operations at the Timber siding or Brewery. L&GRP, courtesy of David and Charles

Midlands or North of England and the South Coast, these together with fast connecting services to Mangotsfield, passed through the station without stopping. However, the local provision remained at a consistent level, with the years around the turn of the century marking the zenith of daytime coverage. The First World War brought this to an abrupt end. In the years which followed, both the passenger usage and train service soon demonstrated the tidal flow associated with commuting: out to Mangotsfield and Bristol in the morning, and back again in the afternoon and evening. There was always a certain amount of long distance travel to the Midlands and the North, the station being particularly useful to people in Twerton and Weston as it saved the journey into town. Travel in the down direction, to Green Park, was much less marked and was frequently used in connection with shopping expeditions or to link up with S&D services, especially in summer.

The hiatus between the closure of Twerton station on the GWR in 1917 and the opening of Oldfield Park station in March 1929 was certainly to Weston's advantage, although as the last-named GWR station had a more frequent and quicker service to Bristol, it syphoned off a number of customers from Locksbrook and East Twerton districts. At breakfast time, a steady trickle of people would be observed crossing the Windsor Bridge on their way to Brook Road and Oldfield Park station. Even so, with many Midland trains running into St Philips station in Bristol,

many shoppers found its greater proximity to Broadmead much more convenient than Temple Meads. The connecting facility at Mangotsfield with expresses going up country, still gave the Midland the edge over the Western, and financially yielded lucrative traffic.

The Second World War boosted traffic considerably with 50 to 60 people leaving on each of the first two morning trains for work in Bristol and, notably, the aircraft factory at Yate. Servicemen too were a regular feature, as on most other stations during these years. Even after the war, factory workers for Mangotsfield, Fishponds and Yate as well as Bristol continued to patronise the station. Up to 40 people would regularly be waiting for the 6.15am, while the 7.20 was also well-supported, with the three-coach train being almost full by the time it reached Warmley. In the late 1940s, the station provided a quick and cheap service for people going into Bath city centre; the fare by train was a penny, while the bus from the Weston Hotel was three-ha'pence. Despite its undoubted convenience, numbers did not recover to previous levels. In spite of this, most daytime local trains continued to call at the station, and this produced an ever-worsening picture in the Passenger Revenue Account Books. Trains from Bristol were booked to stop for two or three minutes at Weston to allow for the collection of tickets before arriving at Green Park. The various changes may perhaps best be appreciated by studying timetables for representative years during the station's life.

	1870	1900	1922	1931	1953
	am	am	am	am	am
	7.50	6.32	8.12	8.11	7.51
	9.55	8.27	10.07	9.28	8.25
	11.02	10.03		11.58	
	pm	pm	pm	pm	pm
TRAINS	12.22	12.02	12.53 SO	12.53 SO	12.28 SX
TO	12.27	1.59	1.51	4.10	12.50 SO
BATH	2.40	3.07	4.11	4.51	2.05 SX
	4.10	4.17	4.48	5.29	2.26 SO
	5.45	5.21	5.29	6.09	3.10 SO
	5.50	6.25	6.07	6.41	5.33
	6.48	7.02	8.17	7.33	6.04 SX
	8.12	8.22	*9.01 SO	8.17	6.43 TC
	8.22	9.36		* 9.00 SO	7.46
		10.00			8.48
	Suns	Suns			
	10.20	10.37			
	11.47	9.22			
	5.27				
	7.37				
	am	am	am	am	am
	7.43	7.44	7.29	6.57	6.19 TM
	8.18	8.46	8.44	7.29	6.56
	9.23	9.50 TH	9.54	8.47	7.24
	10.48	10.04		9.44	8.08
					9.54 SO
					10.02 SX
TRAINS	pm	pm	pm	pm	pm
TO	1.28	12.14	12.14	12.15	12.24 TM
BRISTOL	3.03	1.17	1.39	1.40	2.09 TM
(ST PHILIPS)	4.18	2.10	4.26	4.36	3.39
	6.33	4.29	5.34	5.34	4.34
	7.28	5.30	6.16	6.18	5.42
	8.18	6.34			6.14
		8.19			
		9.34			
		11.04 TM			
	Suns	Suns			
	10.48	8.49			
	4.28	6.44			
	6.33				
	8.18				

SO Saturdays only   TC Through train to Bournemouth   TH Thursdays only
SX Saturdays excepted   TM Temple Meads station   * Calls to set down only

NOTE: All the Bristol trains shown in the 1870 column worked into Temple Meads station, until St Philips opened on 2nd May. This produced a slight restructuring of train times.

Summer-time excursions were a feature of the station, especially during late July and early August. Not only did this correspond with the Bank Holiday weekend, but also with Bath's equivalent of a Wakes Week when the large employer of Stothert & Pitt took its annual holiday, as did large numbers of other workers. Taking 1936 as an example, Westonians were given plenty of variety, and as none of the excursions got back until late evening – and some of them in the early hours – they certainly gave trippers a long day out, even the half days! It may be of interest to look at the first week in August as representative of the destinations available during the holiday peak (the adult fares are shown in brackets).

Sunday 2nd
1) 9.33am half-day excursion to Liverpool (9/6); calling at Stafford (7/–), Crewe (8/–) and Runcorn (9/–), with cheap tickets also to Gloucester, Cheltenham, Birmingham and Wolverhampton.
2) 10.50am half day to Bournemouth (5/–)

Monday 3rd
1) 12.20am full day to Blackpool (14/6)
2) 6.15am full day to Weymouth (7/6)
3) 7.35am full day to Weston-s-Mare (3/6)
4) 7.50am full day to Bournemouth (7/6)

Tuesday 4th
1) 8.27am full day to Weston-s-Mare (3/6)
2) 11.40am half day to Weymouth (5/–)
3) 12.05pm half day to Bournemouth (5/–)
4) 1.30pm half day to Weston-s-Mare (3/6)

Wednesday 5th
1) 11.15am half day to Weston-s-Mare (3/–)
2) 11.35am half day to Weymouth (5/–)
3) 12.05pm half day to Bournemouth (5/–)

Sunday 9th
1) 9.33am half day to Loughborough (7/6) and Nottingham (8/–)
2) 10.10am half day to Weymouth (5/–)
3) 10.20am half day to Weston-s-Mare (3/–)
4) 10.50am half day to Bournemouth (5/–)

An even wider range of destinations was available from Green Park, including a day trip to Dublin to visit the Royal Dublin Horse Show; a combined road/rail outing to the Mendips and Burnham-on-Sea; a visit to the Dockyard at Portsmouth during Navy week; a day trip to Lyme Regis or Seaton; and a half day outing to Southampton Docks to view the Royal Mail Steamer *Berengaria*. All Bath's stations were busy during the week, with platforms thronged with people for the excursions and even thicker on the ground than usual for many of the regular services, on many of which cheaper fares were available to selected destinations. On August Bank Holiday Monday 1933, for example, in addition to very heavy general traffic, the booking office at Green Park sold 470 tickets for Bournemouth, 426 for Burnham-on-Sea and 49 for Wareham, with smaller numbers for Lyme Regis and Seaton. Later in the month, on Thursday 24th, a non-stop evening excursion was organised from Bath to Bournemouth. Leaving Green Park at 3.20pm, it was due into the resort at 5.25, with the return train departing at 10.15pm. The return fare was 3/6.

By the beginning of 1953 the patronage of the station had sunk to alarmingly low levels, with only about a dozen people using the trains on a regular basis, with a further handful doing so rather less frequently. The inevitable finally happened, and Weston closed for passenger traffic in September of that year. The evening of Saturday 19th was wet and chilly, and only a small gathering of 23 people were on the platfrom to witness the sad event. Among them was Arthur Rowett, one of Green Park's foremen, who had walked out to pay his last respects. Most of the people boarded the train in order to take a last ride; and just as the first train to call had been late, so too was the last one 84 years later. Due to leave for Green Park at 8.48pm, it was running 15 minutes behind schedule. One young lady presented the driver with a bouquet of dahlias, and as the train prepared to leave one of the passengers leaned out of his carriage window and blew a loud valediction on a hunting horn. As the train pulled out, its departure was accompanied by a rather down-hearted cheer: no placards, no detonators and no brass bands! As the red tail lamp disappeared into the night and the porter turned out the platform lights, the station quietly died.

As trains continued to run non-stop through the station, the platform edging blocks were soon removed to improve clearance while the platforms themselves quickly deteriorated as the vegetation moved in. Following a period of neglect, the station building found use as a builder's store-cum-workshop. Essentially, the building remained externally unchanged, if increasingly shabby. In recent years a firm of building design consultants has acquired the site and made an excellent job of putting the structure back into order, once again an architectural asset to the locality.

Goods Services. The goods yard at Weston consisted of a single siding with a short spur at the east end. Intended for the handling of domestic coal, the yard's sole facility was a weighbridge and small coal office. There was no loading dock or goods shed; its proximity to the main goods yard at Midland Bridge Road allowed the road haulage of general merchandise to and from there. The coal yard did a brisk trade, and was serviced as required by the daily pick up goods. Much of the coal delivered here originated in the Midlands, and was taken to Bath in the first instance and then brought back on the aforementioned goods. To railwaymen and residents alike the depot was known for years as Jobbins' Yard, named after the coal merchant Charles Jobbins, who lived in the house next to the level crossing and opposite the signalbox. In the days of private owner wagons his deliveries were made in coal trucks which bore the name *CHAS JOBBINS* in large white letters on the sides. The firm employed a coalman, Harold Lapham, to help in the yard and undertake local deliveries. The yard possessed a few hand barrows, with hinged flaps at the front, which could hold a hundredweight of coal. People who lived near the station were able to wheel the coal home, but then had to return to the yard with the empty barrow. Local lads literally cashed in on this inconvenience by going around the streets of Lower Weston and Locksbrook asking people if they wanted any coal fetching from the yard, for which chore they received a tip of a few pence. When Charles gave up running the yard, his place was taken by the elder of his two daughters, Florence. She ran the business with great sagacity. When the goods arrived, she would be out in the yard to make sure the guard stopped the wagon(s) in exactly the desired spot. In appreciation of their co-operation, the regular guards received the present of a hundredweight of coal every Christmas. As soon as a mineral wagon had been unloaded, its prompt removal was requested – even demanded – of the Station Master, for after three days she would be liable to demurrage charges!

The Jobbins family was something of an institution in Lower Weston. Before he took on the coal yard, Charles had followed a career on the railway, culminating in his appointment as Station Master at Weston, a post which he held for 28 years. During the last 13 of these he, somewhat unusually in railway practice, combined the job of Station Master with that of coal merchant. Initially, following his appointment to Weston, the family lived at 1 Hopmead Buildings, one of the company houses on the Lower Bristol Road, but in 1893 moved to 8 Station Road – right next to the level crossing and across the road from The Gatehouse. In 1908 he retired from the railway, but continued with the coal yard; indeed, the business stayed in the family for a long time after his death, the name remaining into the 1960s even after the yard had been acquired by local coal merchants E W & D A Rossiter Ltd.

Before the goods station at Bath opened in May 1870, the inaugural freight on the line worked to Weston only, the 9.30am daily departure from Bristol. Arriving at 10.50, the engine propelled the wagons into the yard over the trailing connection at the east end of the station, performed any necessary shunting to rearrange the train for the return working, and then ran light to Bath. Following hard on the heels of an up passenger train, a light engine left Bath at 4.20pm, arriving at Weston three minutes later. Setting back over the yard points at the west end of the station, the loco was quickly coupled to the ready waiting stock, and was due out again at 4.25pm. Calling at Bitton and Warmley the train terminated at Mangotsfield. This rail-head function was only a temporary expedient, and as through freight services to Bath began to increase markedly, Weston settled into the role of an intermediate depot serviced by a daily pick-up goods, one only in either direction.

Having followed this routine for some 20 years, the west end connection to the yard was removed. The yard could now only be reached by way of the points at the east end, by bridge 39 (over Locksbrook Road). With the installation of two private sidings to the west of the station, and the extra traffic they generated, this alteration forced a revision in the mode of operation as an engine was not able to run round its train (the west end crossover did not then exist). Loaded wagons for the coal yard were brought in on a down freight, which called between 5.50 and 5.55am – just long enough to detach them from the rest of the train and shunt them into the siding. In the afternoon, a train of mineral

Standard class 3 2-6-2 tank engine No 82044 bustles through the gap in Station Road, Weston, with a Green Park to Bristol train, and is about to pass the 133¾ mile-post – this being the distance from Derby. Despite their proximity, residents were so used to the trains that they hardly noticed their passing, even at the dead of night.   30.10.65   J Blake

empties down from Coal Pit Heath called between 2.25 and 2.30 to remove any empty coal wagons before continuing to Bath.

The points down by bridge 39 were a long way from the signalbox, and the levers took some pulling. It was also very difficult for the signalman to see where a shunting engine was in relation to the points, and he relied on a system of hand signals relayed by either the guard or shunter. Even the ground signals here, which had been installed at the time of the modifications already mentioned, were difficult to see from the footplate. The one allowing access to the yard or up main line was between the running lines by bridge 39 and was partly obscured by the raised central girder of the bridge, while that allowing exit from the yard was down by the back wall of the up platform and on a curve! For decades, the working of the yard carried on in a somewhat unsatisfactory manner until the late 1930s when a signalman derailed an engine. The engine had just put some coal wagons into the siding and was returning to the main line. Thinking it was clear of the points, the signalman pushed over the lever in the frame, which changed the points beneath the engine's wheels thereby derailing it. As a result of the enquiry which followed, a

shunting bell was installed to allow proper communications with the signalbox by means of accepted ringing codes.

In addition to private-owner coal, the siding also played host once a year to the station coal wagon. To heat the various rooms in the main building, the station received an annual supply of coal (as did the signalbox in the manner described in chapter 7). In the late autumn a wagon of station coal for locations on the line was made up at Gloucester and sent down to Bath on a regular freight by way of Westerleigh. It was then brought out to Weston by the afternoon pick up goods, or before the last war by the morning Brewery shunt.

The coal yard continued in use for 12 years after passenger services were withdrawn; the facility was only finally closed on Monday 29th November 1965 although the siding remained for another three years. More correctly, rail services were withdrawn from that date as the site continued in use as a coal yard – a function which it retains to this day. Having survived for a further two decades, the superb wooden Midland coal office, with its corbelled slate roof and tall brick chimney, was demolished early in 1986 when a new complex of coal staithes was erected

– but at least they were made of railway sleepers!

Bath Brewery. In 1896 the Bath Brewery Company, formerly of Bathwick Street, opened a large new brewery on the site of an old quarry immediately to the west of the narrow Osborne Road bridge, between the railway and Brassmill Lane. Its massive brick bulk dominated the lineside here to and beyond closure. The company made an application for a private siding, which was eventually brought into use on 10th November 1896. In its heyday large quantities of malting barley and hops were taken in by rail, as also was a certain amount of coal. As with the yard at the station, the traffic was of the 'loaded in/empty out' nature, the beer being distributed mostly locally and by road. With the wind in the right (or wrong?) direction, local residents were very much aware when the firm was having a 'mash'. A considerable amount of traffic was handled at the brewery until about 1920, but following the takeover of the company in 1923 by George's of Bristol, production fell off. Seven years later the Twerton firm of maltsters, James D Taylor & Sons Ltd, acquired the building. Although railwaymen continued to refer to it as The Brewery, technically it was renamed Weston Maltings but still used the railway to bring in malting barley and coal as before.

The Brewery possessed two sidings, which were connected to the up main line by a set of trailing points worked by a ground frame. Unlike the frames in Oldfield Park, this was on a double-track section of line, which could create problems with wrong line working; and unlike those at Green Park station, it was too far from the signalbox to be worked mechanically. The Board of Trade regulations governing the operation of points from signalboxes originally laid down a maximum distance of 200 yards over which they would not permit mechanical leverage. This was subsequently increased to 350 yards, but at twice that distance the Brewery ground frame was obviously far too remote. It was also well beyond Weston's station limits, and so a safe method had to be devised to work the sidings. Until the last couple of decades of the sidings' existence, this was achieved by means of a keyed staff used in conjunction with a wrong line order.

During peak years of production, the volume of traffic was such that a separate trip was warranted. This was known to railwaymen as the Brewery shunt and was done in the morning by one of Bath's yard engines. The end of brewing

and adaptation of the building to a maltings, saw a diminution in traffic and this, combined with the inconvenience of having to work back to Weston, saw the abolition of the morning Brewery shunt. The work was now transferred to the afternoon goods. This incorporation meant that the sidings could be attended en route to Bitton, so that any work at the station would be done first to obviate the need to return. The train would now enter the section to Bitton as a normal up freight train.

As the train did not return to the station, a porter travelled out with it to the brewery. In addition to dealing with the wagon labels, he brought the ground frame key back to the signalbox. It was also part of his remit to bring back any wagon tarpaulins (from both the brewery and timber yard). These were folded to make them more manageable and were carried across his back and shoulders. They were heavy and often dirty, and as it was a long walk back to the station, it was not a popular job!

The timings of the afternoon goods varied but little over the years. Due to the need to maximise access to the main line for the shunting operations at both Weston and Bitton, the most favoured time was the long lull following the departure of the 2.05pm stopping train from Bath. As soon as this train had cleared Weston, the pick-up goods was signalled out of the Midland Bridge yard, leaving at 2.10. Only when its time allocation was halved at Bitton from 1960 was it re-timed to leave at 2.40pm. One winter's day in the late 1940s the train left Bath as usual and shunted the coal yard at the station before moving on to the Brewery. The crew noticed that the building was encased in scaffolding. Uncoupling the Brewery wagons from the rest of the train, the crew prepared to perform the shunt in the time-honoured fashion. As the train backed into the sidings, the guard told the driver to 'take it carefully' as the scaffolding seemed very close to the track. On approaching the building one of the Brewery workers asked if the driver could push a wagon already on the line further down the siding to save them using the capstans to haul it along. This done, the loco rejoined its train on the main line and continued on its way to Bitton, Warmley and Westerleigh. Just after eight o'clock that evening the same engine and crew clanked their way past the Brewery with a heavy freight for Bath. They noticed that arc lights had been rigged up to illuminate the front of the main building, and

The brewery was a prominent landmark in Lower Weston for over 70 years. The capstans seen alongside the tracks were used by the brewery staff to manoeuvre the wagons as required; the grappling hook attached to the vans may be seen to the left of the capstan between the tracks in the foreground of the picture.   16.6.45   National Railway Museum

The line leading into the brewery was on a tight curve, as evidenced by the check-rail behind the van. The extensive site has recently been developed, and is now occupied by smart, modern low-rise advanced factory and trading units.

16.6.45   National Railway Museum

there seemed to be men everywhere. When they reached Bath, the guard was told to report to the Station Master at Weston. Walking out there the man was puzzled, especially when he was asked to make out a report of the work done at the Brewery. What had happened was that as the loose-shunted wagon ran slowly back along the siding, a door-clasp caught one of the uprights on the scaffolding, thereby pulling it out of alignment. This had a dramatic and literal knock-on effect which progressively brought down

much of the steelwork! Because the guard had clambered into the cab of the engine for the ride back to the ground frame, and had not walked back to pin down the wagon brakes, he had not observed the accident. The din on the locomotive footplate drowned out any noise, and the men had set off for Bitton oblivious of the developing mayhem behind them.

From about the mid-1950s the frequency and volume of rail traffic handled at the Brewery decreased significantly. By the middle of the decade the siding was all but out of use. Only when the decision was taken to single the line from Yate to Bath was the Private Siding Agreement formally terminated from 31st March 1968. Five weeks later the connection with the main line was removed, and the latter itself became no more than a long siding all the way from Yate.

Not only was road traffic largely responsible for the demise of the railway, but as if to add insult to injury in this location, motor vehicles have actually invaded the track bed – which is used as a parking lot for a car showroom on Newbridge Road!

Timber Mill Siding. Between the Brewery and the level crossing was another private siding, trailing into the up main line immediately before the bridge under Osborne Road. There had been quite extensive quarrying of stone in this vicinity prior to the opening of the line, and a small cement works, with five lime kilns, had been set up on the edge of the site opposite the *Dolphin Inn* on Locksbrook Road, namely, Henry Shaw & Co's Portland Cement & Blue Lias Limeworks. Soon after the opening of the Bath Branch a siding was laid into these works, the main part of which ran parallel with the up line for a distance of 160 yards. In 1885 the concern was taken over by John Fryer, but railway working timetables continued to refer to the siding as Shaw & Co's siding for the remainder of the 19th century. By 1902 the secondary part of the siding into the cement works had been lifted – the kilns being out of use by then – although the main part was retained to serve J Long's Timber Mill which had been built off Avondale Road in the meantime. This firm, incidentally, had been founded in the same year as the Bath Branch had been sanctioned, 1864. With the change in the type of traffic using the siding, its name was changed, logically, to Timber Mill siding, but was known locally as Long's siding.

Wagon-loads of timber for the yard and saw mills were shunted as part of the afternoon pick-up goods. This could either be done as a separate trip from the station, with the loco propelling any empties back to the up platform to rejoin the rest of the train; or when the goods had finished at Weston yard and was en route to Bitton. Tarpaulined trucks of timber were taken into the siding after any empties had first been removed. As with private sidings elsewhere, road haulage took an ever increasing share of the traffic, and by 1950 the work at Long's was occasional and

small-scale rather than regular and substantial. At the start of the next decade the siding was virtually out of use and, following the necessary formalities, the railway's Permanent Way Department turned up on the second Sunday in February 1962 to lift the connection with the main line.

Rudmore Park. At Rudmore Park the line from Weston traversed the floodplain of the River Avon on a low embankment, crossing first Brassmill Lane and then, a quarter of a mile further on, the river. A number of bridges on the Mangotsfield & Bath Branch, including these two, were not strong enough to take the heavier locomotives introduced in the early years of the London Midland & Scottish Railway; notably, the 2-6-0 Crab (1926), 4-6-0 Royal Scot (1927) and Baby Scot (1930) express passenger engines. As with the Midland Railway's 3-cylinder 4-4-0 compounds, nicknamed Crimson Ramblers, and the S&D 2-8-0 freight engines of earlier years – and the new classes soon to be introduced by William Stanier – they were prohibited from working over the Bath Branch. To remove this increasingly inconvenient restriction, the LMS announced a programme of bridge strengthening and rebuilding, together with the replacement of the turntable at Bath shed – which would be too short to accommodate the new locomotives even if it had been possible for them to reach the city.

The work began in early August 1933 at Brassmill Lane. The intention here was to strengthen the existing rail overbridge by the addition of substantial steel girders. The few train services on Sundays meant that the engineers could have sole occupation of the line for long periods. Following the necessary preparatory work, the main endeavour was undertaken on Sunday 27th. Once the morning passenger train to Bristol had cleared, the engineers' train from Gloucester, with its large contingent of workmen, set about the task. A steam crane was employed in the lifting and positioning of the girders, the morning being spent in dealing with the floor beams and packing the track. The crane had a lifting capacity of some 15 tons on about a 20-foot span, and chugged competently about its business.

After the dinner break, the next task was to deal with the girder which was to form the south side of the bridge. This 2-inch thick steel member had a length of almost 17 feet and a depth of 2 feet, with a substantial railing attached to the top; the

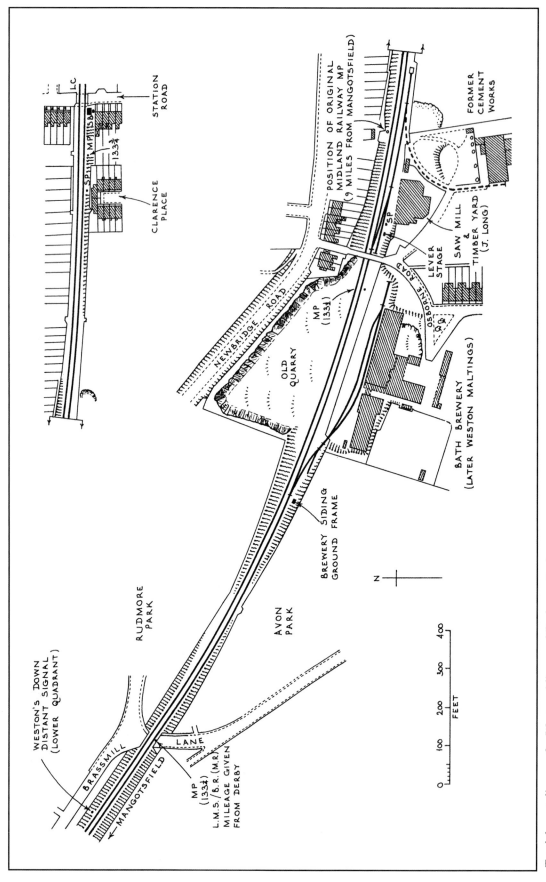

Track layout diagram for Weston sidings and Rudmore Park

Bath Shed covered the majority of services over the Midland line, with Barrow Road (Bristol) the remainder. From the autumn of 1953, the Western Region also became involved, notably with the 5.00pm from Temple Meads, and 6.18 return from Green Park. This introduced Western locomotives and coaching stock, the former generally comprising one of the enormous class of 0-6-0 pannier tanks or, less commonly, Small Prairie 2-6-2 tank engines. Ex-GW single rail-cars – known to Bath locomen as 'Bubblecars' – and 3-car diesel multiple units also made regular appearances. In this picture, taken in May 1957, Small Prairie 4572 is seen approaching the bridge which carried the A4 over the line near Newbridge Turnpike.   Colin G Maggs

whole weighing between 5 and 6 tons. It was presently resting on the masonry abutments, and simply required manoeuvring into position. The crane moved on to the eastern end of the bridge, to enable chains from the jib to be attached to the beam. One of the Gloucester men, H Mander, stood on the girder, grabbed on to the chain, and gave the signal to lift. Meanwhile, two other men, Tom Hollingshead and Norman Chadwick, both from Crewe, were standing on a ladder beneath the bridge ready to guide the structure into place. Slowly but surely it began to rise. Suddenly, the group of men who were standing by watching gave a shout as they noticed that the offside of the crane's undercarriage was beginning to lift off the track, and that the girder was falling back. At the same moment, Mr Mander realised the danger, and moved quickly along to one end of

the beam and jumped off on to the track. Another Gloucester man, H Probert, was at the controls of the crane, and he too realised that something was seriously wrong. He hurriedly left the now noticeably tilting cabin, ran up the sloping undercarriage and jumped on to the down line and safety. Both men were only just in time, for the crane suddenly lurched sideways, sending the heavy girder crashing down some 10 or 12 feet into Brassmill Lane, where it hit the road with such force that it broke in two. The men on the ladder had a very narrow escape, just managing to fall clear seconds before the metal fell.

Fortunately no-one was on the road at the time, and by great good fortune the crane was prevented from toppling right over and thereby causing an even worse accident. As it tipped, the

Freight continued to run over the Midland Line for five years beyond closure to passenger traffic. Motive power was now exclusively the preserve of diesels and, as with steam before, variety was the hall-mark; with Brushes, Peaks, Westerns, Hymeks and Clayton Type Ones all featuring. From 5th May 1968 the section between Weston and Yate was singled – by taking the down line out of use – and in this picture Peak D43 is approaching the A4 bridge from the west just a few weeks later.

Colin G Maggs

near-side edge of the undercarriage caught against another girder, while at the same moment the jib became caught up in the telegraph wires. The weight caused them to become severely distorted, and although a number broke, sufficient remained to hold the jib. Thus it was that the crane came to rest at a precarious angle, looming over the road beneath. As its boiler was still producing steam, there was the risk of an explosion, and the men were warned to keep well clear. Realising this possibility, the fireman on the attendant locomotive grabbed an iron bar, jumped from his cab, ran to the stranded crane and clambered into the steeply leaning cabin. Here, he smashed the pressure gauge, and thereby enabled the steam to escape. Meanwhile, quite a crowd of residents had gathered to see what all the noise and commotion was about! A breakdown gang from Bristol eventually righted the crane and all other bridges were strengthened without further incident over the next few years.

10. Named Trains

The only service actually to carry a nameboard was the 'Pines Express', Green Park's most prestigious train; but in common with custom all over the country, railwaymen gave nicknames to workings which either had locational significance or fulfilled a specific function. These unofficially named trains make up most of this chapter. Unless otherwise stated, the timings referred to in BR days – 1948 and after – are for the period covering 8th June to 20th September 1953. This period not only typifies the variety of work covered by men from Bath in one of the busiest post-war years, but also reflects the traditional pattern of operation on both the Bath Branch and Bath Extension prior to the gradual slimming down of services which significantly changed train diagrams and crew rosters. It is also a year in which most of the named trains were still running. A full timetable of train movements at Bath is printed in the appendix at the end of the chapter.

PART 1: PEOPLE, PERISHABLES & PARCELS.

The 'Pines Express'. Linking the south coast resort of Bournemouth with the industrial Midlands and North of England was the famous 'Pines Express', a train which was instituted in 1927 and took its name from the pine plantations which are a characteristic feature of the sandy heathlands between the valley of the Dorsetshire Stour and the coast, and through which the S&D line passed near Broadstone. Initially the 'Pines' was a lightly-loaded train, six coaches (including the restaurant car) being the norm. Later, during the peak summer weeks this would be increased to eight or more, and thus required double-heading over both the S&D and LMS. As a rule, the express was brought up from Bournemouth by one of Bath shed's 2P 4-4-0s, and departed over the LMS behind another. One of the restricting factors placed on motive power over the Bath Branch was the existence of a number of weak bridges on the section between Bath and Bitton, mostly over the River Avon. On reaching Gloucester, the Bath engine was uncoupled and moved out of the platform to allow a new engine and crew to set back and continue the next stage to Birmingham. As the northbound and southbound expresses met in the vicinity of Gloucester, a separate engine and crew was required to work back with the latter. This was another of Bath's 2Ps, whose turn of duty, or diagram, began with an early morning stopping train from Green Park to Bristol St Philips. Having stabled the coaches, the engine went to Barrow Road shed nearby to turn before running to Temple Meads to work the 9.10am stopping train to Gloucester. Arriving at Eastgate station there was plenty of time to shunt the carriages, use the turntable and prepare the engine for the run south with the 'Pines'. The express was brought into Gloucester from Birmingham by men from Saltley shed, whose engine was now taken off to allow the Bath loco to back on. The run down to Bath demanded some smart work by the footplate crew; by the late 1930s the train was allowed only 31 minutes to cover the 31½ miles between Eastgate and Mangotsfield North Junction. The start away from Gloucester with a heavy train could be quite taxing but once past the 1¾-mile climb to Tuffley Junction, the gradient eased off and a long straight section began. The loco which had come in with the up 'Pines' worked back to Bath later in the afternoon on another service.

The run between Bath and Gloucester was enjoyed by drivers as it gave a chance for some fast running on the Midland main line. For the five miles between Standish Junction and Tuffley Junction the tracks of the LMS and GWR ran parallel, and thus provided the possibility of racing a rival company's trains. One driver recalled his first acquaintance with the diminutive Collett 0-4-2 push-pull tank engines used on the Gloucester Central–Chalford shuttle. As the two lines converged on Standish Junction, the Midland's was on a rising gradient and the Great Western's on a falling one, which gave the latter an immediate advantage on northbound trains! The driver was surprised by a sudden clattering and bustle alongside his engine as an auto-train pulled level and then overtook. He was not a little chagrined, but nonetheless impressed!

One of the regular guards on the 'Pines' in the 1930s – indeed, the regular guard – was Fred Toller. Originally he worked from Bournemouth to Bath and back, but as this gave considerable

The 'Pines Express' circa 1929 approaching Bath Junction in the charge of 4-4-0 No 39. The general loading in the early years was only six coaches, which avoided the need to pilot the train north from Evercreech Junction.

L&GRP, courtesy of David and Charles

dead time at Green Park, the roster was extended to Gloucester. In his manner and bearing he resembled something like an Admiral of the Fleet, and as he worked this train day after day, did extremely well out of tips – they certainly kept him in tobacco. Christmas was particularly lucrative. Many of the first-class passengers travelled on the train several times a year, and always made sure that 'their guard' received a seasonal appreciation. This took the form of bottles of whisky, hampers of food, cigars and money. No wonder he was keen to hang on to the roster, and that others were equally keen to see him reassigned! In addition to his concern for the welfare of the first-class passengers, he was a stickler for time-keeping; a job at which he was remarkably good. Passengers were entrained or detrained quickly but courteously, and station staff chivvied along with their handling of luggage. He always did his bit to keep the train moving, adhering rigidly to the timings shown for the booked stops, including the mere one minute allowed at Shepton Mallet on the northbound journey. On one occasion this produced an interesting confrontation between himself and

one of the Bath drivers who was going to Dorset on holiday and wished to alight at Broadstone. At the time, the Broadstone stop was by request only, so at Green Park the guard was duly informed that the train would be required to stop. Guard Toller, however, replied that as the man only had a privilege ticket and was not a fully-paying member of the public, he was not a *bona fide* passenger and consequently could not expect the train to make a stop which would needlessly delay it! However, he had not reckoned with the fraternity which existed between locomen, for the driver promptly walked up to the engine and had a word with his colleague on the footplate. The 'Pines' stopped at Broadstone! Fred was furious; indeed, so angry was he that his authority had been subverted that he made an official complaint, and the Bath driver was called to account. In order to safeguard his interest he brought in a union representative on the interview, which was just as well, as the case went all the way to Derby for adjudication. Here, the company ruled in the driver's favour, stating that a passenger was anyone in possession of a valid ticket – and that

Sir William Stanier's Class Five 4-6-0s (known as Black 5s) made their first appearance on service trains over the S&D in 1938. Six of these locos were allocated to Bath shed; one of them – No 5440 – arrived in Bath on 30th April. On the following Monday she worked the down 'Pines' without assistance, and is seen here with that train in Lyncombe Vale. Notice the smoke billowing from Devonshire tunnel, centre-left.   2.5.38   L&GRP, courtesy of David and Charles

included railway privilege tickets!

The up 'Pines' called at Green Park at around 12.30 each weekday, the southbound express arriving about two hours later. This mode of operation continued until the late 1930s, when the loco then worked through between Bath and Birmingham, although the crews continued to change over at Gloucester. By 1938 the last of the weak bridges in the Avon Valley had been strengthened, and more powerful engines were now assigned to the turn, notably the Stanier 4-6-0 Black 5s. The express was suspended during the Second World War and not reinstated until 1949, from which time it consisted of 9, 10 or 11 coaches, the latter figure being the more usual during the summer and at other peak times like Easter, Whitsuntide and the Christmas/New Year period. The timings varied by only a few minutes over the post-war years, and the train always worked into the longer Departure platform – although even here there was an overhang which left the rear two or three vehicles on the river bridge.

In post-war years, the northbound 'Pines' left Bournemouth West at 9.45am, and called at

Poole, Blandford Forum, Stalbridge, Evercreech Junction and Shepton Mallet before arriving at Green Park at 11.56am. The major part of the express, including the restaurant car, worked to Manchester Mayfield. Mayfield was a sort of overspill station to relieve pressure on the main London Road terminus at busy times, especially for arrivals (like Green Park, it also had its roof glass blown out during the last war). Although it was connected to London Road by a footbridge across the intervening Fairfield Street, it could be disconcerting for passengers expecting to arrive at the main station. London Road was renamed Piccadilly in September 1960. The two coaches for Sheffield were detached at Birmingham New Street, while the Liverpool portion, also two coaches as a rule, was separated at Crewe. On Mondays and Fridays during the summer of 1953 a relief 'Pines' was provided, thereby allowing the Lancashire and Yorkshire portions to run as separate trains. On these days the usual arrangement was for the Manchester/Liverpool service to leave Bournemouth at 9.45 with up to 11 coaches, including the restaurant car. This was the advertised 'Pines'. Ten minutes later the

From the summer of 1954 Standard class 5 locos began to make appearances as 'Pines' train-engines, although the trusty 2Ps continued to act as pilots. However, various other combinations were to be seen, which was one of the attractions of the line to the railway enthusiast. In this picture, one of Bath shed's three Standard 5 4-6-0s, No 73052, is acting as pilot to Black 5 4-6-0 No 44917. With their uniform rake of red and cream coaches, they make a splendid sight as they sweep down the bank through Lyncombe Vale in March 1956.

R E Toop

Sheffield portion left, running almost to the same schedule and arriving in Green Park at 12.09pm. Typically, the relief 'Pines' comprised eight coaches, but with no restaurant car, the load of 240 tons meaning that the loco should not require a pilot to assist over the Mendips. The actual timings and loadings of this train varied to suit circumstances at other times of the year.

The locomotive assigned to the S&D leg of the journey in post-war years was involved in a 24-hour diagram, which utilised crews from Bath, Templecombe and Branksome. It left Bath in charge of the 2.40am 'Down Mail' to Bournemouth, the Bath crew changing over with colleagues from Templecombe at the lower platform there. The Branksome men took over the engine at their small m.p.d. and worked the up 'Pines' in the morning and returned with the down in the afternoon. An eight-coach train, of about 270 tons maximum, was considered to be the upper limit for the classification of engine normally assigned, a Black 5 or West Country Light Pacific in the early 1950s. As the train was almost always over this limit, Templecombe shed provided a pilot engine to assist on the climb up thenorthern flank of the Mendips north of Evercreech Junction. Invariably a 2P, the pilot left the m.p.d. at Templecombe Lower at 10.15 and ran light to Evercreech, where it set back into the middle road and waited for nearly half an hour for the 'Pines' to arrive.

The footplate crew who were to work the train north from Bath booked on duty at 10.30am and had an hour to prepare the engine for the journey. A wide variety of motive power was used on this diagram, the engine having arrived in Bath earlier in the morning with the 12.37am Leicester parcels (6.09 in Green Park). With final preparations complete, the driver walked to the shed telephone between Nos 3 and 4 roads and asked the signalman in the Station box to change the points on the loco road and pull off the signal. At around 11.40 the engine moved off

Pounding through the Vale with the down 'Pines' are Templecombe-based 2P 40601 and Bath-based West Country Pacific 34042 *Dorchester*. This was very much the classic formation of the express in the early 1950s. The Pacific is passing over the three-arch bridge 12.   3.6.53   Hugh Ballantyne

shed, climbing the short distance to the loco road. From here, she moved back towards the top shed until she was clear of the double-slip points. With these changed, she moved over to the up main line to await the arrival of the train, which ran past on the down line, swung through the facing crossover near the signalbox and eased gently into the Departure platform.

One important duty which was performed at Green Park until the mid 1950s was the topping up of the gas reservoir tanks on the restaurant car of the northbound train. The black, twin-cylinder, six-wheeled gas tank wagon was a familiar sight at the station, in its customary position against the buffer stops in the carriage siding. Just after 11.30 the shunting engine from the Midland Bridge Road goods yard ceased its duties there and was dispatched to the station to attend to this job. The tank engine drew the wagon along the siding until it reached the

approximate place opposite which the driver expected the restaurant car to come to a stand. The five minute stop-over was ample time for the coach to be 'gassed up', by means of flexible valved pipes, after which the tank wagon was propelled back to the buffer stops until the next day. Periodically, the wagon would be taken over to the Midland's own gas works at Barrow Road, Bristol, to be replenished. A simple exchange at Green Park ensured that a serviceable vehicle was always available there.

As passengers alighted or entrained, the northbound crew eased their engine back on to the coaching stock, where the passenger shunter was waiting to couple it up. Leaving Bath at 12.01pm, the men worked the express as far as Gloucester. As the train drew out of the station, the two engines which had brought it in remained momentarily at the buffer stop end of the platform before setting off for the shed. As

With its reporting number indicating a destination in the London Midland Region, Royal Scot class No 46157 *The Royal Artilleryman* leaves Bath for the North with the relief 'Pines'.   2.6.62   the late Ivo Peters

the 'Pines' passed the Station signalbox, the signalman returned the starting signal to danger, and as soon as the last coach had cleared the points he pulled it off again to permit the coupled engines to draw clear of bridge 43 before crossing to the turntable line. Here the locos were uncoupled, then individually turned and transferred to the lower shed to be prepared for the return journey. In the case of the train engine this involved setting back on to No 2 road beneath the coaling stage, for coal would be required not only for the trip down to Bournemouth, but also for the final return leg of the diagram with the 9.28pm Poole–Bath freight (arriving back at 2.39am).

Providing everything was running to time, the men on the Midland stage had a wait of just over an hour and a quarter at Gloucester between trains, the southbound 'Pines' being scheduled to arrive at Green Park at 2.58pm. As soon as the train had cleared the platform for its sojourn

over the S&D, the men took their loco on shed, where they set about getting her ready for the 10.15pm 'Perishables' to Derby. Having turned the engine first and taken her down to the lower shed, the smokebox and fire had to be cleaned, the tender replenished and the motion oiled, and finally the fire had to be built up again to keep the boiler pressure nicely simmering for the new crew that evening. The men finally booked off duty at 6.30pm.

About 10 minutes or so before the down 'Pines' was due into Bath, the coupled pilot and train engines were signalled off shed to wait on the up main line for its arrival. Although a stop-over of seven minutes was provided on the southbound journey, a late running train could be dealt with in just three. The up 'Pines' generally kept very good time, as did the southbound as a rule, although with a greater distance to cover before reaching Bath, and with connections and carriage attachments to be made, there was a greater opportunity for delay. With the lunch period over, there was no need to call on the services of the gas tank wagon, so removing another potential delaying factor. Trying to make up lost time was a matter of pride for most drivers, as well as a stricture laid down by management.

The first booked stop on the down 'Pines' over the S&D was Evercreech Junction, to detach the pilot, take on water if necessary, and make a connection with a stopping train which followed it down to Bournemouth. Passengers wishing to filter into the Southern Region at Templecombe had to change at Evercreech and take the slow train, as the 'Pines' ran straight on to Blandford Forum, Broadstone, Poole and Bournemouth. Once the express had cleared back from Cole signalbox, the pilot engine duly returned light to Templecombe shed. On arrival at the south coast resort – the Torquay of Hampshire as it was known – the Branksome crew took the loco on shed and left it simmering in readiness for a new set of men to take it over to work the 9.28pm freight. Templecombe men first took the engine light to Poole yard to collect the ready assembled train, and from there on to Templecombe Junction, where they were relieved by a Bath crew who then completed the journey – the second round trip for the engine.

As on the northbound leg, a relief train ran on Mondays and Fridays, leaving Green Park 12 minutes ahead of the 'Pines' proper. Providing the load was kept to no more than eight coaches, the southbound train would not require a pilot, the same engine and crew working the service as had brought in the up relief. If for any reason the load exceeded the maximum on the southbound run, Bath shed would have to requisition a spare engine and crew to pilot the train either to Shepton Mallet or Evercreech Junction, depending on how urgently the loco was needed back at Bath. Some drivers would absolutely insist on a pilot as soon as the load was exceeded, with sometimes chaotic results on summer Saturdays when there was hardly anything to spare, while other men were prepared 'to have a go with nine on' depending on their confidence in the particular engine allocated to the job.

A notable feature of the 'Pines' was the provision of a restaurant car, although it was not the first service on the Midland or S&D at Bath to be so equipped. It was in fact the named descendant of the Bournemouth–Manchester express introduced on 1st October 1920, and known to railwaymen as the 'Manchester Diner', or simply the 'Diner'. As with the initial 'Pines' it was a lightly-loaded train – generally six coaches hauled by a 2P – and carried the restaurant car as far as Birmingham. The leading coach was for Bradford, the next for Liverpool and the remainder for Manchester. The pattern varied slightly according to holiday requirements, as indeed did the timings over the years. The First World War saw a curtailment in services in general and of restaurant car workings in particular, while there was a substantial and understandable time lag in restoring a normal service after a war which had been so tragically expensive in both manpower and materials. Various modes of express working to and from Manchester were tried out from 1921. The following year, this saw the up express into Bath at around 12.30, with the down train two hours later. In the summer of 1922 the restaurant car on this service only worked on the Midland stage of the journey, being attached or detached at Bath. The coach was stabled in the Gas siding, where the chef would begin preparing lunch in mid-morning, the smell of cooking wafting across the Midland shed area. The aroma so intrigued one young fireman recently transferred from the small shed at Wimborne, that one morning he decided to investigate. Clambering into the coach, he peered into the tiny kitchen area, stared at the gas cooker, and asked 'What's that then, mate?' 'Pastry' came the curt reply. Looking at the ancient blackened baking tray, with contents to match, the fireman retorted 'Is that what you call it?' This elicited the comment 'Well I'll put some flour around it to make it look white and it'll be all right'. The man left the coach with a strong preference for his own sandwiches!

The 'Pines Express' was such a part of the railway scene at Bath that its demise was unthinkable, and surely could not happen? On 1st February 1958 the Western Region of British Railways took over the management (mismanagement?) of both the lines to Bath. Some railwaymen were pessimistically predicting that they would be shut within a year. Although their worst fears were not realised, it certainly proved to be the beginning of the end. The real bombshell came on Wednesday 20th June 1962, when BR announced that the 'Pines' was to be routed away from the city from early September, to travel via Oxford instead. This caused a storm of protest locally, but the management remained adamant. When asked if this decision had any

The gas tank wagon was a familiar sight against the buffers on the carriage road at the station. Its function in servicing the restaurant car on the northbound 'Pines' became redundant in the mid-1950s, and it is seen here stored away in Tommy's siding – still bearing the initials LMS.

Real Photographs/Ian Allan

implications for the future of Green Park, a spokesman at Bristol replied tersely that, although no definite decisions had been taken, 'I should think things will begin to accelerate with this announcement'. To make matters worse, 1962 was also to be the last year of the summer through trains from the Midlands and the North of England to Bournemouth. The last 'Pines' left Green Park for ever on Saturday 8th September hauled by 2-10-0 Standard class 9 *Evening Star*, the emotions of the many who watched it being a mixture of affection and sadness.

The 'Derby Perishables'. This train actually had two nicknames, one on the S&D and another on the Midland. It originated at Templecombe, from where it departed at 8.25pm and rolled into Green Park's Departure platform at 9.58pm. Meat and, more seasonally, vegetables and fruit were conveyed in great quantity by this train, with rabbits, watercress and strawberries being prominent examples of these three types of traffic. Vans were brought to Templecombe from the Southern Region as far west as Axminster in Devon, and a number of locations in Hampshire and Dorset. In practice, it was much more than a

perishables train: livestock (mainly cattle) was carried from Sturminster Newton on market day; general parcels and parcel-post was sent up from Bournemouth; mails were put on at Wincanton; and at Evercreech Junction vans were attached from the Highbridge Branch (notably GPO parcels, and footwear from Clark's factory at Street). Of all the traffic carried, however, it was the rabbits that were pre-eminent; in hot weather, one would be very much aware of their presence! Hung from wooden dowelling by their legs, the hundreds – even thousands – of carcasses were conveyed in large baskets to markets in the Midlands and the North.

The 'Perishables' required careful marshalling and forward planning, determined by the work to be done at the various locations en route. Thus for example, vans for Gloucester had to be next to the engine at Templecombe so that they would be at the rear of the train when it left Bath on the Midland leg of its journey. At Templecombe, the engine was positioned on the outer line alongside the S&D platform line, with wagons being attached to it by the station pilot either from the yard or from the 5.18 and 6.40 locals from Bournemouth. Men from Bath undertook most of the work involved in this train's long sojourn, whilst maintaining the old S&D/LMS divide. On leaving Templecombe, the formation displayed typical S&D complexity. The locomotive had left Green Park earlier in the day with the 8.15am stopping train, and had been gainfully employed with a Templecombe crew in the interim. The footplate crew worked out to Templecombe with the 3.15pm stopping train from Bath – the loco of which was taken to the m.p.d. to be disposed – whilst the brake vehicle and guard had worked south on the 4.37pm stopper from Green Park. S&D railwaymen nicknamed the 8.25 the 'Perisher', and it was invariably a heavy train. As the loadings were often greater than was permitted for a single engine between Evercreech Junction and Masbury Summit, assistance was necessary. This was generally provided by an engine on shunting duties at the Junction. If for some reason no loco was available, Control was asked to make arrangements to send a light engine down from Bath. Around Christmas time, traffic was exceptionally heavy, so much so that the 'Perisher' ran in two parts.

While the train lumbered its way through the North Somerset Coalfield, the men who were to work it north from Bath were booking on duty and checking the engine, which had already been got ready by one of the preparation gangs and left standing on either the Gas siding or Tommy's siding near the top shed (it had arrived in Bath in mid-afternoon with the down 'Pines'). From here, the loco moved directly over to the up line, and waited by bridge 43 for the 'Perisher' to run past and into the station. After a stop of 17 minutes, to permit the handling of traffic from Bath, the train was off once more, with its new engine and crew. On the Midland stage of its journey the 'Perishables' was known to railwaymen now as the 'Rabbits' due to their prominence in the total composition of the traffic; an unusual instance of one train being known by two names. Even when this traffic was diverted on to other lines following the closure of the S&D, the equivalent train was still referred to as the 'Rabbits' in the Midlands.

The first booked stop from Bath was at Gloucester. The train drew into the loop at the city's Eastgate station in order to take on water and, if time allowed, for the crew to have a quick cup of tea while the station pilot attached or detached vans as required. Sometimes the pilot was not to be seen, and the yard inspector asked the train crew if they would do the work. Regulars on this run got wise as to the reason for the absence of the engine in cold weather especially. The pressing engagement which required the presence of the pilot elsewhere generally turned out to be a warm shunters' cabin beyond the station! If the crew of the train engine refused to do the shunt, a delay would ensue while the pilot was summoned.

From Gloucester the 'Rabbits' ran non-stop to Bromsgrove, where a banker was required to assist up the famous Lickey Incline. If there was time, water would be taken on here, for with only a short stop at Birmingham and no water crane conveniently situated, it was important to have sufficient to get to the water troughs at Tamworth. This intention was sometimes thwarted, for if the train was signalled straight through Bromsgrove and the signalman let the banker out on to the main line as soon as the train had passed, the train crew felt the engine buffering up at the rear even before they had come to a halt, and were storming off up the bank without even stopping. Arriving at Birmingham's New Street station, the Bath crew handed over the train to colleagues from Derby. A meal break in the smoky gloom of the cabin at New Street was taken before it was time to return to the platform and take over the 12.37am Leicester to Bath parcels train. After the last war, the arrangements for working the parcels were modified. The 'Rabbits' ran into New Street as before, but the crew had to make their way to Landor Street sidings to pick up the return working, which now used the Camp Hill avoiding line, by-passing New Street to the east. They would either catch a lift on a light engine working back to the nearby Saltley shed, or would wait for the shuttle bus service which was provided by the railway and linked the various locations. Arriving at Landor Street, there was time for a wash and a meal – if everything was running to time – and then they would walk over to the trackside to take over from the crew bringing the train in.

The 'Rabbits' was the only working which involved Bath men travelling north of Gloucester on Mondays to Fridays in the summer of 1953. On Saturdays, however, men would regularly work passenger excursions and relief trains through to Birmingham, Derby and Sheffield. Return workings of Wakes Week specials to the North could occasionally take men to Crewe or even as far as Blackpool. Lodging would be necessary on a number of these trips. Before nationalisation, three of the night-time freight departures from Bath – 12.20am, 4.00am and 9.15pm – had involved lodging at Birmingham. The Railway Lodging House in Birmingham was by all accounts a dreadful place, 'a proper dump' as one man put it. It was situated in an uninspiring part of the city, alongside a busy railway and a gas works, thereby being continuously permeated by the smell of gas and the noise of trains. Crews requiring to stay there would pick up a lodging ticket from the foreman at Saltley shed, before making their way to the house. The accommodation was little better than a barracks, with beds housed in wooden cubicles about six feet wide and only marginally longer than the bed itself. Quite often men had to wait for a bed, which more than likely would still be warm from the previous occupant. Food was not provided, so men had to take their own and also do their own cooking if they wanted a hot meal. Eight hours after registering, the men were called in readiness for the next turn of duty. The lodging allowance at this time was 2½d an hour, just about one penny in decimal currency! There was no railway lodging house in Bath for men from the North and Midlands who worked in on summer or other seasonal expresses (the regular work was covered by Bath shed). If visiting locomen required accommodation, they would consult a list posted in the m.p.d. which informed them of households which would take them in. These were often 'railway' households themselves, and were predominantly in Oldfield Park and Twerton.

The Leicester Parcels. The men on the 'Rabbits' roster were spared the need to lodge, coming back with the Leicester parcels train, which reached Green Park at 6.09am, a time which varied only slightly over many years. As the men had been on duty for over eight hours, they were relieved on arrival at Bath by one of the shed's relief links. As the original crew walked back to the m.p.d. to book off duty, the station's passenger shunter uncoupled the engine from the stock which it had brought into the Arrival platform, thereby allowing it to draw forwards to the buffers and run round the train as it was used to shunt the stock rather than one of the yard engines. Traffic terminating at Bath was propelled into the Dock siding, while vans for dispatch via the 6.55 and/or 8.15am S&D passenger trains were left on the river bridge for collection later by the engines concerned. When this work was finished, the Leicester parcels loco was taken on shed to be serviced in readiness for its return journey with the midday 'Pines'. On this diagram, therefore, the elite express engines of the Midland Region found themselves involved in humble shunting duties. Great care had to be exercised when working into the Dock siding, for although there were no restrictions placed on the class of MR loco permitted to enter it, there was a pronounced kink in the orientation of the track just beyond the single-slip crossover. On Saturday 7th January 1961 the Leicester parcels had been brought in by 4-6-0 Jubilee class No 45557 *New Brunswick*. During shunting operations, the engine became derailed right at the entrance to the siding, thereby causing it additionally to block the Arrival platform. This had two repercussions. Of immediate concern was the loss of one of Green Park's only two platforms. It could hardly have happened at a more inopportune time, for as it was just after 7.00am the Arrival platform was at a premium, being used by departures at 7.23 and 8.11, and arrivals at 7.49 and 8.22. The other problem was the indisposition of the engine, which of course was rostered to work back with the northbound 'Pines'. The foreman at Bath shed got on to his opposite number at Barrow Road in Bristol to see if they had a spare engine suitable for working the express, but found no joy there. Bristol Control was asked to make enquiries in their area, but also drew a blank. The only spare engine with adequate power at Bath was 7F No 53807, but its use on the 'Pines' could not be entertained, if only because it was not fitted with carriage steam heating apparatus. It was decided to take Standard class 5 No 73028 away from its booked allocation to the 9.03am Bristol to Bournemouth semi-fast (9.53 off Bath) and give it to the 'Pines' roster. The 7F then worked the 9.53; cold comfort indeed!

The 'Fish and Chip Special'. The timings and destination of the last S&D departure from Green Park varied over the years, and was generally timed to leave between 8.00 and 9.00pm. The provision of a late train began in the 1930s with the appearance of what railwaymen and passengers alike called the 'Fish and Chip Special'. On Wednesdays, Bath's market day, and Saturdays a train left Green Park at 11.00pm calling at all stations to Midsomer Norton (thereafter returning to Bath as empty carriage stock). On a Saturday night it was customary for the young blades from Radstock, Shoscombe and Wellow to have an evening on the town. This consisted of a visit to a cinema, and/or a few beers and then a stop for fish and chips on the way to the station. With their suppers finished soon after leaving Bath – as evidenced by a goodly collection of lineside chip papers – it occasionally happened that some merry individual decided that it would be great fun to pull the communication cord in one of the tunnels. Needless to say this was most definitely not appreciated by the train crew, 'a proper nuisance' as one driver put it – or words to that effect!

An excess of alcohol was not restricted to the younger passengers, although the older ones were usually more quiet or simply fell asleep! One chap just managed to make it to the station one Saturday night before collapsing in an insensitive heap. The station foreman and guard debated what to do with him. Finding a ticket for Radstock in his coat pocket they decided to get him on the train, no easy task when he was flat out. A four-wheeled luggage trolley was commandeered and the drunk lifted on to it, before being wheeled recumbent to the waiting train. Here he was lifted into the guard's compartment, where an eye could be kept on him, and unceremoniously dumped on the floor. On reaching Radstock he was manoeuvred somewhat awkwardly off the train and left for the porter there to deal with.

On another Saturday night, passengers found four coaches waiting in the platform; actually they were separate sets of two coaches each. The set nearest the buffers had been positioned ready for the Sunday morning Bristol train, and so people were directed into the front set for the S&D departure. However, a young courting couple were so engrossed in each other's company that this direction failed to register, and they got into one of the rear carriages. Oblivious to everything outside their compartment, they did not hear the train pull out of the station, and were only apprised of the fact a little later by one of the staff!

The 'Fish and Chip Special' was taken off during the last war, and in the years which followed was timed to leave at 10.00 and to run on all weekdays. Its nickname still stuck to the Saturday working, however. While not advertised as a through train, the coaches for the 10.00 were provided by the last train from Bristol. This left St Philips station at 9.15pm and arrived in Green Park's Arrival platform at 9.51pm. The passenger shunter uncoupled the tank engine at the buffer stop end of the train – usually just two coaches – and then coupled the tender engine for the S&D working (this was one of Templecombe's 2Ps or 4Fs which had come into Bath earlier in the evening in charge of the 4.15pm ex-Templecombe stopping train; 6.03 in Green Park). It was one of the few passenger trains on the Bath Extension to be worked by men from Templecombe rather than Bath, and as it had no direct balancing working for the coaches – there was one more down passenger train than up – they came back attached to the first up train the next morning. This was more than a mere administrative convenience as it reflected the fact that the 7.00 from Templecombe (8.42 in Bath) was an extremely well-patronised service, and would often arrive at Green Park full and standing (throughout the 1950s anything from 60 to 90 people would be waiting at Radstock alone).

In its first years as the 10.00, the train called at all stations to Binegar from where it ran empty to Templecombe. The service was well used on Saturday nights still, although was just a bit inconveniently timed for people who wished to spend a full evening in the city – but at least it was only a four or five minute dash from the Beau Nash and Little Theatres and a little more from the Odeon and Forum! In the early 1950s the train was extended to Shepton Mallet before running empty carriage stock, and by 1955 ran as an advertised service for the full 37 miles to Templecombe, thereby extending the delights of the city to people further south – providing passengers for Evercreech, Cole and Wincanton remembered to tell the guard they wished to alight, as these were request stops! By 1957 the train was retimed to leave at 10.25pm, a time which remained until its demise in 1965. Following the withdrawal of the 9.15 from Bristol, in September 1953, the two carriages for this train were obtained from the 6.05pm Binegar local.

The 'Sunshine Special'. This was a summer-time excursion from Bristol to Bournemouth, running to a faster schedule than the regular morning through passenger service and consequently providing a longer day out at the coast. It was a long-established train and was known to men on both the Midland and S&D lines as the 'Sunshine Special' – or often simply the 'Sunshine'. In the 1930s it ran every weekday during the peak

Caprotti class 5 4-6-0 No 44755 has just been uncoupled from the 'Sunshine Special', having brought it over from Bristol (8.20am ex Temple Meads). The engine which will take it on to Bournemouth is seen blowing off furiously at the other end of the train.   25.7.59   Hugh Ballantyne

summer weeks, leaving Green Park at around 9.15am with stops at Shepton Mallet, Wincanton and Poole before reaching Bournemouth West 2¼ hours later. The return excursion left at 7.45pm and ran into Bath just after ten o'clock. For a time, the outward journey was part of a hectic and demanding roster for the crew. They were relieved on arrival at Bournemouth and promptly walked round to an adjoining platform to take over the return working from Templecombe colleagues, which was due out only 10 minutes or so after the arrival of the 'Sunshine'. There was no time for a brief spell of relaxation or even a meal break before the men were off with an express passenger train which ran to a tight schedule back to Bath, where arrival was a few minutes before 2pm.

After the war the 'Sunshine' continued to run, but now on Saturdays and Sundays only in the summer and at other peak times like Whit Sunday/Monday and the August Bank Holiday. The Saturday train left Temple Meads at 8.20am and picked up passengers at stations to Mangotsfield before running non-stop to Bath. Departure from Green Park varied by only a few minutes over the years – 9.05 to 9.10 – the train then running through to Evercreech Junction,

where the pilot engine was detached. From there the 'Sunshine' was only scheduled to make advertised stops at Wincanton, Blandford Forum and Poole, but the express nature of the train was more apparent than real as unadvertised stops had to be made at Templecombe Junction, Stalbridge, Sturminster Newton and Shillingstone in order to cross with up trains on the single line Dorset section of the route. The Sunday 'Sunshine Special' was introduced after the war, and as it stopped at more locations to pick up day-trippers – Radstock, Midsomer Norton and Shepton Mallet – was the main working to which the nickname applied in the 1950s. The train left Bristol at 9.30, its departure from Bath varying between 10.05 and 10.13. The loading was sufficient to require a pilot as far as Shepton Mallet, from whence it returned tender first to Bath shed.

The return working in the evening left Bournemouth at 7.05 and reached Bath at 9.40; continuing to Bristol 10 minutes later. This roster involved a long day for the crew, having booked on duty at around 9.00am and off again over 13 hours later. Unfortunately they could not benefit from overtime pay as the working was classified as a split-shift or short-break turn, with an enforced rest period at the south coast terminus. On a beautiful summer's day the family of some of the men would sometimes travel down as passengers and meet up with the menfolk on the beach an hour or so later (after the engine had been stabled at Branksome shed). By the late 1950s the pattern of summer Sunday working had improved somewhat; until then the 'Sunshine' had been the only passenger train over the S&D on Sundays. Bath now had its own Bournemouth train. It left at 9.30 and called at the same stations as the 'Sunshine' had previously, which permitted that service – still 9.30 from Bristol – to be speeded up: a journey time of 2 hours 16 minutes between Bath and Bournemouth made it a few minutes faster than the 'Pines'! This improvement, however, was short-lived. The summer of 1961 was the last year in which Sunday trains were run on the Somerset & Dorset.

PART 2 : MAIL & MERCHANDISE

The 'Down Mail'. The 2.40am train from Bath to Bournemouth was unique in a number of ways. In the first place it was the only down freight train to run the entire length of the line and, indeed, was the only one whose diagram began at Green Park station rather than the yard. It was also one of the S&D's most enduring trains, its timings hardly varying over decades. As it conveyed mail vans it was known to generations of railwaymen as the 'Down Mail', or more simply the 'Mail' (although it was essentially a goods train). Another distinguishing feature was that the loco booked on this turn was part of the 'Pines' diagram, whilst for a number of years the train was powered by no less than three engines on leaving Bath. All in all, an exceptional train!

The preparation for the working began the previous evening, with the positioning of the mail van(s) at the station. The S&D possessed a few large six-wheeled brake vans, which had been purpose-built at the company's Highbridge works for carrying secure loads in addition to their customary function. They contained a special compartment in which the mail bags were locked. As the station was closed at night, a particular mode of operation was followed. With the stock from the last passenger train of the day berthed by about 11.00pm, the station area was clear of possible conflicting movements for several hours. The requisite number of vans – usually only one or two – were collected from the

yard by the engine crewed by the shunt gang, who had booked on duty at 9.45pm. The vans were propelled from the up main line along the engine release road, over the river bridge, and into the Dock siding. As soon as the vans had been uncoupled, the engine returned to its normal shunting duties in the Midland Bridge Road yard.

The GPO vans gained access to the Dock platform by way of the sloping approach road leading up from the double gates on James Street West. Anything up to four vans would arrive from Manvers Street Sorting Office sometime after 2.00am, the bags being loaded on to the train by Post Office personnel. The guard was then responsible for locking the vans. Departure from Green Park was at 2.40, but much had yet to be done before the train entered the section to Midford. For many years two engines were allocated to this train, a train engine and a coupled engine (generally referred to as the '2.40 coupled'). The crew booked to work the latter reported for duty in the time office at 1.10am in order to prepare their engine, and about an hour or so later took it over to the station to pick up the vans. At the prescribed time the engine and vans left the Dock siding, crossed the river bridge and joined the up main line near the signalbox. From here they continued out to Bath Junction, coming to a stand clear of the three-way point connecting the up line to both up and down side yards. They would wait here for the train engine to run out along the loco road from the shed and into one of the S&D yard sidings. The crew for this loco had booked on at 2.10am, their loco having already been prepared.

Both before and during all this activity, the third engine to feature in the working had been busy, namely the midnight banking engine. This loco had been assembling the train in the S&D yard, and as soon as the train engine arrived from the shed, the yard shunter changed the points and waved the banker out – the engine pulling the wagons along the loco road until it was well clear of the exit points. Coming to a stop, the engine remained coupled to the brake van as it was required to bank to Combe Down tunnel. The Junction signalman now changed the points to enable the coupled engine to propel the mail vans over the down line and buffer them up to the remainder of the train on the loco road. With this done, the engine was uncoupled and drew forwards into the sidings. The train-engine now

One of the 6-wheeled 20-ton goods brake vans used to carry mail bags on the 2.40am Bath to Bournemouth mail/goods.

Real Photographs/Ian Allan

set back on to the train, to be followed in turn by the coupled engine, which was to act as pilot. With all these manoeuvres complete, the exit points were changed and, with the ground signal and S&D starting signal showing 'clear', the assemblage departed at 2.52am: coupled engine, train-engine, mail vans, goods wagons, brake van and banking engine. Although there was adequate motive power at the head of the train, the banker was needed in order to combat draw-bar strain (whilst the coupled engine was needed for subsequent duties elsewhere).

The train stormed up the 1:50 gradient to Combe Down tunnel, where the banker was detached and returned light to the Junction. Meanwhile, the 'Mail' continued double-headed to Radstock. Here, the train was brought to a stand by the station's outer home signal, to allow the leading engine to be uncoupled, draw forwards into the platform, and then set back into the sidings. As soon as the running line was clear, the signal came off and the train-engine pulled the wagons forwards until the brake van

was comfortably clear of the yard points (this often took the front part of the train on to the level crossing over the A367). The coupled engine now moved out of the yard to couple to the rear of the train to act as the banker up the long slog to Masbury Summit. The night shift was a busy time for Radstock shed's own banking engines, and the two tank engines assigned to this work were already otherwise committed.

The rearranged train now surged away from Radstock, with the coupled engine remaining attached to the rear as far as Shepton Mallet. Here, it was detached while the train engine was taking water at the column at the south end of the platform. The 'Mail' left with just the one engine to haul it down the bank to Evercreech Junction. Once it had cleared Shepton, the coupled engine drew forwards to take on water and wait for the 'Mail' to clear the section before proceeding light engine to the Junction. Using the turntable at Evercreech, the engine then coupled up to the wagons waiting for it in the north sidings, and worked tender-first with a freight to Templecombe. In this way, the engine got to Templecombe – without needing to turn there – in time to work back to Bath with the first up passenger train of the day.

Another distinguishing feature of the 2.40 was that it was the longest surviving lodging turn on the S&D, lasting down to the last war. Bath men worked the 'Mail' right through to Bournemouth. Having taken the engine to Branksome Shed, and ensured that the fire was in good order and the water topped up, they booked off at about 10.00 and made their way to a private lodging house in the town for a meal and a sleep. Returning to Branksome at around 7.30pm, they collected the engine for the return working, a through freight to Bath, which got back to the Midland Bridge Road yard in the early hours.

By the mid-1940s this method of working had been greatly simplified, due to a change in the handling of the traffic previously assigned to the coupled engine. Now the train-engine collected the vans from the station at around 2.20am, its crew booking on earlier than formerly to allow for this. In order to avoid the need for banking from Radstock, the train was made up as a single load, while Templecombe shed provided the engine for the first up passenger train. On Monday mornings the 'Mail' was the first train to run over S&D metals for almost 24 hours. If it was considered that the track might be greasy after rain, or affected by frost or black ice in cold weather, the yard shunting engine was sent up to Combe Down tunnel to sand the line.

The 'Mail' ran to the same schedule as before, but this time the engine and crew went separate ways at Templecombe, the Bath men changing with colleagues from Templecombe at the lower platform, where the train stopped for two minutes. The 'Mail' continued to Bournemouth, the vans returning later in the morning on a through freight from Poole to Evercreech Junction and thence on to Bath ready to repeat the operation again that evening. The crew, meanwhile, returned to Bath with the first up passenger train of the day, i.e. 7.00am from Templecombe, 8.42am in Green Park.

The 'Up Mail'. Two trains qualify for this title! Some men used the appellation in respect of the 3.35pm semi-fast passenger train from Bournemouth to Bristol, especially on the Midland line from Bath when it ran non-stop to Mangotsfield to make a connection with a North of England express. As the 3.35 conveyed mails

from the south coast destined for the Midlands and the North, it was imperative that this connection was made and crews were urged to keep to time. On the single line sections south of Templecombe, the running of this train was given precedence over others, even the southbound 'Pines', should the diagrammed crossing at Blandford have to be rearranged due to the late running of the express. On Mondays to Fridays it was common to see a van attached to the rear of the train on the S&D – front on the Midland section – but this carried parcels; the mail bags were conveyed in the luggage/guard's compartment of either or both of the brake-end coaches of the 3-set which comprised the train for much of the year.

The train was due into Green Park at 6.56pm, with departure for Bristol nine minutes later. It was now in the charge of one of Bath's tank engines as a rule, and was the final stage in its crew's roster. Arriving at Mangotsfield, the procedure followed was characteristically involved! A generous time allowance was provided to allow for the transference of the mail from the Bournemouth train in platform 4 to platform 1, and for passengers to make their way through the gloomy and dank subway. As the 'Mail' came to a halt, another engine would be waiting on the line (the back road) on the other side of the island platform, near the signalbox. The van was uncoupled from the carriages and then drawn by the Bath engine out on to the down main line until it had cleared all the pointwork near the junction. The signalman now set the connection from the down main to the up siding, and the engine propelled the van into the back road behind platform 1, and then back out on to the long spur which ran parallel with the up main line. Meanwhile, the other engine came out of its siding and set back on to the coaches in platform 1 and completed the journey to St Philips.

As soon as the northbound express came to a halt in platform 1, the up siding points were changed and the Bath tank engine pushed the van out and buffered it up to the rear coach. The van was coupled and then the engine uncoupled, easing back to await 'line clear' to Bristol. Running light engine to St Philips, it collected the carriages from the sidings which were to form the last service of the day on the Midland line. Leaving St Philips at 9.15pm, the train called at Fishponds, Staple Hill and Mangotsfield before running non-stop to Green Park, where it arrived at 9.51pm. As the Bath crew had done a little more than eight hours on duty, they were relieved on arrival. The new set of men now used the tank engine as station pilot, that is, to shunt at the station as required which included putting away the coaches from the last S&D arrival at 10.29. In the last few years, when the last Bristol arrival was at 8.50, the shunting duties were done by the loco which brought in the 'Perishables' train from Templecombe. This alteration also affected the working of the van attached to the 'Mail'. The loco taking the train on from Bath was now diagrammed to work right through to Bristol, though a generous wait was still provided at Mangotsfield for the connection. Under this new arrangement, Barrow Road shed sent a light engine up to Mangotsfield when required to deal with the van – which was now marshalled at the rear of the train from Bath (front from Bournemouth). On arrival in platform 4, the van was uncoupled and left behind when the train continued its journey. The light engine now came out of the siding by the signalbox, collected the van and attended to the shunt.

The other contender for the title of 'Up Mail', especially with S&D footplatemen, was the 9.28pm Poole–Bath freight. Although it did not carry mail, or even empty mail vans, it was hauled by the engine which was working back to its home shed at the end of a two round-trip diagram which began with the 'Down Mail'. The 9.28 was a heavy train, one notable commodity being ball clay from East Dorset. Banking assistance was necessary between Evercreech Junction and Binegar, and this train was more likely than most to 'lose it' on the descent to Radstock. Men were particularly unhappy if a West Country 4-6-2 was hauling the train. Not only was their pulling ability on the up grades in question, but they had inadequate braking power to cope with the loads regularly assigned to this train. There were occasions when the Bath men who took over the 'Up Mail' at Templecombe Junction refused to work beyond Evercreech unless the load was lessened: they knew only too well what difficulties lay ahead otherwise.

The 'Ghost Train'. Through the 1930s and much of the 40s the first freight train out of Bath on the S&D line was the one minute past midnight, known as the 'Ghost Train' due to its proximity to the haunting hour! It was often the heaviest southbound freight of the day, and required banking up to Combe Down tunnel and again from Radstock up the southern slopes of the Mendips to the summit at Masbury. Even with this assistance the climb on the 1.50 out of Bath could be a struggle, and on more than one occasion the train stuck in the vicinity of Claude Bridge. On the descent of the Mendips south of Masbury the train was difficult to hold – even for a 7F. The continuous down grade beyond the summit was briefly checked by a climb through Shepton Mallet. Most southbound freights were booked to take on water here. The water was consistently pure and clear, militating against priming and so popular with enginemen. Beyond Shepton station the line passed beneath the bridge carrying the Great Western's East Somerset line, and then had a short climb to Cannard's Grave. From here there was a 3¾ mile descent at 1:50 to Evercreech Junction, and crews on the 'Ghost Train' had their work cut out to prevent the wagons taking the train. On this section the driver began applying the steam brake, while the fireman screwed down the brakes on the tender and the guard wound on the handbrake in his van. Running down a steep gradient with a heavy train and the brakes full on created quite a spectacle. Bluish-white flames and sparks from the loco's wheels cascaded like catherine-wheels, giving off a continuous glare at night, the intensity of which was such that objects could be clearly seen at quite a distance from the line. Crews on the 'Ghost Train' would regularly see rabbits running for cover and animals up to two fields away as clearly as in the day. Running through Evercreech New station it was even possible to tell the time showing on the church clock a quarter of a mile from the line. On reaching the Junction, men would not be at all surprised to find that the brake blocks had virtually been worn down to the hangers, and it was by no means uncommon to damage the steel wheel tyres as well.

There were many instances of the 12.01 running away on this section. Generally, a driver sensed when the wagons were about to take the train, and knew there was nothing he could do about it except to keep the whistle blowing to alert the signalman at the Junction. The nickname of this train became even more apposite when the crew 'lost it' on the bank: the screaming whistle and impressive display of sparks in the blackness and silence of the early hours could be an eery sight to the uninitiated! It could also be pretty unnerving on the footplate and for the guard in his swaying van at the rear of the train. During the Second World War the train was almost always overloaded, carrying military materials in addition to its normal types of traffic (such as barbed wire for the south coast defences soon after Dunkirk). Under these conditions, drivers were not really taken by surprise when the train ran away; the only question was whereabouts it would come to a halt, and whether the level crossing gates would be closed across the road at Evercreech Junction station. One of the longest overruns at the Junction was made by the 'Ghost Train'. Losing the train soon after passing Cannard's Grave, the train progressively gathered speed and roared through Evercreech New with sparks streaming from the brake blocks of both the loco and brake van. With whistle shrieking its warning to the station signalman, the train swayed round the sharp curve leading to the junction with the Highbridge Branch, and rocked over the points at well over the prescribed 25 mph, the crew bracing themselves for a half-expected derailment. Holding the track, the train surged on towards the station. Screeching over the road and on along the straight beyond, it only came to a halt on the rising gradient at Bruton Road level crossing 1¼ miles further on. The wheels of the loco had developed distinct 'flats' and she was obviously unable to continue the journey.

From Templecombe, the crew returned to Bath with a northbound freight, arriving in the Midland Bridge yard just after 6.45am. In the early and mid 1950s the train only ran as required, and was retimed to leave Bath at 12.30am. Being a request train it was only run as a single load, that is to say, its loading would not exceed the ability of the allocated engine on the up grades, and so avoid the need to have banking engines waiting to assist. Control would advise the m.p.d. if the train was required, this generally being three to four hours in advance of the scheduled time. This then gave the shed foreman time to organise a spare engine and a set of men from the depot's spare link.

The 'Four o'Clock Light'. Running as either a light freight or light engine, this was the only working on the Midland line not to traverse the full length to Mangotsfield. Running on all six weekdays, it was booked to run non-stop to Warmley, and was the first leg of a roster which kept the train crew particularly busy. Despite its woefully inadequate yard – perhaps because of it – a number of freight trains called at Warmley. The traffic was substantial, principally connected with three nearby firms: the colour

manufacturers West of England Ochre & Oxide Co Ltd; Haskins' Warmley Pottery which made drain and sanitary pipes; and Hollybrook Brick & Tile Works. There was also much general coal traffic for local merchants, of whom there were three between the wars: Sidney Fussell, the Lacey Brothers, and Joseph Peacock. The ochre traffic was distinctive, if seasonal, the red staining of the yard sleepers being physical evidence of this. Ochre was imported from the Near East to Avonmouth twice a year, in spring and late summer. It was taken from the docks in several wagon-loads at a time, and railed to Westerleigh, where it was marshalled and sent on to Warmley by way of a Bath freight. At these times the yard, which was normally busy anyway, was absolutely packed. This traffic ceased in the late 1930s, although it continued at the firm's Bitton works. The footplate crew of the 'Four o'Clock Light' booked on duty at 3.30am, to find their engine prepared and waiting for them: it was invariably a six-coupled class 4. Coming off-shed 15 minutes later, the loco was taken over to the Midland Bridge Road yard to collect any wagons and the guard. Leaving at the appointed time, the train ran along the goods road to Bath Junction, where it was switched to the up main line and thence out through Weston to Warmley (20 minutes being allowed for the 8½ mile journey). The main purpose of the working was to shunt the yard at Warmley: dealing with the loaded traffic brought in by down freights in the early hours and previous evening, and assembling the empties for dispatch. Thus, although timetables showed the trip from Bath as a freight train, it was common to find that the engine ran alone, or light to its destination. When this occurred, the guard travelled on the footplate – his presence was still necessary as he was required to work the yard ground frame and attend to the shunting. With the work complete, the loco left the sidings by way of the diamond crossing at the station end of the yard, and returned tender-first to Bath. This could be an extremely unpleasant experience for the crew in the depths of winter when it was raining or an icy easterly wind was blowing – especially for the guard who was without the customary warmth and protection of his van, a fact which caused some locomen a certain wry satisfaction!

If there was traffic either to take to, or bring back from, Warmley, then a brake van had to be attached to the 'Four o'Clock'. Now and again the odd box van or two, or two or three wagons of clay for the Pottery, would be waiting in the yard for the engine, having arrived in Bath from the S&D in the early hours. Running as a light freight, the guard now travelled in his van at the rear. With no cross-over at Warmley, the loco could not run round its train. Thus, if there was no return traffic, the loco had to propel the brake van back to Bath. This was an unusual manoeuvre over such a distance, but the van had to be brought back as it was required for the 7.00 freight to Bristol. A white lamp had to be displayed on the van, and a red one on the engine. Sometimes the yard was so full of traffic that it was not possible to use the diamond crossing to regain the down main line. This meant that the engine and van had to run on to Mangotsfield, cross tracks there, and then work back to Bath.

Should there be traffic booked for the return run, an alternative procedure had to be followed. Upon completion of the shunting, the loco left the wagons and brake van in the siding nearest the main line, and ran light the short distance to Mangotsfield to change tracks, returning on the down line to Warmley station, from where it could set back into the yard. The vehicles were coupled up and the train left for Bath.

After the last war this working was retimed to leave later – in the 1953 timetable extract printed in the appendix for example it was at 5.30am – although it continued to be referred to by most railwaymen as the 'Four o'Clock Light'. It also remained the beginning of an interesting roster, the second leg of which was the 7.00 freight from Bath to Bristol St Philips; one of only two through freights each weekday between the cities. Although it was not a heavy train – consisting generally of 25 wagons or so – many, or sometimes all, of the vehicles were vacuum fitted. Much of the traffic consisted of box vans of perishables, which had reached Bath earlier via the S&D. Having secured its train in the extensive goods yard at St Philips, the engine and brake van set off for Westerleigh Sidings to collect a coal train for Stapleton Road gas works, which was reached via Mangotsfield, Fishponds and Kingswood Junction. From the gas works the crew returned to Westerleigh to pick up a freight for Bath. This was booked to run ahead of the midday passenger train from Bristol, but it often happened that the men were required to undertake an additional trip working on the main line before returning home, and consequently the final time of arrival was subject to considerable variation.

The 'Road Box Train'. Freight trains which call at all stations are commonly referred to as pick-up goods trains. The 5.50am S&D departure from Bath was one such, calling at all the stations which possessed a general freight facility down to Templecombe (except Evercreech New, which was served by its own local trip from the Junction in the afternoon). It also called at Moorewood sidings between Chilcompton and Binegar for quarry traffic. This distinctive train was known to S&D railwaymen as the 'Road Box Train'. Road boxes were closed or box vans, which were required for specific purposes at each location and thus gave the train its individuality. For example, a firm at Norton St Philip very occasionally shipped out agricultural and related machinery from the small yard at Midford; lawnmowers were a particular feature of this, and a number of road box vans were sent out on this train to deal with it. Along the line at Wellow, a carpenter, smith and barrow maker, Herbert Gainey, specialised in the manufacture of wheelbarrows between the wars, and these too required box vans. The absence of a loading dock or goods shed here created difficulties for handling certain types of merchandise: thus the wheelbarrows would be lined up on the down platform, and loaded directly from there. As far as Midford and Wellow were concerned, this was not only the sole down freight of the day to call, but was the only freight. This meant that any northbound traffic from these villages had to be conveyed by the 5.50 to Radstock and then sent back from there.

With many stops to make, and different layouts to shunt at each, the train had to be assembled in a precise order. This was undertaken by the banking/shunting engine in the S&D yard. It was marshalled in such a way that the Midford wagons would be next to the engine upon departure, with the Wellow ones behind them; then the Radstock vehicles behind them, and so on. The locomen booked on duty at 5.20 and found their engine already prepared and waiting for them. Leaving the shed 15 minutes later, they trundled out to the yard. It was unusual for the 'Road Box Train' to require banking to Combe Down tunnel, and so when the shunting engine had drawn the wagons out of the yard on to the loco road, it was uncoupled.

Shunting at Midford was a straightforward affair, the goods yard there being on the single track section and trailing to the direction of travel of the 5.50. As the train did not convey a shunter, the guard performed these functions in addition to working the ground frame controlling the yard points (the frame being unlocked by inserting the single line token into the tablet machine inside the lever hut). Dealing with goods at Wellow was more complex as the sidings were on the up side of the layout, and thereby required the engine to run round the inward wagons – which had been detached from the rest of the train, and then use these to draw out any outward ones first. In later years there was less and less work to do at these first two locations, so that the train ran straight on to Radstock. The stop here in any event was long enough for the crew to have their breakfast – for some the proverbial fry-up on the shovel – before the 'Road Box Train' resumed its leisurely peregrination south. By the very nature of its role it was a slow train, and did not reach Templecombe until 1.30 in the afternoon. To avoid overtime or lodging for the men, they changed over with the team who were working the 6.05am freight from Templecombe to Bath. As the two trains met at Shepton Mallet, the crews changed over there, the Bath men getting back home at 12.23pm (and signing off duty at 1.20pm).

The 'Engine and Van'. This was the name given to the daily pick-up goods over the Midland line to Westerleigh. Leaving the Midland Bridge Road yard at 2.10pm, it called at all stations with a freight facility : Weston, Bitton and Warmley. The locomen booked on duty one hour before departure, checking the engine before moving off shed (little preparation was necessary as the engine had only recently returned with a freight from Westerleigh, at the end of a turn of duty which involved departures from Bath over the Midland line at 5.30 and 7.00am). A Fowler 0-6-0 4F was invariably assigned to the 'Engine and Van', although from the end of the 1950s a 7F made increasing appearances on this turn.

The train left the yard five minutes after the 2.05pm Bath to Bristol passenger in order to maximise the availability of the line for shunting manoeuvres in the hour and a half lull between passenger workings. The term 'Engine and Van' was so entrenched that it even appeared as the formal description of the 2.10 in the shed Train Arrangements book, although only applied to the working between Bath and Bitton – which might seem curious seeing that this was the only goods to call at Weston. While the train might well be an engine and van either to or from Weston, the term was often a misnomer. As traffic for Bitton and Warmley could be sent out by morning services, there were few if any vehicles for these locations on the 2.10, and as the traffic handled at Weston became increasingly light and sporadic in later years, the term grew to have greater accuracy!

If there was no traffic at Weston, the train would run straight on to Bitton – subject to the clearance of the preceding train. There was invariably work to do at Bitton, for which an hour was allocated (between 3.00 and 4.00pm). Bitton did a brisk trade in freight, its spacious yard possessing a large stone-built goods shed, the only intermediate station on the Bath Branch to have such a facility. In addition to coal, which was considerable in volume, and general merchandise, which was the mainstay of most rural rail heads, Bitton also handled its own particular traffic. In season, it dispatched flowers and mushrooms from local nurseries and market gardens. Cattle specials were occasionally worked in, as was ochre. Huge rolls of paper were brought in for the Golden Valley paper mills, while sheet metal came in for the engineering firm of Torrance & Sons. Although a large part of this traffic had worked into Bitton by the one up and one down goods to call in the morning, the shunting and collecting of trucks was done by the 'Engine and Van'. Any wagons standing on the up main line during shunting operations had to be moved soon after 3.30, as the line was required by a Bath to Bristol passenger train. Within a few minutes of this stopper clearing back from Warmley, the pick-up goods set off once more.

Arriving at Warmley at 4.10, the train had a stop-over of 65 minutes. There was always a good deal of work to do here, and as soon as the crew had completed this there was time for a tea break. Whereas the 2.10 frequently ran between Weston and Bitton with only five or six wagons, by the time it left Warmley it could have as many as 40. The weight of the train, together with a rising gradient, caused the train to pull on to the main line at a slow pace, which permitted the guard to change the points as soon as the brake van had cleared them, and jump aboard while the train was still moving to avoid the inconvenience of having to stop.

On reaching Westerleigh at 5.38 there was a chance for the crew to have another short break before leaving again for Bath with the 6.30pm

The 'Engine and Van' approaching the old Turnpike at Newbridge in April 1956. The loco is 7F No 53802 and the brake van an ex-GWR 'Toad'. Both of these were somewhat atypical at this date, as the loco was generally a 4F and the van a standard ex-LMS type.
Colin G Maggs

freight. On these out-and-back turns to Westerleigh it was the practice for engines to run chimney-first from Bath and work into the up-side yard at their destination. Due to the absence of a turntable, the loco had to return tender-first, leaving from the down-side yard.

The number of wagons which could be carried on any particular service depended upon the type of traffic and class of engine, but whatever the calculated loadings, the absolute upper limit permitted was 50.

The 'Burton'. The 6.30pm Westerleigh to Bath freight was a heavy train, and although it carried local traffic for Warmley and Bath, much of it was destined for the S&D. By far the most notable commodity carried was beer from Burton-on-Trent, and earmarked for places as far away as Portsmouth, Southampton, Exeter and Plymouth (a legacy of the ties between the old Midland Railway and the London & South Western). A train conveying wagon-loads of beer left Burton

every weekday morning and ran to Westerleigh via the Camp Hill–King's Norton avoiding line at Birmingham. It had some fast point-to-point running and generally kept very good time, arriving at Westerleigh at about 6.00 (having been brought on from Gloucester by a Bristol crew). About twice a week the normal loadings were supplemented by wagons for the Navy at Portsmouth. It is hardly surprising that men on the Midland referred to this train as the 'Burton'. The vans for Bath and beyond were marshalled straight away, with up to 30 trucks being attached. Some of the beer was in bottled form and thus crated, but most of it was in barrels, these being conveyed in ordinary box vans or in mineral wagons with tarpaulins stretched over the top. During peak periods barrels were also carried in cattle wagons. Leaving the down sidings at 6.30, the train made a 10 minute stop at Warmley, and reached Bath Junction at 7.27pm. The long-distance beer traffic was marshalled in the S&D

yard, the usual service by which it was forwarded being the 10.35pm to Templecombe as this allowed it to be fed in to workings on the Southern Region. This was the train known by S&D men as the 'Burton', again due to its prominence in the composition of the train. On a Saturday night it was essential that the 6.30 from Westerleigh waited for the 'Burton' as the 10.35 was the last S&D working from Bath until Monday morning. On other weekdays a missed connection did not matter, as the beer could go out on the Dorset on the 3.30am to Evercreech Junction, from where a forwarding service to Templecombe and beyond was available.

The beer traffic was amongst the first to be diverted away from the Midland and S&D when the Western Region took control of operations, an early indication to railwaymen of the way things were to develop over the next few years. Indeed, many men felt that the Western still bore them malice going back to the days of inter-company rivalry in the 1860s and 70s. The deliberate policy of diverting through traffic away from the Bath Branch/Bath Extension infuriated railwaymen, for they could see that in many cases it was not done for any sound commercial reason, as with an incident which happened at Westerleigh soon after the takeover. A goods inspector – a newly arrived Western man – noticed that 10 wagons of coal destined for Sherborne had been attached to one of the morning freights to Bath. Here, in time-honoured fashion, they would have been shunted in the S&D yard, taken on to Evercreech Junction and then on to Templecombe and finally Sherborne. Despite these three breaks of journey, they would have reached their destination early the next morning. The inspector ordered the shunter and footplate crew to remove them from the formation, stating that it was now policy for through traffic for the Southern to go via Stoke Gifford and the WR line through Bath Spa to Salisbury. Out of interest, the driver later made enquiries in the messroom at Templecombe of the length of time the consignment actually took: it was 12 days!

The 'Market'. The mid-afternoon S&D freight departure from Bath was known to railwaymen down the line to Evercreech as the 'Market'. With the exception of Masbury, it called at all stations between Radstock and Evercreech Junction, its nickname perhaps being coined through its analogous function of bringing home the goods after a day at market, and, as with markets, the train carried a wide range of goods, with no one commodity predominating. The 'Market' was generally lightly loaded at the start of its journey, but as it performed a useful pick-up facility for general goods en route, soon acquired much more traffic. Its timing from Bath varied by only a few minutes over a considerable number of years; in 1950 for example it was 3.45pm. Over an hour was spent in the yard at Radstock, and two hours in Shepton Mallet, in both cases allowing other down trains to pass. Evercreech Junction North signalbox was reached some $5\frac{1}{2}$ hours after leaving Bath, the crew setting the wagons back into the north sidings before turning the engine in readiness for the return journey with a northbound freight, the 10.00 from Evercreech.

The loading of the 10.00pm freight was generally sufficient to warrant assistance up to Binegar. The procedure for attaching the banking engine followed a set pattern for this train. Leaving the up yard at 9.55pm, the train drew sufficiently far along the up main line for the brake van to clear the assemblage of points near the junction with the Highbridge Branch. This enabled the banker to move out and couple to the rear. Quite often the banking engine had been taken to the station to fill up at the water column at the north end of the up platform prior to the climb up the bank; the engine returning along the main line, to wait by the junction bracket signal. Once the train had come out of the yard and the points had been changed, the banker moved up and coupled to the brake van. This done, her driver sounded a whistle 'crow' to indicate his readiness. As soon as the driver of the train-engine answered the crow, the freight set off at full tilt on the 1:50 climb to Cannard's Grave. The banker was detached at Masbury, for which two minutes was allowed, the train then continuing to Bath, where arrival was scheduled for 11.45pm.

In the early 1950s the 'Market' was retimed to leave Bath at 5.00pm. The stop at Evercreech New was cut out, and the stops at Radstock and Shepton Mallet greatly reduced. Now taking less than three hours to complete the journey, the crew were still able to work back with the 10.00pm freight.

The 'Fitted'. From the late 1950s the 7.25pm S&D freight from Evercreech Junction up sidings to Bath came to be known as the 'Fitted' due to the prominence of vacuum-fitted wagons in the formation. It was not a particularly heavy train by S&D standards, and did not require banking from the Junction, but it did carry important through traffic for the Midlands and North. As this was to be forwarded from Bath on the 9.15pm to Birmingham, it was essential that the train kept to time. The absence of a banker saved a few minutes at Binegar, where the assisting engine on other workings was detached and thus required the train to stop. The 7.25 had for long been the fastest of the up freights, and from 1957 was speeded up further, taking 17–20 minutes less that other fast freights. The 'Fitted' arrived in Bath's Midland Bridge Road yard at 8.48pm, which gave adequate time to deal with the transfer of the through traffic.

As with the other northbound S&D freights, a set ritual was followed at Bath to deal with the wagons. Having accepted the train from his colleague in the Junction box, the signalman in the Station box pulled lever No 25, which set off a gong mounted on a sturdy wooden post near the entrance to the Midland Bridge Road yard. This alerted the crew on the shunting engine that the freight was on its way from Midford and that they were required to take the engine along the goods road to the spur at the Junction in readiness for the impending arrival (if on other occasions the yard inspector wished to summon the shunters, checkers, etc. he could operate the gong manually by pulling a special chain. During the last war, incidentally, the gong had been used to warn of an air raid; it was rung in repeating cycles of 12 – four sequences of three – the men in the yard area then making their way to the shelter behind the present Stothert & Pitt canteen building). With 15 minutes allowed for a freight to run between Midford and Bath, there was plenty of time for the shunting engine to leave the wagons it was dealing with, and amble over to the Junction. Here, the goods road points were set for the spur when 'normal', the signalman pulling off two ground signals to indicate to the driver that he 'had the road'. With the shunter on the spur, the points were changed and the signal pulled. As this was the only signal for incoming freights, it was slotted by Bath Station, so that only when both signalman had pulled their respective levers did the arm move to 'off'. As soon as the 'Fitted' came to a stop, the train engine was uncoupled and released to the m.p.d. as quickly as possible to allow the shunting engine which had by now coupled to the rear to deal with the train. To expedite matters, all the other traffic for the 9.15 was ready and waiting in one of the long sidings by the signalbox. The shunter now propelled the through wagons from the S&D train into the siding and coupled them to the remainder of the formation. Traffic which was either terminating or being remarshalled at Bath was pushed into another siding to clear the goods road for the loco diagrammed to work the 9.15.

The roster of which the 'Fitted' was part was unusual for Bath shed in that it began with the men travelling out on a passenger train to pick up their charge. This was known in railway parlance as travelling on the cushions. Booking on at 12.55pm, the men walked briskly to Green Park station to climb aboard the 1.10 stopping train to Templecombe, on which they travelled to Midsomer Norton to effect a changeover with colleagues from Radstock shed. This was part of a complicated working, beginning with the 3.30am down freight from Bath, and involved three sets of men and a change of engine half way through! The Radstock men were subsequently conveyed home by the next up passenger train. At 4.05, the Bath men left Midsomer Norton with a coal train from Norton Hill Colliery, which required the assistance of one of Radstock's 0-6-0 3F tank engines as far as Masbury Summit. The train engine had run tender-first from Evercreech Junction to Midsomer Norton, so that on its return there with the coal train it required turning before working back to Bath with the 'Fitted'. The Junction possessed a balanced turntable, so that precise positioning of an engine was necessary to make its operation easier, otherwise it could be hard work – as a number of bad backs over the years testified. To spread the weight as evenly as possible, men liked to have a full tender of water, and took advantage of the water stop at Shepton Mallet with the coal train to fill right up.

In 1958 the complex diagram of the 3.30 was changed, cutting out the involvement of Radstock shed. Hereafter it consisted of two straightforward out-and-back turns for the engine, with a different crew on the second leg, namely 3.30am from Bath (9.50 return), and 2.00pm from Bath (8.48 return).

The 'Avonmouth'. The out-and-back freight working to Avonmouth on Mondays to Fridays began with the 8.20pm departure from Bath's Midland Bridge Road goods yard. This was a substantial train, conveying loaded wagons and empties from all over the Bath Control District, and beyond, to Avonmouth Dock via Mangotsfield, Kingswood Junction, Ashley Hill

Junction and the former LMS/GWR joint line through Clifton. The return working was particularly heavily laden, as frequently witnessed by sagging wagon springs. All manner of merchandise was carried with grain, sugar, fertiliser and fruit being some of the most regular.

Leaving Avonmouth (Old Yard) at 11.00 for the return journey, the train reached Bath at 1.00am. In traversing the Avonmouth to Clifton section, the train had to slog up through the mile-long unventilated Clifton Down tunnel. Conditions here were not as unpleasant as Combe Down tunnel as it was slightly shorter, the gradient less steep and the bore wider (being double-track). Nonetheless, the fumes could still be bad when travelling slowly. About 100 yards from the eastern portal on the up line, the train passed over a treadle which activated loud clapper boards, the function of which was to inform the crew of their proximity to the tunnel mouth. One night when the 'Avonmouth' was pounding up through the tunnel, a wagon coupling broke. Feeling his van moving backwards, the guard hurriedly screwed down his hand brake, inserting his brakestick and tightening it as much as he could. Realising that this was not holding the breakaway wagons, he grabbed a hand lamp and clambered off the van. With great presence of mind in the unpleasant conditions in the tunnel, he began to pin down the wagons' brakes as they rumbled past. Even this action was unable to hold them, and they rolled back out of the tunnel and down towards Sea Mills, leaving the guard marooned and somewhat shaken. Catch points and a sand drag existed near Sea Mills to cover just this sort of eventuality, deflecting the breakaways from, and thus protecting, the main line and minimising the damage to both the wagons and the track.

At Ashley Hill Junction the Bath train took the Midland line up the bank through Eastville to Kingswood Junction. With a rising gradient of 1:57, a 4F could make heavy weather of the climb. For one of Bath's 4Fs the combination of the load and gradient proved too much. Near Stapleton Road Gas Works the right hand crank pin sheered off from the valve gear and twisted the connecting rod outwards, causing it to lodge

against the opposite track. In the final few years of the 'Avonmouth', a 7F was often allocated as they were more used to this type of work, and now had fewer commitments to their own line, although sometimes even these powerful 2-8-0s had their work cut out.

If the 'Avonmouth' could have its problems, it could also have its perks. One of the regular commodities conveyed from the Docks was bananas. Before loading them into the railway box vans, it was customary to hold back any which were just past their best: they would blacken and go soft before they reached the shops. As an alternative to dumping them, train crews would sometimes be offered a whole stalk, or they casually suggested that it seemed a pity to dispose of them when they were just perfect for eating! The booty was concealed somewhat bulkily beneath a coat, conveyed back to Bath shed, and carried home as discreetly as possible. Families and neighbours did very well for bananas for the next day or two!

Much of the traffic brought in by the 'Avonmouth' was forwarded on the S&D by the 3.30am departure – also from the S&D yard. Between Avonmouth and Bath the traffic had been classed as 'mineral' and had been limited to 22 wagons and a brake van due to the gradients, but on the S&D it was redesignated as 'general merchandise' (i.e. class 3), thereby permitting more wagons to be carried and thus precipitating the tendency of overloading which was so common on the night-time Dorset freights. Regularly leaving with 40 to 42 wagons on, the 3.30am would require banking to Combe Down tunnel even if it was carrying all legitimate class 3 traffic.

The 'Avonmouth', along with the other trains described in this chapter, give only a glimpse of the enormous volume and variety of work undertaken by train crews based at Bath. They form only a part of the daily routine and for a fuller appreciation of the total scenario, attention is drawn to the timetables for the summer of 1953 printed on the following pages. This shows that, in a very real sense, there was indeed 'Life on the Railway'!

Train Departures: Summer 1953

						MONDAYS TO FRIDAYS

GN PK STN	MBR YARD	S&D YARD	BATH JN			DESTINATION
–	12.20	–	12.22	MX	G	Empties to Washwood Heath
–	–	12.30	12.32	Q	G	Templecombe
–	2.44	–	2.46	MX	G	Westerleigh
2.40	–	2.52	2.54		G	Bournemouth (conveys mail)
–	–	3.30	3.32		G	Evercreech Jn (AE to C.Dn tnl)
–	4.00	–	4.02		G	Empties to Washwood Heath
–	4.35	–	4.37	MX	G	Westerleigh
–	–	5.00	5.02		G	Evercreech Jn (AE to C.Dn tnl)
–	5.15	–	5.17	MO	G	Warmley
–	5.30	–	5.32	MX	G	Warmley
–	5.35	–	5.37	MO	G	Westerleigh
–	–	5.50	5.52		G	Templecombe
6.15	–	–	6.17		P	Bristol (Temple Meads)
6.52	–	–	6.54		P	Bristol (St Philips)
6.55	–	–	6.57		P	Bournemouth
–	7.00	–	7.02		G	Bristol (St Philips)
7.20	–	–	7.22		P	Bristol (St Philips)
–	–	7.25	7.26		G	Bath Co-op siding
8.04	–	–	8.06		P	Bristol (St Philips)
8.15	–	–	8.17		P	Templecombe
–	–	8.55	8.57		G	Evercreech Jn (AE to C.Dn tnl)
–	9.23	–	9.25		G	Westerleigh
9.55	–	–	9.57		P	Bournemouth
9.58	–	–	10.00		P	Bristol (St Philips)
–	10.45	–	10.47	FX	G	Empties to Washwood Heath
–	–	11.20	11.22		G	Evercreech Jn (AE to C.Dn tnl)
12.01	–	–	12.03		P	'Pines Express' Manchester
12.14	–	–	12.16	MF	P	Sheffield
12.20	–	–	12.22		P	Bristol (Temple Meads)
–	–	12.35	12.37		G	Evercreech Jn (AE to C.Dn tnl)
–	1.00	–	1.02		G	Westerleigh
1.10	–	–	1.12		P	Templecombe
1.58	–	–	2.00		P	Gloucester
–	–	2.00	2.02	Q	G	Evercreech Jn (AE to C.Dn tnl)
2.05	–	–	2.07		P	Bristol (Temple Meads)
–	2.10	–	2.12		G	Westerleigh
2.53	–	–	2.55	MF	P	Bournemouth
3.05	–	–	3.07		P	'Pines' Bournemouth
3.15	–	–	3.17		P	Templecombe
3.35	–	–	3.37		P	Bristol (St Philips)
4.26	–	–	4.28		P	Bournemouth
4.30	–	–	4.32		P	Bristol (St Philips)
4.37	–	–	4.39		P	Templecombe
–	–	5.00	5.02		G	Evercreech Jn
5.38	–	–	5.40		P	Bristol (St Philips)
6.05	–	–	6.07		P	Binegar
6.10	–	–	6.12		P	Bristol (St Philips)
7.00	–	–	7.02		P	Bournemouth
7.05	–	–	7.07		P	Bristol (St Philips)

GN PK STN	MBR YARD	S&D YARD	BATH JN			DESTINATION
–	–	7.15	7.17		G	Templecombe (AE to C.Dn tnl)
–	8.20	–	8.22		G	Avonmouth
–	–	8.55	8.57		G	Evercreech Jn (AE to C.Dn tnl)
9.05	–	–	9.07		LE	Barrow Road m.p.d.
–	9.15	–	9.17		G	Water Orton
10.00	–	–	10.02		P	Shepton Mallet
10.15	–	–	10.17		PS	Derby
–	10.30	–	10.32		G	Bristol (St Philips)
–	–	10.35	10.37		G	Templecombe (AE to C.Dn tnl)
–	11.29	–	11.31		G	Westerleigh
–	–	11.50	11.52	Q	G	Evercreech Jn (AE to C.Dn tnl)

EXPLANATION OF REFERENCES

MF	Mondays and Fridays only	G	Goods train
MO	Mondays only	P	Passenger train
MX	Mondays excepted	PS	Perishables train
FX	Fridays excepted	AE	Assisting engine
Q	Train runs as required	LE	Light engine

GN PK STN	MBR YARD	S&D YARD	BATH JN			DESTINATION	
–	–	12.30	12.32	Q	G	Templecombe	
2.35	–	–	2.37		P	Bournemouth	(341)
2.45	–	–	2.47		P	Bournemouth	(339)
–	2.44	–	2*49		G	Westerleigh	
2.40	–	2*55	2.59		M	Poole	
3.15	–	–	3.17		P	Bournemouth	(345)
4.10	–	–	4.12		P	Bournemouth	(W132)
–	5.30	–	5.32		G	Warmley	
6.15	–	–	6.17		P	Bristol (Temple Meads)	
6.52	–	–	6.54		P	Bristol (St Philips)	
6.55	–	–	6.57		P	Bournemouth	
7.20	–	–	7.22		P	Bristol (St Philips)	
–	–	7.25	7.26		G	Bath Co-op siding	
8.04	–	–	8.06		P	Bristol (St Philips)	
8.15	–	–	8.17		P	Templecombe	
9.05	–	–	9.07		P	Bournemouth	
9.50	–	–	9.52		P	Bristol (St Philips)	
9.55	–	–	9.57		P	Bournemouth	
10.30	–	–	10.32		P	Sheffield	(224)
10.32	–	–	10.34		P	Bournemouth	(213)
11.28	–	–	11.30		P	Bradford	(228)
11.50	–	–	11.52		P	Manchester & Liverpool	(234)
12.00	–	–	12.02		P	Bournemouth	(227)
12.05	–	–	12.07		P	'Pines' Manchester	(236)
12.20	–	–	12.22		P	Bristol (Temple Meads)	
12.35	–	–	12.37		P	Leeds	(238)
12.50	–	–	12.52		P	Cleethorpes	(246)
1.05	–	–	1.07		P	Manchester	(250)
1.10	–	–	1.12		P	Templecombe	
1.55	–	–	1.57		P	Derby	(254)
2.05	–	–	2.07		P	Bristol (Temple Meads)	
2.12	–	–	2.14		P	Bournemouth	(241)
2.15	–	–	2.17		P	Sheffield	(256)
2.30	–	–	2.32		P	Bournemouth	(243)
2.50	–	–	2.52		P	Bournemouth	(245)
3.10	–	–	3.12	Q	P	Birmingham	
3.35	–	–	3.37		P	Bristol (St Philips)	
3.40	–	–	3.42		P	Bournemouth	(W220)
4.25	–	–	4.27		P	Bournemouth	(W242)
4.30	–	–	4.32		P	Bristol (St Philips)	
4.36	–	–	4.38		P	Bournemouth	(W196)
4.47	–	–	4.49		P	Templecombe	
5.30	–	–	5.32		P	Bristol (Temple Meads)	
5.38	–	–	5.40		P	Bristol (St Philips)	
6.10	–	–	6.12		P	Bristol (St Philips)	
7.00	–	–	7.02		P	Bournemouth	
7.05	–	–	7.07		P	Bristol (St Philips)	
–	–	8.55	8.57		G	Evercreech Jn (AE to C.Dn tnl)	
9.58	–	–	10.00		P	Bristol (Temple Meads)	
10.00	–	–	10.02		P	Shepton Mallet	
10.08	–	–	10.10		P	Bristol (St Philips)	
–	10.20	–	10.22		G	Bristol (St Philips)	
–	–	10.35	10.37		G	Templecombe (AE to C.Dn tnl)	
–	11.29	–	11.31		G	Westerleigh	
–	–	11.50	11.52	Q	G	Evercreech Jn (AE to C.Dn tnl)	

GN PK STN	MBR YARD	S&D YARD	BATH JN		DESTINATION
				SUNDAYS	
–	12.20	–	12.22	G	Empties to Washwood Heath
–	2.44	–	2.46	G	Westerleigh
8.00	–	–	8.02	P	Bristol (Temple Meads)
10.08	–	–	10.10	P	Bournemouth
7.05	–	–	7.07	P	Bristol (Temple Meads)
7L15	–	–	7.17	LE	Evercreech Jn
9.50	–	–	9.52	P	Bristol (Temple Meads)

EXPLANATION OF REFERENCES

Q	Train runs as required	G	Goods train
L	Motive power depot	P	Passenger train
*	Waits for line clear	M	Mail train
AE	Assisting engine	LE	Light engine

Train Reporting Numbers on Saturdays shown in brackets

Train Arrivals: Summer 1953

MONDAYS TO FRIDAYS

BATH JN	S&D YARD	MBR YARD	GN PK STN			PLACE OF ORIGIN
12.04	–	–	–	Q	LE	C.Dn tnl
12.55	1.00	–	–	MX	G	Avonmouth
1.47	1.56	–	–	MX	G	Westerleigh
2.08	–	2.09	–	MX	G	Templecombe
2*38	–	2.39	–	MX	G	Poole
3.23	–	3.24	–	MX	G	Evercreech Jn
3.44	–	–	–		LE	C.Dn tnl
4.33	–	4.34	–	Q	G	Evercreech Jn
4.53	4.55	–	–	MX	G	Westerleigh (LE coupled)
4.58	–	4.59	–	MX	G	Templecombe
5.14	–	–	–		LE	C.Dn tnl
6.07	–	–	6.09	MX	PC	Leicester
6.28	6.30	–	–		G	Warmley
6.43	–	–	6.45		P	Bristol (Temple Meads)
7.52	–	–	7.54		P	Bristol (Temple Meads)
8.09	–	8.10	–		G	Bath Co-op siding
8*12	8.35	–	–		G	Westerleigh
8.26	–	–	8.28		P	Bristol (St Philips)
8.40	–	–	8.42		P	Templecombe
9.09	–	–	–		LE	C.Dn tnl
9.47	–	–	9.49		P	Bristol (Temple Meads)
10.24	–	10.25	–		G	Evercreech Jn
10.58	–	–	11.00		P	Bournemouth
11.30	11.32	–	–		G	Westerleigh
11.34	–	–	–		LE	C.Dn tnl
11.54	–	–	11.56		P	'Pines' Bournemouth
12.07	–	–	12.09	MF	P	Bournemouth
12.10	12.15	–	–		G	Westerleigh
12.22	–	12.23	–		G	Templecombe
12.29	–	–	12.31		P	Bristol (St Philips)
12.49	–	–	–		LE	C.Dn tnl
1.36	–	–	1.38		P	Templecombe
1.51	–	–	1.53		P	Bournemouth
2.06	–	–	2.08		P	Bristol (Temple Meads)
2.14	–	–	–	Q	LE	C.Dn tnl
2.15	–	–	2L20		LE	Westerleigh
2.46	–	–	2.48	MF	P	Sheffield
2.56	–	–	2.58		P	'Pines' Manchester
3.25	–	–	–		G	Westerleigh
3.43	–	–	3L45		LE	Westerleigh
3.49	–	3.50	–		G	Evercreech Jn
4.09	–	–	4.11		P	Bristol (Temple Meads)
4.19	–	–	4.21		P	Gloucester
4.21	–	–	4.23		P	Bournemouth
5.34	–	–	5.36		P	Bristol (St Philips)
5.49	–	5.50	–		G	Evercreech Jn
6.01	–	–	6.03		P	Templecombe
6.05	–	–	6.07		P	Bristol (St Philips)
6.44	–	–	6.46		P	Bristol (St Philips)

BATH JN	S&D YARD	MBR YARD	GN PK STN			PLACE OF ORIGIN
6.54	–	–	6.56		P	Bournemouth
7.05	–	–	–		G	Bristol (St Philips)
7.27	–	–	–		G	Westerleigh
7.32	–	–	–		LE	C.Dn tnl
7.47	–	7.48	–		G	Evercreech Jn
7.47	–	–	7.49		P	Bristol (St Philips)
7.59	–	–	8.01		P	Binegar
8.49	–	–	8.51		P	Bristol (St Philips)
8.59	–	9.00	–		G	Evercreech Jn
9.01	–	–	9L03	FX	LE	Westerleigh
9.09	–	–	–		LE	C.Dn tnl
9.49	–	–	9.51		P	Bristol (St Philips)
9.56	–	–	9.58		PS	Templecombe
10.27	–	–	10.29		P	Bournemouth
10.49	–	–	–		LE	C.Dn tnl
11.43	–	11.45	–		G	Evercreech Jn

EXPLANATION OF REFERENCES

MF	Mondays and Fridays only	G	Goods train
MX	Mondays excepted	P	Passenger train
FX	Fridays excepted	PC	Parcels train
Q	Train runs as required	PS	Perishables train
L	Motive power depot	LE	Light engine
*	Waits for line clear		

BATH JN	S&D YARD	MBR YARD	GN PK STN			PLACE OF ORIGIN	
12.04	–	–	–	Q	LE	C.Dn tnl	
12.55	1.00	–	–		G	Avonmouth	
1.47	1.56	–	–		G	Westerleigh	
2.28	–	–	2.30		P	Sheffield	(341)
2.38	–	–	2.40		P	Derby	(339)
2.59	–	–	3.01		P	Bradford	(345)
3.41	–	3.42	–		G	Evercreech Jn	
3.53	–	–	3.55		P	Manchester	(W132)
4.36	–	4.37	–	Q	G	Evercreech Jn	
4.53	4.55	–	–		G	Westerleigh	
4.58	–	4.59	–		G	Templecombe	
6.28	6.30	–	–		G	Warmley	
6.43	–	–	6.45		P	Bristol (Temple Meads)	
6.56	–	–	6.58		PC	Leicester	(P477)
7.52	–	–	7.54		P	Bristol (Temple Meads)	
8.09	–	8.10	–		G	Bath Co-op siding	
8.26	–	–	8.28		P	Bristol (St Philips)	
8.40	–	–	8.42		P	Templecombe	
8.58	–	–	9.00		P	Bristol (Temple Meads)	
9.47	–	–	9.49		P	Bristol (Temple Meads)	
10.21	–	–	10.23		P	Bournemouth	(224)
10.25	–	–	10.27		P	Birmingham	(213)
10.58	–	–	11.00		P	Templecombe	
11.18	–	–	11.20		P	Bournemouth	(228)
11.39	–	–	11.41		P	Bournemouth	(234)
11.48	–	–	11.50		P	Nottingham	(227)
11.54	–	–	11.56		P	'Pines' Bournemouth	(236)
12.23	–	–	12.25		P	Bournemouth	(238)
12.38	–	–	12.40		P	Bournemouth	(246)
12.51	–	–	12.53		P	Bristol (St Philips)	
12.58	–	–	1.00		P	Bournemouth	(250)
1.03	–	–	1.05		LE	Barrow Road m.p.d.	
1.39	–	–	1.41		P	Templecombe	
1*40	–	–	1L45		LE	Westerleigh	
1.47	–	–	1.49		P	Bournemouth	(254)
2.03	–	–	2.05		P	Cleethorpes	(241)
2.08	–	–	2.10		P	Bournemouth	(256)
2.13	–	–	2.15		P	Sheffield	(243)
2.27	–	–	2.29		P	Bristol (Temple Meads)	
2.41	–	–	2.43		P	Bradford	(245)
2.54	–	–	2.56	Q	P	Bournemouth	(264)
3.11	–	–	3.13		P	Bristol (St Philips)	
3.28	–	–	3.30		P	'Pines' Manchester	(W220)
4.09	–	–	4.11		P	Bristol (Temple Meads)	
4.15	–	–	4.17		P	Liverpool	(W242)
4.21	–	–	4.23		P	Bournemouth	
4.29	–	–	4.31		P	Manchester	(W196)
5.09	–	–	5.11		P	Bournemouth	
5.34	–	–	5.36		P	Bristol (St Philips)	
6.01	–	–	6.03		P	Templecombe	
6.44	–	–	6.46		P	Bristol (St Philips)	
6.54	–	–	6.56		P	Bournemouth	
7.05	–	–	–		G	Bristol (St Philips)	
7.47	–	–	7.49		P	Bristol (St Philips)	
8.49	–	–	8.51		P	Bristol (St Philips)	

BATH JN	S&D YARD	MBR YARD	GN PK STN			PLACE OF ORIGIN
9.09	–	–	–		LE	C.Dn tnl
9.49	–	–	9.51		P	Bristol (St Philips)
9.51	–	–	9.53		P	Bournemouth
10.27	–	–	10.29		P	Bournemouth
10.49	–	–	–		LE	C.Dn tnl

SUNDAYS

BATH JN	S&D YARD	MBR YARD	GN PK STN			PLACE OF ORIGIN
12.04	–	–	–	Q	LE	C.Dn tnl
1.37	1.46	–	–		G	Westerleigh
2.38	–	2.39	–		G	Evercreech Jn
3.28	–	3.29	–		G	Poole
4.53	4.55	–	–		G	Westerleigh (LE coupled)
5.23	–	5.24	–		G	Templecombe
10.00	–	–	10.02		P	Bristol (Temple Meads)
10.28	–	–	10.30		P	Bristol (Temple Meads)
11.58	–	–	12L00		LE	Shepton Mallet
9.22	–	–	9.24		P	Bristol (Temple Meads)
9.38	–	–	9.40		P	Bournemouth

EXPLANATION OF REFERENCES

Q	Train runs as required	G	Goods train
L	Motive power depot	P	Passenger train
*	Waits for line clear	PC	Parcels train
		LE	Light engine

Train Reporting Numbers on Saturdays shown in brackets

On the last day of public service, Saturday 5th March 1966, the Great Western Society ran a special over both the Midland and Somerset and Dorset lines. The train was brought into Bath over the former by Warship diesel-hydraulic D828 *Magnificent* – which truly lived up to its name on this occasion. Stanier 8F No 48706 took over the train at Green Park for the journey south.

J Blake

One of the solid, powerful Standard class 4 2-6-4 tank engines which appeared at Bath for the last 30 months or so, prepares to take out the packed penultimate train to Templecombe on Saturday 5th March 1966, the last day of public service. J Stamp